Turbulence
Over the
Middle East

Turbulence Over the Middle East

*Israel and the Nations
in Confrontation
and the Coming Kingdom
of Peace on Earth*

LOUIS GOLDBERG

LOIZEAUX BROTHERS
Neptune, New Jersey

FIRST EDITION, JULY 1982

Library of Congress Cataloging in Publication Data

Goldberg, Louis, 1923-
    Turbulence over the Middle East, or, Israel and
the nations in confrontation and the coming kingdom
of peace on earth.

    Bibliography: pp. 281-287
    Includes indexes.
    1. Bible—Prophecies—Near East. 2. Near East—
History—Prophecies. 3. Israel—History—Prophecies.
I. Title.
BS649.N45G64   236   82-15251
ISBN 0-87213-240-4   AACR2

PRINTED IN THE UNITED STATES OF AMERICA

CONTENTS

ILLUSTRATIONS

5

ACKNOWLEDGMENTS

In a project such as this book entails, one finds himself indebted to so many people. I am grateful for a Jewish background in an orthodox home which gave me a love for the Torah (the Hebrew Scriptures, or Old Testament) and particularly the hope of a restored Israel, where Jewish people will once again live in peace on their own land endowed to the seed of Jacob because of God's promises. This hope was highlighted every year at the Passover table when we all chanted at the end of the meal, "This year we celebrate it here, but next year in Jerusalem." It was a hope instilled in me by my earliest teachers.

I am also indebted to my teachers in the seminaries where I attended, Dr. Arnold Schultz at Northern Baptist Theological Seminary and Dr. Alva McClain of Grace Theological Seminary who, while fair with all the different views of eschatology (the doctrine of end things), nevertheless gave me an appreciation for the restoration of Israel in accordance with the promises that God made with the prophets and other sacred writers of His people. I make no attempt to disparage any eschatological view different from my own because I do not feel that one's view of eschatology is a test for fellowship within the body of Messiah. However, with humility of heart and in accordance as God has given me to understand the Scriptures, I do set forth a premillennial approach in eschatology.

I also am indebted to so many congregations and conference platforms where there has been the opportunity to present in part the material included within this book. I have learned much from those who listened to the messages and then sought me out to raise questions which made me constantly think through what the Scriptures do teach concerning Israel and its future, the coming lineup of the nations, and the kingdom of God on earth. My students in the classroom have also taught me much as I have listened to their questions and have had opportunity for an interchange with them.

Finally, I realize that in many ways I have entered into the labors of those who have gone before me in dealing with the area of eschatology. My only hope is that the labors expended in bringing forth such a book will enable the reader to understand more clearly the teaching of the prophetic Word.

My thanks also go to my typists, Callie Knicely and Gay Hoch, who have gone through three or four generations of manuscripts, no small task in producing the final one.

Finally, I am thankful and grateful to my wife, Claire, for her understanding while I was doing the research to bring together the materials to produce this book.

FOREWORD

Occasionally a book appears from the press which says something. This latest work from the pen of my friend Louis Goldberg is that kind of a book.

There are many prophecies in the Bible which contain no mention of Israel. However, prophecy in its fullest sense must include the nation of Israel and certain specified geographical areas. Omit Israel from the Bible prophecy and you are left with an imcomplete picture of the future.

Here the reader will find fresh material on "the day of the Lord," which Dr. Goldberg shows to be the key to prophecy. His study on the three covenants—the Abrahamic Covenant, the Davidic Covenant, and the New Covenant—were a blessing to me personally as I read the manuscript.

The chapter entitled, "God and the Arab Peoples," contains helpful material seldom dealt with by prophetic teachers.

The value of the book is enhanced by numerous maps and diagrams. It will provide the reader with the proper perspective of Israel's future in the plan of God.

LEHMAN STRAUSS

PREFACE

Most of us who travel by air usually enjoy smooth flights which whisk us hundreds of miles to our destination as if we are sitting quietly in our living rooms. We are grateful to modern scientific advances which enable us to enjoy such conveniences.

There are occasions, however, when airplane flights are not so smooth. Turbulence in the air can cause the aircraft to encounter "bump," and the pilot usually searches for a level of altitude, either up or down, to avoid the small bumps of turbulence and provide as smooth a ride as possible.

Once in a while nature has a way of really stirring up the atmosphere with terrific storms, and anyone ever caught in such a storm never will forget the turbulence caused by the furious winds. I once was on a plane from Chicago to Salt Lake City, and no sooner were we airborne than we ran into a kind of storm I had never encountered in a number of years of air travel. For almost three hours, until almost at our destination, the storm buffeted the plane; the pilot could not find a level where we could avoid the worst of the turbulence. There were not only the "bumps"; but as we were buffeted by the winds, the plane pitched to the left and right, dipping toward the front of the craft and then to the rear. Anything loose in the cabin went flying; the stewardesses who attempted to serve luncheon could only strap themselves into their seats and let the food and everything else go. In the cabin there was an eerie silence; and not a few of the passengers bowed their heads and were, no doubt, praying to God that He would enable them to get out of that predicament safely.

As I thought of that plane ride many times afterward, I could not help but make comparisons between the severe turbulence affecting the plane and the political and military turbulence of events in the Middle East. For centuries Jerusalem, supposedly the city of peace, has been subjected to violence beyond description. In the ancient world, the Assyrians were at the gates of Jerusalem; then the Babylonians, Persians, Greeks, Seleucid-Syrians, and Romans all had their control of

11

the city. Most of these peoples made the streets of the city of peace run with the blood of the people of Israel. The Byzantine Christians after Rome made the temple site a rubbish heap, and the Arabs, in turn, arabized Jerusalem and the land of Israel. In the Middle Ages, the knights of Christendom again made the streets of Jerusalem run with the blood of Jews, Christians, and Muslims. The Turks then retained control in 1517, and Jerusalem was a part of the backwash of nations until the modern era.

In the turbulent events leading to World War I and subsequent to that conflict, the Middle East was very much in the picture. The West perceived that whoever controlled this area held the lifeline to the connection between the three major continents of Europe, Asia, and Africa. World War II only accentuated the importance of that lifeline as Nazi Germany tried desperately to get to Egypt and the Middle East through North Africa. After World War II, oil became one of the dominant diplomatic, political, and economic dimensions of the Middle East. Up to the modern era, we see how turbulent the events have been in the Middle East with important implications for Israel and Jerusalem. In particular, Israel in the modern period has had to fight for the right to exist in her own land, with frightful loss of life for both Israelis and Arabs.

As we attempt to assess the future prophetic events for Israel and the nations of the Middle East, the prophets paint the picture of horror beyond description: power struggles by the nations, wars which will kill thousands and even millions, and Israel who will experience her greatest pressuring in history in her own land in the day of Jacob's trouble. The turbulence among the nations in the prophetic sense will be worse than that plane ride which threw us all over the sky. These events will take place before the Prince of Peace comes to take His rightful place on David's throne to rule in God's kingdom of peace on earth.

I have not tried in this book to be all-inclusive with the prophetic Scriptures. My main interest is to give the reader a topical approach to the study of prophecy. In the first chapter, consideration is given to the covenant made with Abraham's descendants, Israelis and her neighbors. Without an understanding of the covenants, we cannot have a grasp of how history unfolds as well as the purposes in history. In the second chapter I have provided a key for interpreting prophecy which will enable the student to place the major events yet to unfold.

In the third chapter my main interest is to give the reader a picture of modern Israel and its concerns: its build-up in the modern period before statehood, events since 1948, and some of the experiences which will take place within the land in the future.

No study of prophecy should ever be undertaken without taking into consideration the Arab peoples and their place in God's scheme of things, and this I try to handle without getting into too many details in chapter 4. Successive chapters are a study of the build-up of the power blocs of nations as we come to the end of the age, and also the great wars this earth will yet have to face. I have considered what will happen to the nations in connection with Israel because I feel that the promises God made with Israel puts her in the center of the platform of history and prophecy, and the nations relate to Israel within the framework of God's covenants with His people. A chapter is given over to the plight of Israel, her suffering in the day of Jacob's trouble, and the sinister figures of the antichrists who wreak such havoc. There is a consideration of the judgment seat of Christ and experiences of Christians at that time.

Finally, I have also tried to show God's ultimate program for Israel and the nations in His kingdom of peace before the eternal state. There is a bright day yet to come on this earth, God's utopia which the prophets have pictured. It is an experience which man will never achieve with his own efforts, terms, and ideologies.

The practical value of a prophetic study dealing with turbulent events yet to come must also target the individual response to Jesus the Messiah. The impending events, such as the return of Christ for His body of peoples, make it paramount that we know Him and not be left behind to enter earth's worst scene yet to be played out, assuming one will even live to that time. And for us as believers, these turbulent events, some of which are already being felt and which will have such horrible results in a coming hell on earth, call for the greatest commitment on our part to our Lord for His service in evangelism and the world thrust of the great commission for the nations.

1

INTRODUCTION

Israel

Wilt rise again in glory,
    Though dark thy present night;
Wilt yet complete thy story,
    Thine enemies despite,
To prove thy past a prelude
    To future fair and bright.

After the dirge of sorrow—
    The gladsome bridal song;
After the night—tomorrow,
    When righted every wrong,
And hopes fulfilled, awaited
    So eagerly, so long.
                    Max Reich

The study of Bible prophecy is a detailed and difficult study. For the new believer, the attempt to understand the historical background of the prophetic portions of the Bible and then to correlate them into a chronological pattern of the future may seem a hopeless task. For the more advanced student of the Bible there still may be a problem of fitting the prophetic pieces together.

If believers can have difficulties understanding the prophetic message, what might strangers to the Bible think when references are made to the "little horn" of Daniel, or to the judgment of "bowls" of the book of Revelation? I can well remember when as an unbeliever, I was asked to go to a service for the first time and was waiting near the church for my friend who had invited me. Assuming that I was a believer, a Christian approached me and began to tell me of the pastor's message that very morning on the "beasts" of Revelation. Can you imagine what I thought? I was ready to run home, thinking that all believers were somehow "way out." Fortunately my friend showed up at that moment and prevented my flight!

15

There are words in our language which run in pairs. We speak of fellow and girl, husband and wife, brother and sister, lox and bagels, corn beef on rye, and so on. From a religious point of view, Israel's sages remarked on the peculiar arrangement of the limbs of the body which run in pairs (*Midrash Genesis Rabbah* 14:9).[1] In the same way, one pair of words go together naturally: Israel and prophecy.

What is Israel without prophecy? It would have no meaning. How can we speak of Israel and omit altogether the revelation of God, or even minimize the Word of God, especially those portions which have prophetic import for Israel? Secular people may question the importance of Israel in its modern setting and explain its presence from a sociological or political position. Modern man may very well ask how a Creator God who is supposed to rule the universe evenhandedly can choose for Himself one particular people in one special land. And many Christians can also question the position of the State of Israel, which represents a distinct and God-elect people. The answers to these questions, however, lie in the Biblical doctrine of election as regarding Israel after the flesh. Indeed, although God's dominion and power are worldwide, His favor, self-revelation and providence concerning modern Israel are not to be seen as some strange quirk of history, but as the prophetic expression of His elective divine will.

On the other hand, how can we speak of prophecy without also at the same time mentioning Israel? We do have a small number of prophecies regarding individuals in the Hebrew Scriptures (Old Testament) which have no relation to Israel, and there are many Biblical prophecies concerning Messiah; but prophecy in its fullest extent must include the people of Israel as well as the land of Israel.

We need also to recognize that Biblical prophecy contributes immeasurably to the Bible's philosophy of history.

---

[1]*Midrash Rabbah, Genesis* Vol. I, Rabbi Dr. Freedman ed., (London: Soncino, 1939), p. 116.

What is history apart from the declaration of the revelation of God? Dates are numerous and the names of the men of history abound. We try to relate various events within the movement of history in accordance with various theories explaining the ebb and flow of history. But when men are finished with their theorizing, history still has a way of appearing disjointed and without any specific goal. Humanistic views of history do not have a purpose, an end result. The Bible, however, does present reason and purpose in the movement of history with an end result which God has definitely in mind. The revelation of God becomes necessary to reveal this purpose so as to make it meaningful.

Before we examine God's purposes and end result within history, which are the theme of this book, we need to see the prophetic portions of the Old Testament which spell out a Biblical philosophy of history. Central to this philosophy are the covenants or agreements God made with Israel, in some instances thousands of years ago. It is the divinely appointed covenants that put Israel in the very center of history, make Israel a part of the flow of history, and also indicate some of the purposes in the historical process God has in mind. We want to note, therefore, some of these agreements which are still in effect from today's point of view, and which will have even greater meaning in the days ahead as history unfolds.

Abrahamic Agreement

The initial prophecy that we will observe is the covenant with Abraham where he was uniquely encountered by God about four thousand years ago. This covenant is the first one in a series of agreements ratified with Israel which also have meaning and significance in international history. In every one of the covenants God makes His statement as to the covenant, and then spells out the terms.

Regarding the Abrahamic covenant, God took the initiative and declared of Himself, "I am God Almighty"

(Genesis 17:1), a testimony particularly to His omnipotence and sovereignty. Based on these attributes, as well as His capacity to know all future events beforehand, God also issued the statement of this agreement:

And I will establish My covenant between Me and you (Genesis 17:2a).

A number of terms unfold the divine intent in this covenant. The *first* of these terms describes Abraham's descendants:

And I will multiply you exceedingly (Genesis 17:2);
And I will make you exceedingly fruitful (Genesis 17:6).

This term promises descendants without number for Abraham. We need to remember, however, that we cannot limit ourselves to just one family of the patriarch's descendants because this is a *general* term which applies to *all* of the seed of Abraham.

Therefore, included in this promise was Isaac and the line that came from his son Jacob. But this term also includes the other seed of Abraham. It has meaning for Ishmael as well:

And as for Ishmael, I have heard you; behold, I will bless him, and will make him fruitful, and will multiply him exceedingly (Genesis 17:20).

But Isaac and Ishmael were not the only two sons of Abraham. In the round of life, when Sarah died, Abraham married again; and with Keturah, Abraham had six other children (Genesis 25:1-2), and the promise in the first term was already in the process of fulfillment. But the extent of the promise does not stop here.

As this first term works itself out in history, we find two main lines of progeny developing. The first is the line of Isaac and Jacob from whom come the people Israel.[1] The other line consists of Ishmael, the six sons of Abraham from Keturah in his later life, and one of the two grandchildren of the patriarch, Esau. Many of the descendants of these individuals

---

[1]This is the proper designation of the seed of Jacob, although today these people are known as Jewish people.

across the centuries intermarried and became, for all practical purposes, the Arab peoples as we speak of them today in the geographical areas of Israel, the West Bank, Jordan, parts of the areas of Lebanon, Syria, and northern Arabia.[2] In a general sense, all the seed of Abraham must be included in the first term to comprise the modern Arab Semitic peoples in the geographical areas mentioned, and Jewish people.

The *second* of these terms specified by God mentions nations and kings:

I will make nations of you, and kings shall come forth from you (Genesis 17:6).

(Note also Genesis 17:4-5.) Here again is a *general* term that applies to *all* of the seed of Abraham. In the line of Isaac and Jacob, and in the ensuing development of the nation Israel, there were many illustrious kings: David, Solomon, Asa, Jehoshaphat, Hezekiah, and Josiah. Some of these kings were spiritually minded and led the nation in spiritual revival.

But there were illustrious kings in the other line. Concerning Ishmael, God promised:

I will multiply him exceedingly. He shall become the father of twelve princes, and I will make him a great nation (Genesis 17:20).

Of Midian there came a large clan of people (Genesis 25:2-4), and of Esau came the people of Edom. What we need to recognize is that, besides Ishmael, many nations eventually developed from this genealogical line of Abraham. Among these nations many illustrious kings came and went, and what we frequently overlook is that the Arab peoples have played their part in the history of and contribution to mankind. For example, history reveals the significant role Arab peoples have played in Europe in the day when the

---

[2]By no means do I try to make these identifications simple. Of Abraham's nephew, Lot, came Ammon and Moab (Genesis 19:31-38). Other folk also must be included in the ethnic mix of this region. When Samaria was conquered by the Assyrians, the latter brought many of their own people into this area and intermarried with many of the people of Israel there (2 Kings 17:24), and the descendants became the Samaritans of Jesus's day. Today many of these very descendants are the Palestinian Arabs of the West Bank.

latter was in the depths of the Middle Ages; it was the Arab peoples who brought culture to Europe through their philosophers, scientists, and writers. (We shall discuss this more at length in chapter four.) What God said to Abraham in His agreement concerning nations and kings was fulfilled and still is in the process of fulfillment; the backward glance in history reveals the greatness of both lines, and the modern look at these peoples indicates that many of today's events revolve around them.

We come to the *third* term in this covenant where God now declares to Abraham:

And I will establish My covenant between Me and you and your descendants after you throughout their generations for an everlasting covenant, to be God to you and to your descendants after you (Genesis 17:7).

In a very general way, this is also a promise which applies to *all* of the descendants of Abraham, both lines already indicated.

We must hasten to add, however, that a particularization now enters into the picture which becomes quite specific for the one line of Isaac and Jacob. This is explained:

But Sarah your wife shall bear you a son, and you shall call his name Isaac; and I will establish My covenant with *him* [italics mine] for an everlasting covenant for his descendants after him (Genesis 17:19).

But My covenant I will establish with Isaac, whom Sarah will bear to you at this season next year (Genesis 17:21).

This very special message now contrasts Isaac and Ishmael.

By the third generation from Abraham there is a further contraction of this term within the Abrahamic agreement. In particular, God's promise says, not only to Abraham and uniquely to Isaac, but also ultimately to Jacob:

Your name is Jacob;
You shall no longer be called Jacob,
But Israel shall be your name
(Genesis 35:10).

Then God adds:

> I am God Almighty;
> Be fruitful and multiply;
> A nation and a company of nations shall come from *you*,
> And kings shall come forth from *you* [italics mine]
>   (Genesis 35:11).

Since this is a continuation of the Abrahamic agreement, already promised to Isaac, we note that God promised His continued presence with the line of Isaac as well as Jacob for as long as there is a history of the human race. It is the specific promises to Isaac and Jacob that give meaning to the protection of Abraham's seed in Genesis 17:7.

This third term guarantees that there will always be an Israel on this earth's scene. We cannot ever forget that God's purposes within the human arena are entwined with the descendants of the patriarch, Israel. With history as our witness, and considering all that has ever happened to God's people Israel in the course of the countries of their dispersion, there is testimony that God's hand has always been with them. Many may not like some of the things they see in the present State of Israel, but we must recognize the presence of Abraham's Almighty God with Israel because of a promise He made with the patriarch in a particularization concerning the line of Isaac and Jacob.

One more term regarding this covenant specifies land in the Middle East:

> On that day the LORD made a covenant with Abram, saying,
> To your descendants I have given this land,
> From the river of Egypt as far as the great river, the river Euphrates (Genesis 15:18).

This is the piece of real estate associated with this covenant. All of Abraham's people are to live in a certain geographical area, but the line of Isaac and Jacob has its land specified very clearly.

The question can correctly be asked as to whether the land described in Genesis 15:18 is for all the seed of Abraham or not. The answer is negative. There is the specification of a particular piece of land for Isaac:

> And the LORD appeared to him and said, "Do not go down to Egypt; stay in the land of which I shall tell you. Sojourn in this land and I will be with you and bless you, for to you and to your descendants I will give all these lands, and I will establish the oath which I swore to your father Abraham" (Genesis 26:2-3);

and for Jacob:

> And the land which I gave to Abraham and Isaac,
> I will give it to you,
> And I will give the land to your descendants after you
> (Genesis 35:12).

Therefore, God's directive concerning land in this covenant applies in a specialized sense to the line of Isaac and Jacob in perpetuity. The question of a right to land for Jacob's line is settled on the basis of God's Word, and this declaration should be sufficient insofar as Christians are concerned. One cannot speak of the Abrahamic covenant without at the same time *bringing* to the forefront the right to title of a particular piece of land in the Middle East.

People, however, do ask, "What about the other line? Do not Abraham's descendants apart from Isaac and Jacob also have a land?" Assuredly there is a phrase mentioned in a very general way which suggests a possible answer to this question. When Abraham settled the inheritance claims with his six sons, he gave gifts to the sons of Keturah while he was still living. Then, he sent them away from his son Isaac eastward to the *land of the east* (Genesis 25:6). Since God spelled out the specific land that was to belong to the line of Isaac and Jacob, then the very general distinction "land of the east" is taken to mean east of Israel's land, or actually the rest of the geographical area as a part of the Middle East reserved for Abraham's other line. Please note carefully, however, that the Middle East is the home for *all* the seed of Abraham, but that the seed of Jacob has its particular share.

David's Agreement

Another of the agreements God had with Israel was a specific one with King David. The prophet Nathan once came to this king some three thousand years ago and declared:

When your days are complete and you lie down with your fathers, I will raise up your descendant after you, who will come forth from you, and I will establish his kingdom (2 Samuel 7:12).

I will establish the throne of his kingdom forever (2 Samuel 7:13b).

These passages form the statement of the Davidic agreement. The terms of the covenant are further specified:

And your *house* and your *kingdom* shall endure before Me forever: your *throne* shall be established forever [italics mine] (2 Samuel 7:16).

The three terms of house, kingdom, and throne are designed by God to have far-reaching consequences. In an interesting revelation with interesting implications from today's point of view, God said that of the line of David there will be a house, that is descendants; there will be a kingdom over which David's descendants will reign; and there will be a throne upon which David's descendants will sit. Since God took the initiative with David as previously with Abraham, we can then say that this agreement with David parallels that of the Abrahamic one. David, however, did not understand all the implications and he exclaimed:

Who am I, O Lord GOD, and what is my house, that Thou hast brought me this far? (2 Samuel 7:18)

In tracing David's line we can appreciate how God's promise unfolds. As the historical kingdom of the Old Testament ran its course, the first commonwealth[1] was disrupted when the Solomonic temple was destroyed by the Babylonians in

---

[1]Israel's history is designated in commonwealths, the first one ended in 586 B.C. with the loss of the first temple; the second in 70 A.D. with the loss of the second temple; currently, the third commenced in 1948.

586 B.C.[1] But while there were no kings of the house of David ruling in the second commonwealth (because of a curse placed on this kingly line, Jeremiah 22:30), commencing with the inception of the second temple in 536 B.C., the actual line of David never ceased. Near the end of the second temple period, in the first century A.D., Jesus appeared as the Messiah and both Matthew and Luke trace His genealogy back to David.

Joseph of the line of Solomon gave Jesus the inheritance right to sit on the throne of David (Matthew 1:6-16), but there can be no biological tie between Jesus and the foster father because of the curse. Mary provides Jesus with proper identity credentials whereby Jesus is linked to David other than the line of Solomon (Luke 3:23-31).

Jesus as Messiah, therefore, has the right to sit upon the throne of David, and since He is of the house of David He has authority to rule in the kingdom promised by God to David as well as to the nation Israel. While the fullness of the Messianic kingdom has not yet taken place, and consequently David's throne remains unoccupied, there is yet coming the day when Jesus will take His rightful place on His throne.

One also sees the divine purpose to which God is moving within history: the Messianic kingdom on earth comprised of Israel and the nations.[2] A political ideology of kingdom and king might not be compatible with the current political optimum of government by a democracy. Democratic governments seek to avoid the extremes of dictatorships on the one hand and anarchy on the other, and this political arrangement is the best protection in a world of unregenerate men. But there is coming a day when the democracy option will be

---

[1] Jewish reckoning is B.C.E. (before the common era) for B.C. (before Christ) and C.E. (common era) for A.D. (anno Domini, in the year of the Lord) since in the latter sense Jewish people do not acknowledge Jesus as Lord.

[2] The term Messianic kingdom is employed to describe all the conditions promised by the prophets of the Old Testament rather than "millennial" which refers only to the length of time of this kingdom on earth.

changed. It is God's purpose that David's greater Son rule over His kingdom on this earth to insure justice and righteousness among nations. Therefore, we need to keep in mind that God made a statement to David, and the terms spell out the perpetuity of his throne, his house, and his kingdom that will one day see their greatest fulfillment amid utopian conditions for which men have always longed.

The New Covenant

Still another agreement has consequences for Israel, and all peoples, in the statement of the New Covenant, issued some two thousand six hundred years ago:

Behold, days are coming, declares the LORD, when I will make a new covenant with the house of Israel and with the house of Judah (Jeremiah 31:31);

But this is the covenant which I will make with the house of Israel after those days, declares the LORD (Jeremiah 31:33a).

God took the initiative again to announce His intentions for His people Israel.

The Mosaic Constitution. We need, however, to obtain some background as to some of the purposes God has in mind regarding the New Covenant. God gave Israel the Mosaic constitution as well as a kingship, and provided His people every opportunity to develop under this specialized agreement. There was nothing wrong with the constitution itself, and many people made an attempt to live within its principles of righteousness and justice; many in Israel knew the Lord and lived godly lives in Old Testament times. But tragically there were also very real problems when at times many people lived at low spiritual levels, and the kings were not godly at all. The prophets were well aware of these conditions and preached their messages to their generations, calling for atonement of the person and for the application of the principles of justice, equity, and righteousness.

But the prophets also began to spell out the days of a coming Messianic kingdom. Within this new arrangement, people were pictured as knowing the Lord, and the king was to be a perfect one, David's greater son, the Messiah. This king is presented as the most excellent monarch in history, ruling in a utopian set of conditions, not initiated by men but instituted by God Himself. Therefore, the Prophet Jeremiah stressed the point as the *first* term of the New Covenant as a comparison with the Mosaic constitution:

Not like the covenant which I made with their fathers in the day I took them by the hand to bring them out of the land of Egypt, My covenant which they broke, although I was a husband to them, declares the LORD (Jeremiah 31:32).

The New Covenant is not the Mosaic one; an entire new set of conditions was in view.

Possibility of Fulfillment of the New Covenant. The fullness of the Messianic kingdom could have been initiated if the nation Israel, through its leadership, had received the Messiah when He came. All during Jesus's ministry He demonstrated His claims to be Messiah by His work and teaching, and finally He presented, at His trial, His Messianic credentials to the high priest. After all the witnesses had been dismissed because their testimony was not considered plausible, the high priest asked Jesus two questions:

I adjure You by the living God,[1] that You tell us whether [1] You are the Messiah, [2] the Son of God (Matthew 26:63).

Jesus replied to the two questions. Concerning the first one He declared:

You have said it yourself (Matthew 26:64).
I am (Mark 14:62).

But to the second crucial question, Jesus did not answer on

---

[1]The characteristic phrase under trial which required a defendant to tell the truth. We see it today, possibly preserved from the first century, in the Mishnah which was compiled at about 200, Sanhedrin chapter 4, H. Danby, trans. (London: Oxford University Press, 1933), pp. 386-388.

His own; rather, He used the declaration by Daniel which He paraphrased to describe His own identity:

> I kept looking in the night visions,
> And behold, with the clouds of heaven
> One like a Son of Man was coming,
> And He came up to the Ancient of Days
> And was presented before Him (Daniel 7:13).

Nevertheless I tell you, hereafter you shall see THE SON OF MAN SITTING AT THE RIGHT HAND OF POWER, AND COMING ON THE CLOUDS OF HEAVEN (Matthew 26:64).

The reply left no doubt in the high priest's mind as to what Jesus was trying to say, yet the answer by the Messiah is so mysteriously unique that it can only be interpreted that He had every right to bring in the kingdom. There was the distinct possibility that the nation Israel at that time could have accepted Jesus as the Messiah, and had He been received, atonement would have been made for sin, and the kingdom could then have been instituted.

Tragically the facts of history are otherwise.

What Was Established. The *second* term of the New Covenant spells out the totality of the spiritual and moral dimensions:

> I will put My law within them, and on their heart I will write it: and I will be their God, and they shall be My people. And they shall not teach again, each man his neighbor and each man his brother, saying, 'Know the Lord,' for they shall all know Me; from the least of them to the greatest of them, declares the LORD, for I will forgive their iniquity, and their sin I will remember no more (Jeremiah 31:33-34).

When most of Israel's leadership turned from their king, it did not thwart fully the purposes of the Lord. The Messiah Jesus became the atonement for our sins, and died, was buried, and also rose in His resurrection from the dead. The second term of the New Covenant became a reality. Individuals of Israel in the first century did accept Jesus as their Messiah and Redeemer. We can never forget that what is referred to as the flower of the early Church is, in reality, ethnic Jewish believers who affirmed the hope of Israel in Jesus as their Messiah. Therefore those of Israel's ranks as believers enter into the fullness of spiritual blessings of the second term (Hebrews 8:8-12), and Gentile believers are also included to enjoy the same blessings (Ephesians 2:13f).

The tragedy is that the decision by the leadership of Israel in the first century brought about a negative divine action as to national position. Some forty years later in 70, the Herodian temple was destroyed, bringing the second temple period to an end. After a second Judean revolt against Rome in 132-135, there began a worldwide dispersion of Israel. However, even though Jewish people were scattered, God never forsook them! There is always the possibility for individual Jews to enjoy peace of mind and heart and enter into the experience of atonement when the claims of Jesus the Messiah are recognized. The tragedy is that Jewish people too often never have a clear picture of who Jesus is, especially at those times when the unregenerate and even ungodly element in Christendom did untold and indescribable harm to the sons of Israel. Yet God always has His individual godly believers who with humility share the Messiah Jesus. Some day we will rejoice with what God already knows as to the great numbers of Jewish people who found Messiah during the period of the *galut* (Jewish dispersion across the centuries).

What Was Not Established in Our Age. The *third* term of the New Covenant referred to in Jeremiah 31 relates to physical and material blessings, and is seen in a number of areas:

1. The restoration of the tribes which had ceased to be a political unit (from Jeremiah's view in his day) with the fall of Samaria. Jacob is to be recalled to its ancient homeland (Jeremiah 31:10-12).

2. The restoration of Judah (in Jeremiah's day, the desig-

nation of the leading tribe in whose territory Jerusalem was located). Both Judah and its cities will once again be in its homeland also (Jeremiah 31:23-24).

3. A further reference to the restoration of all twelve tribes where they will be welded together as a single people (Jeremiah 31:27-28).

4. The promise by God within this term relates to the existence of all the seed of Israel and guarantees it within human history (Jeremiah 31:35-37). If one were to destroy the universe or juggle its governing laws, then the entire New Covenant would be destroyed, thereby ending Israel's existence.

5. The mention of the city of Jerusalem (Jeremiah 31:38-40), and a quick glance declares that its boundaries are specified in a counterclockwise direction beginning with the northeast point of the wall, the tower of Hananel, today called the "crow's nest." More about this city will be indicated later on.

6. There are also descriptions of tremendous material blessings as a part of this term, crops in abundance, the enjoyment of these blessings, etc., (Jeremiah 31:12, 24-28). These blessings are not to be dismissed or spiritualized. Neither do they apply within the body of Messiah because God has *not* promised physical blessings in abundance to believers today, except our needs (Philippians 4:19). If we do enjoy them in our age, it is only the grace of God. The point of the matter is that believers in this age have suffered much and have been deprived in every way except in the spirit. But the New Covenant has something quite different in this respect insofar as material blessings are concerned.

Rather, what is demonstrated in God's purposes is that the fullest extent of this third term of the New Covenant is yet to be realized, and the day will yet come when the *combination* of both spiritual and material blessings will be enjoyed by Israel and the rest of the nations. This combination of New Covenant blessings will yet be ratified with a totally re-

Figure 1

The Covenants and Their Terms Which God Made With Israel and the Fulfillments

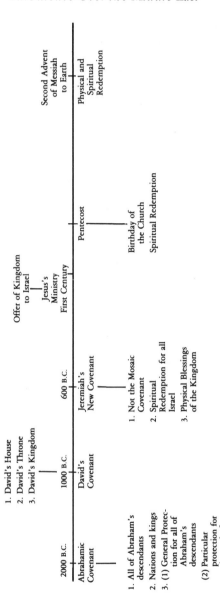

2000 B.C.	1000 B.C.	600 B.C.	First Century	Pentecost	Second Advent of Messiah to Earth
Abrahamic Covenant	David's Covenant	Jeremiah's New Covenant	Jesus's Ministry / Offer of Kingdom to Israel	Birthday of the Church / Spiritual Redemption	Physical and Spiritual Redemption
1. All of Abraham's descendants	1. David's House	1. Not the Mosaic Covenant			
2. Nations and kings	2. David's Throne	2. Spiritual Redemption for all Israel			
3. (1) General Protection for all of Abraham's descendants	3. David's Kingdom	3. Physical Blessings of the Kingdom			
(2) Particular protection for the seed of Jacob					
4. Promise of land to the seed of Jacob					

deemed Israel in, hopefully, the not too distant future when Jesus the Messiah will be acknowledged as King. This is an area to be explored further in chapter nine.

It is these three covenants—the Abrahamic, the Davidic, and the New—which enable us to proceed with the theme of this book as we examine the rest of the Scriptures to see how God will bring about the fulfillment of His prophetic Word. I do believe we live in the days of prophetic anticipation and that the events of the modern period are none other than Messianic times. God has a purpose toward which He is moving regardless of what man will say or do.

The author sat one evening in one of the main halls in Jerusalem and heard Shlomo Goren, who at that time was the chief of chaplains. For forty-five minutes he spoke of the Biblical materials that relate to these days. That man, with his soft eyes and face framed by a grey beard, standing as though an Old Testament prophet had stepped out of the pages of the Scriptures, said to the audience, "These are the days of the foot of the Messiah. There are dark days ahead but there is no turning back. The day is coming," he declared emphatically, "when the Messiah will come here and the kingdom will begin." Can you imagine the effect that went through the listening audience? But what do these statements mean to believers now? One cannot afford to close his eyes as to what God is doing with the modern people Israel for their rendezvous with divine purposes.

Let us therefore proceed to an examination of what I feel to be the key of prophetic interpretation in chapter two.

2

THE KEY FOR PROPHETIC
INTERPRETATION

> There is no royal road to the scientific study of prophecy.

> Watchful care and accuracy in dealing with words, fidelity to the text . . . and honest determination to be led by the Spirit of Truth and not by a foregone theory—these are the requirements of the man who would deal thoroughly and loyally with the prophetic Scriptures.   R. Girdlestone

As difficult as the prophetic study of the Scriptures can be, I do believe that there is a key to this study which has been a great help to enable one to place properly in sequence the great events yet to happen in the future. I am referring to the key phrase, "the day of the Lord," as the best means of correlating prophetic events. I am sure you have seen the full phrase, or the simple description, "the day," as you have read your Bible very carefully.

"The day of the Lord" is the phrase which the prophets used to define the experiences of the people of Israel just prior to, and during the reign of Messiah on earth. As to how this phrase came into being, the writers of the Old Testament do not go into any explanation, and we are left to ourselves to surmise its origin. I think, however, that as we know some of the facets of the cultural background of Israel we can find the clue for application of the use of the phrase.

The Jewish Twenty-Four-Hour Day

The prophetic phrase could be a takeoff from the Jewish twenty-four-hour day. In the Biblical backgrounds of Israel, and in the Jewish religious culture today, the day begins at about 6:00 P.M sundown, give or take an hour or so, depending on the time of the year. The first part of the day is actually for rest, a most sensible procedure!

The second part of the day therefore, is light, or the brightness of the day.

Figure 2—The Jewish Twenty-Four-Hour Day

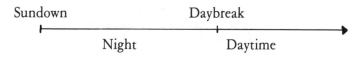

The Prophetic Day of the Lord

Now it is the sequence that becomes important here. Just as there is a definite pattern in the Jewish twenty-four-hour day, so it is the sequence that becomes important as it applies to the experiences of Israel in connection with the coming of the Messiah. The Jewish twenty-four-hour day can be linked to the prophetic day of the Lord:[1]

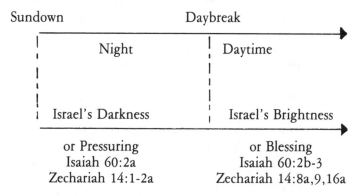

Figure 3—The Link Between the Jewish Twenty-Four-Hour Day and the Prophetic Day of the Lord

---

[1] I am indebted to Alva McClain, *The Greatness of the Kingdom* (Grand Rapids: Zondervan, 1959), page 178, for the suggestion to link the Jewish twenty-four-hour day and the prophetic day of the Lord to indicate the sequence of the pressuring and blessing experiences Israel will yet pass through in future events.

It remains now to take two representative passages from Scripture to demonstrate the claims that have been made. The first of these is seen in Isaiah 60:1-3. The prophet begins by making a general statement as to Israel's future blessing during the Messianic reign:

> Arise, shine; for your light has come,
> And the glory of the LORD has risen upon you
>   (Isaiah 60:1).

The pronouns "your" and "you" refer to Isaiah's people as he talks of Israel's future brightness. But before there is to be a glorious Messianic reign, there will also be a time of unprecedented terror on earth for all peoples as well as Israel. The prophet declares (referring to figure 3):

> For behold, darkness will cover the earth,
> And deep darkness the people (Isaiah 60:2a).

In verse 2a Isaiah pictures the extreme horror that will be the experience of the nations, including Israel. The symbols depicted by the four horsemen of the book of Revelation (Revelation 6:2-8), respectively, conquering army commanders with their armies, war, famine, and death, graphically describe the horror on earth. Israel will also have her experience in this catastrophe. (I am not spelling out details here but only generally describing it. As the picture unfolds, the pieces will be put together.)

This period of darkness is short-lived however. The scene changes in the prophet's view:

> But the LORD will arise upon you,
> And His glory will appear upon you.
> And nations will come to your light,
> And kings to the brightness of your rising (Isaiah 60:2b-3).

While peace will come to all nations when the Messiah destroys His enemies and stops the carnage on earth, yet the scope of the prophetic day of the Lord centers largely around Israel, and the nations are seen only with respect to Israel's pressuring and blessing. This was the prophetic view of the international scene in the Old Testament, and it will once again be the scene with respect to the prophetic events of the day of the Lord.

Therefore the pronouns, "you" and "your" are a reference to Israel in her restoration. Israel will yet have the glory of God resting upon her, and nations which once despised Israel will find blessings and glory as they relate and attach themselves to Israel. But note however the sequence: the darkness followed by the brightness, the judgments followed by the blessings. It is the sequence, as a take-off from the Jewish twenty-four-hour day, which gives us direction in understanding the prophetic day of the Lord.

Let us take another representative Scripture passage which illustrates the claim for Israel's experiences in the day of the Lord:

> Behold, a day is coming for the LORD when the spoil taken from you will be divided among you. For I will gather all the nations against Jerusalem to battle, and the city will be captured (Zechariah 14:1-2a).

In these two verses and in several others in this chapter, there is the description that Jerusalem and Israel will suffer at the hands of the nations who will invade the land of Israel. The reference to destruction and gloom depict the horror which will occur during the darkness of the day of the Lord, which is the first part of the day.

The period of gloom is only for a short period of time. This same chapter of Zechariah also describes Israel in her glory in the second part of the day of the Lord (see figure 3):

> And it will come about in that day that living waters will flow out of Jerusalem. . . . And the LORD will be king over all the earth; in that day the LORD will be the only one, and His name the only one. . . . In that day there will be inscribed on the bells of the horses, "HOLY TO THE LORD" (Zechariah 14:8a,9,20a).

Zechariah was not speaking merely of a restoration from Babylon from the point of view of his generation. Rather, his sights were set for the future when all the tribes of Israel, not just Judah, will yet be restored to full favor with the Lord to enjoy the greatest of all blessings. The presence of the Messiah on earth, reigning as the Lord, will bring about the best of that which men have ever hoped for, for Israel and all the nations. This will be the experience of the second part of the day, the Messianic kingdom. Once again we note the sequence of events, first, the day of pressuring and terror, and then the day of blessing, which follows the sequence of darkness and brightness in the Jewish twenty-four-hour day.

Other prophetic Scriptures can be demonstrated in practically the same way, although not all of them will show both parts of the day; some Scriptures will mention only the terror yet to be experienced by Israel, while other passages will paint the picture of Israel's glory yet to come.

The Time of Israel's Day of Jacob's Trouble

The big question now remains: "When will Israel experience the period of great pressuring and horror?" But one is immediately prone to ask, "Hasn't Israel suffered enough?" In tracing the past sixteen centuries of Jewish history, especially during the period of the Middle Ages, we can point to numerous occasions when Jewish people suffered greatly. This century alone has seen terror and degradation because of the death of the six million in the holocaust on the continent of Europe. The suffering is still not over for those Jewish people who wish to exit from some of the eastern European countries, especially the Soviet Union. As soon as one indicates his intention to emigrate, he is stripped of all rights and is persecuted. And now do we dare to talk of more pressuring of Israel, especially in the land of Israel? However, while retaining a sensitivity for Jewish experiences, we yet need to follow what the Scriptures teach. Our task therefore is to find the starting point for the final pressuring experience for Israel that will lead to the day of Israel's glory, and one sees an amazing correspondence between the concept of the day of the Lord and Israel's future experiences.

Jesus as the Messiah. We turn to the book of Revelation for the clues to this most important period of history. In chapter 12 of the final book of prophecy in the Bible, the Apostle John gives us three major symbols representing very real people. The first two of these figures are provided:

And a great sign appeared in heaven: a woman clothed with the sun, and the moon under her feet, and on her head a crown of twelve stars; and she was with child; and she cried out, being in labor and in pain to give birth (Revelation 12:1-2).

At first sight we might be puzzled with John's imagery, but the best rule of the interpretation of Scripture is to let it interpret itself. By no means are we to read into the Word of God, or spiritualize it, in accordance with some subjective or preconceived fancy.

If we drop down to verse 5 in this chapter, we note:

And she [the woman of verse 1] gave birth to a son [verse 2] a male child, who is to rule all the nations with a rod of iron; and her child was caught up to God and to His throne (Revelation 12:5).

Without laboring the point, the son here is Jesus the Messiah. He is the one who is yet going to rule all the nations with a rod of iron (Psalm 2:9); but from John's point of view, and ours as well, this kingly rule is still to come. While Jesus today sits at the right hand of the throne of God (Hebrews 1:3), He still waits for the opportune time when He will reign in the fullness of His kingdom on earth.

Israel Depicted by the Woman. Furthermore, once having identified the "male child" as Jesus the Messiah, we can also claim that the peculiarly described woman is Israel. The crown of twelve stars represents the twelve tribes, while the sun and the moon depict, respectively, Jacob and his wives, who brought forth the twelve sons, who in turn fathered the twelve tribes of Israel. This description reminds us of the dream which Joseph had of the sun (Jacob), moon (Leah, because by that point Rachel had died), and the eleven stars bowing down to him (Genesis 37:9), for which his brethren despised him.

Satan as the Dragon. There is also a third figure which becomes crucial for discovering the point in history when Israel will be pressured:

And there was war in heaven, Michael and his angels waging war with the dragon. And the dragon and his angels waged war, and they were not strong enough, and there was no longer a place found for them in heaven [that is, the dragon and his angels], And the great dragon was thrown down (Revelation 12:7-9a).

John does not leave us to guess as to the identity of the "dragon" as he defines him to be:

The serpent of old who is called the devil, and [even] Satan, who deceives the whole world; he was thrown down to the earth, and his angels were thrown down with him (Revelation 12:9b-c).

At a certain point in history, therefore, still in the future, there is to be a cosmic battle between the forces of light and those of darkness. There will be no question as to the outcome inasmuch as it will be in the purposes of God to finally rid Satan and his forces from His presence. Once Satan and his hosts (Ephesians 6:12) are put out of Heaven and pushed to earth's domain, they will nevermore return to the heavens.

It comes as a surprise to some Christians that Satan does have access to the presence of God. But Scripture does point out this possibility without going into the details of explanation. Satan, in the presence of God, accused Job (Job 1:6-10; 2:1-4); Peter describes Satan as our adversary (1 Peter 5:8); and John indicates that one of the functions in which Satan engages is to be a deceiver, even in the presence of God. This activity by Satan will continue until the day when there is a divine show of force finally to oust Satan from the heavens. For this reason the heavens are told to rejoice (Revelation 12:12). At the same time, however, a warning is issued to those who live on earth:

Woe to the earth and the sea; because the devil has come down to you, having great wrath, knowing that he has only a short time (Revelation 12:12b).

When the Day of the Lord Commences. In this historical period yet to come, Satan has a number of activities, but for our purposes in this discussion concerning the day of the Lord, we shall limit ourselves to the experiences of Israel. We do want to see Satan's attitude to Israel as described by John:

And when the dragon saw that he was thrown down to the earth, he persecuted the woman [Israel] who gave birth to the male child. And the two wings of the great eagle were given to the woman, in order that she might fly into the wilderness to her place. . . . And the dragon was enraged with the woman (Revelation 12:13-14a, 17a).

Once he is thrown out from God's presence, Satan's special target of attack is Israel. All of Satan's fury is directed against God's special people, attempting to bring about their disappearance from the face of the earth. This action also gives us a clue as to the reason for the way Israel has suffered in the past. Many of the persecutions against Jewish people can be attributed to Satan working through ungodly people. But the special pressuring of Israel in the first part of the day of the Lord is because Israel's archenemy knows he has only a short time before his confinement. Satan will try to make God out to be a liar by destroying the presence of Israel. So many of the promises of God are related to Israel for the Messianic reign of Jesus, and if there is no Israel, then how can the promises be kept? The special strategy of Satan then is to make Israel his target. However, God's purposes are also served because it will be just this satanic strategy that will bring all Israel to the Lord.

Not only is Israel the target of attack, but believers in Israel are especially singled out!

And the dragon was enraged with the woman, and went off to make war with the rest of her offspring, who keep the commandments of God and hold to the testimony of Jesus (Revelation 12:17).

In Revelation 7 we shall note how one hundred forty-four thousand Israelis will become believers, but it will be their evangelistic ministry that will be responsible for thousands of other Israelis who will also find salvation. It will be these believers who will understand the strategy of Satan and seek to warn their countrymen. For this knowledge, and for the preaching of salvation, Satan will try his hardest to obliterate them.

The Time Period of the First Part of the Day. The establishment of the length of this pressuring of Israel is important since the existence of Israel is at stake. For how long does this rage with the woman (Israel) go on? The Apostle John indicates:

She [woman] was nourished for a time and times and half a time, from the presence of the serpent (Revelation 12:14b).

Again, we might be puzzled by John's reference to "time" and "times," and once again the Scripture itself gives us the clue for interpretation. We back up to verse 6 to note also that the woman (or Israel) seeks refuge in the wilderness for the reason described in verse 14:

And the woman fled into the wilderness where she had a place prepared by God, so that there she might be nourished for one thousand two hundred and sixty days (Revelation 12:6).

When describing the prophetic-day year in terms of days, the Scriptures use 360 days to the year. In applying the 360-day figure in relation to the 1,260 days of verse 6, we discover a time period of three-and-a-half years. This is the time length which helps us to understand the "time" of verse 14. We can now say that "time" refers to one year, "times" indicates the dual or two years, while "half a time" is one-half year. This totals three-and-a-half years. We can therefore conclude that the first part of the day, the time of darkness and pressuring for Israel, will be a period of three-and-a-half years. Satan will bring everything to bear in a time of horror against the Jewish people in Israel. But note that the starting point in history for this pressuring of Israel is still future, occurring only when Satan is thrown out of Heaven after a great cosmic battle. The following diagram, Figure 4, demonstrates the take-off of the prophetic day of the Lord from the Jewish twenty-four-hour day, and then ties this sequence to an actual future period of history.

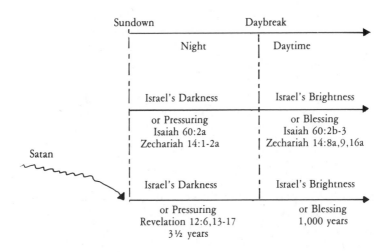

Figure 4—The Link Between the Jewish Twenty-Four-Hour Day, the Prophetic Day of the Lord, and Israel's Pressuring

Satan's Man and His Ultimate Authority. Now so far in Revelation we have been talking about symbols. How do we translate symbols into actual concrete situations? Satan is a spirit and to accomplish his work on earth he needs human instruments. The tragedy many times, however, is that Satan's human subjects are not even aware that they are his unwitting tools. We have to recognize that Satan, even today, has his principalities standing by the side of human leaders and influencing their decisions that are opposed to God's will. (See Daniel 10:13,20 which describes emissaries of Satan who influence earthly leaders, activities which lie within the permissive will of God.) Satan will certainly have his antichrist in the future to wreak havoc on mankind, and particularly Israel.

In Revelation 13:1-10, John describes some of the activity of the political antichrist. While we will speak more at length about this enemy of God in successive chapters, it is enough to indicate here that this political antichrist will eventually take the control of a revitalized Roman empire and then wield massive power and authority. But God will limit the time in which this evil person will operate. The Apostle John describes his character and power, but for our purposes now he also spells out the period of time of his activity:

And there was given to him a mouth speaking arrogant words and blasphemies; and authority to act for *forty-two months* was given to him (Revelation 13:5).

It is the time period that is interesting. How long is forty-two months? It adds up to three-and-a-half years in which the political antichrist will exercise his total power.

This dictator will not give believers any rest at all. John speaks of this future reign of terror which will be launched against God's own people:

And it was given to him to make war with the saints and to overcome them (Revelation 13:7a).

The believers living in this period are going to have a difficult time for effective testimony. Israel, as we have seen, is going to have a most difficult time, and many Israelis will die. But the believers in Israel will be a special target, and many of them, including many believers in the rest of the world, will perish as martyrs. One good reason why the saints are singled out is that they, of all people, will understand the true character of the antichrist and the purposes of Satan in using his man. When they try to expose the evil designs of Satan, the man of sin will be impelled to hunt down and kill them. But the most important aspect of antichrist's ministry is that he will be the human instrument for Israel's darkness and extreme pressuring. The time period for his total power will be limited to three-and-a-half years, when he reigns during the first part (darkness) of the day of the Lord. Satan will have his man, but praise the Lord, the time of horror will be a short, fixed one.

The Time Period Prior to the Day of the Lord. We need now to examine additional references to time periods in association with the day of the Lord so as to account for many prophetic events yet to occur. John again has predicted some of the events as well as time periods that figure so importantly in Israel's future:

And there was given me a measuring rod like a staff; and someone said, ''Rise and measure the temple of God, and the altar, and those who worship in it'' (Revelation 11:1).

The startling information is that John talks about a sanctuary which will already be in existence in this future historical period. It will be a place where religious Jewish people will be worshiping. This is not a reference to the temple which Jesus knew, since John wrote the book of Revelation at about 90-95 A.D., at least twenty years *after* the second temple was destroyed in 70 A.D. We shall be discussing further this temple and place of worship in chapter five, concerning Israel's experiences prior to the coming of Jesus the Messiah.

The point to make there is that Israel will have a sanctuary in a very strategic time period. John now adds:

And leave out the court which is outside the temple, and do not measure it, for it has been given to the nations; and they will tread under foot the holy city for *forty-two* months (Revelation 11:2).

In a vicelike control of Israel and Jerusalem, Israel will be pressured by blocs of nations. The control will be for a time period of three-and-a-half years, the time already mentioned in Revelation 13:5, and in Revelation 12:6,14. The political antichrist will be the leader who will desecrate the sanctuary and then tighten the noose around Israel's neck, and it will appear he will attempt ultimately to destroy God's people. But the Lord will not permit this total destruction.

Another time period which John mentions is also important:

And I will grant authority to my two witnesses, and they will prophesy for twelve hundred and sixty days, clothed in sackcloth (Revelation 11:3).

But immediately we have to ask ourselves a question, "Is the time period of forty-two months of verse 2 the same as the period of 1,260 days in verse 3?" Or, because of the difference in terminology, did John mean to distinguish between the periods? The only way to solve the problem is to examine the context in this chapter, and the identification of the witnesses becomes extremely important.

The world conditions in the period described here picture an extremely difficult situation for preaching the gospel message. In fact, drastic means have to be employed in order that this message of salvation might not be hindered:

And if anyone tries to harm them [the two witnesses], fire proceeds out of their mouth and devours their enemies; and if any one would desire to harm them, in this manner he must be killed (Revelation 11:5).

Preaching the gospel will be a frightful and dangerous experience, and believers will be special targets for persecution and execution. This is only one indication of the terror yet to come on the earth. I am not a gloom-and-doom type of person and always try to be positive; yet we need to pay special attention to what the Scripture says of future world conditions in a day of horror on earth. Yet I dare say this could be a day when multitudes will be saved in spite of all the satanic pressure against divine proclamation.

John provides us with a description of the functions of these witnesses, who are in reality the leaders of a world evangelization program.

These have the power to shut up the sky, in order that rain may not fall during the days of their prophesying; and they have power over the waters to turn them into blood, and to smite the earth with every plague, as often as they desire (Revelation 11:6).

The functions of ministry are quite descriptive and suggestive. Who once had the power to shut up the sky so that it did not rain? This certainly reminds us of the Prophet Elijah. Who was the individual who long ago had control over plagues to discomfit a people? We can hardly keep from thinking of the contests of Moses on behalf of God with the gods and goddesses of Egypt. Can we then say for sure that we positively identify the two witnesses as Elijah and Moses? This chapter in Revelation does not say so specifically, and herein lies our problem. It is always wise policy that if the Scripture does not identify and name the people it is talking about, then it is best not to read into the Word of God, unless we have good reason to do so.

But perhaps we can find reasons for making an identification. The Prophet Malachi does give us the clue, inasmuch as he was the last prophet before the four-hundred years of divine silence with Israel, the period between the closing of the Old Testament and the opening of the New Testament. The words of this prophet are actually the last prophetic message long before the days of Jesus the Messiah. What then can be the message of hope for a people before the Messiah was to come? Malachi's comments are interesting:

> Remember the law of Moses My servant, even the statutes and ordinances which I commanded him in Horeb for all Israel. Behold, I am going to send you *Elijah* the prophet *before* the coming of the great and terrible day of the LORD. And he will restore the hearts of the fathers to their children, and the hearts of the children to their fathers (Malachi 4:4-6).

Malachi declares that the prophet Elijah will yet return and have a preaching ministry among Israel. The effect will be to unite whole families as believers in a testimony concerning the coming of the Messiah, who will then institute the Messianic reign. This is the message of the Prophet Malachi as he sees it from the vantage point of his day.

However, from our day, we must keep in mind what happened in the coming of John the Baptist and Jesus the Messiah. Of John the Baptist, Jesus had described him as "Elijah who was to come" (Matthew 11:14). But we need to understand the meaning of and distinction in Jesus's words as he spoke of John the Baptist in the *spirit* of Elijah, and not actually of Elijah. There are two reasons why we take this view:

1. The presence of John the Baptist, performing many of the functions which Elijah was to do, became a testimony to Israel to identify the ministry of Jesus. In other words, John the Baptist became the test case of the seriousness of intentions of the people Israel concerning Jesus. If Jesus had been accepted and recognized by the nation as a whole, then God would have subsequently sent Elijah himself to continue the ministry as described by the Prophet Malachi. The fact that Israel's leadership did not recognize the claims of Jesus certainly did not thwart the purposes of God. John the Baptist, in the spirit of Elijah, still remains as a witness concerning Jesus as the Messiah.

2. From our view today we can see the truth of what Malachi was saying concerning the appearance of Elijah. If Israel had recognized Jesus, the day of the Lord would have taken place in the first century, many of the events alluded to above from the Scriptures would have happened then. The fact is that Israel, as a nation, did not see in Jesus the Messianic king; therefore all of the events of the day of the Lord, the appearance of a literal Elijah, etc., are all future from our view today. The significant key word for the arrival of Elijah is just *before* the terror of Israel is to be initiated. This would mean that the Old Testament prophet Elijah is to have a preaching ministry in a time period prior to Israel's darkness and pressuring, and consequently Elijah's coming is still future.

Now, as we return to Revelation 11:3, and from what we have discussed already, I am asserting that Elijah comes in a time period *before* the first part of the day of the Lord. This would mean that the time periods of Revelation 11:3 and 11:2 are *different*. Revelation 11:2 describes the first part of the day of the Lord when Israel will be pressured in the day of darkness. But Revelation 11:3 depicts a period of ministry by two witnesses, one of whom is Elijah, already pointed out by Malachi as having a specific leadership function before Israel's pressuring. Accordingly, Figure 5, gives us the relation of the time periods, a period prior to the day of the Lord, and the day of the Lord itself, and their setting in history in the future.

Figure 5—Israel's Pressuring and Period Before Her Pressuring

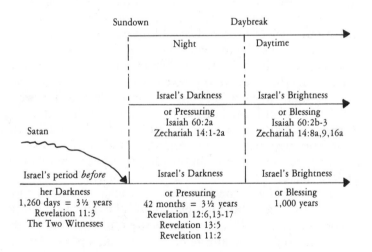

Something should be said regarding the second witness. While I feel that we have made a good case for one of these witnesses as Elijah, yet I think that we have no scriptural clue as to the identity of the second witness. I know the suggestions; e.g., 1, Moses, because of the description of the function, similar to that of Moses's ministry in pronouncing the plagues; or 2, Enoch, since both Enoch and Elijah did not actually die, then it is necessary for these two to actually return and die as human beings. But I must insist that the sure and safe guide to follow for the interpretation of Scripture is what the Scripture says of itself; therefore, if the Scripture is silent as to the identity of one of these witnesses, then we should be silent also. We should not identify in this instance Moses or Enoch on the basis of deductive reasoning.

It remains now to put together the events of these three-and-a-half-year time periods. The two three-and-a-half-year periods, adding up to one seven-year period, are in reality the seventieth week of Daniel. Daniel himself indicates that this period is divided into two three-and-a-half-year periods (Daniel 9:27). Both Daniel and John refer to some of the same events that occur in this seven-year period, and we shall refer to them in later chapters. However, by starting with John's instead of Daniel's descriptions of establishing the two three-and-a-half-year periods, we arrive at a clearer picture of how to put together the time periods and identify the events included in them. The additional information in Revelation 11—12 makes it easier to understand Daniel 9:27.

Figure 6 indicates the relationship of major events in connection with the tribulation period and the day of the Lord:

The point marked "today" in figure 6 is where we are at the present time. The rapture has not yet taken place, but we do feel it is near, as we shall point out in subsequent chapters in this book. As believers today, we look forward to the rapture, carefully explained in 1 Thessalonians 4:16-17. Those to be caught up in the rapture comprise the body of Christ: the dead in Christ, and we who are alive and remain. My position

Figure 6—The Tribulation Period, Daniel's Seventieth Week and the Day of the Lord

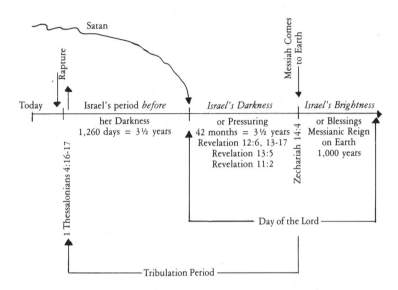

of the rapture as it is explained here, that is, prior to the period of the tribulation, will be discussed further in chapter eight. But it is necessary to distinguish between a return of Christ in two steps: 1, when He comes to take His body; and 2, when He returns to earth to institute the fullness of His kingdom. Now, once the rapture occurs, God turns to Israel again, and believers among Israel will spearhead one of the greatest movements of world evangelization. God is today fashioning Israel for this effort, as we shall be discussing these in chapters three and seven. This great drive to reach the nations of the earth will continue all through the ''before'' period, that is prior to the first part of the day of the Lord.

When we come to the midpoint of the tribulation period, Satan is thrown down to earth after a great cosmic battle, and then there commences the darkness of the day of the Lord, and the first part of that ''day.'' Israel is pressured by the nations in what Jeremiah referred to as the experience of Jacob's trouble (Jeremiah 30:7). The pressuring ceases only when Israel calls for divine help in her hour of greatest trial. It is at this point that Jesus the Messiah returns to earth to begin the redemption of the remnant of the people of Israel (Zechariah 14:4). With Him also come the hosts of the Lord (Revelation 19:11f), as well as the body of Christ. Only then can the brightness of the day of the Lord begin, lasting for one thousand years, and in the second part of the day, this time period will contain the greatest and most blessed experiences for man on this planet.

The One Thousand Years of Messianic Blessing

I have made the statement that the brightness of the day of the Lord is to be a literal one thousand years in length. Obviously not all Christians will understand it in this way. Amillennial scholars have insisted that the ''thousand years'' are not to be taken literally. Their view of the coming of Christ marks the point when the kingdom of this world will become the kingdom of Christ, who will then reign forever and ever (Revelation 11:15). Christ's kingdom is seen as eternal, and the amillennialist will not admit any limited literal thousand-year glorious kingdom on earth as a substitute.

The premillennialist does not deny an eternal kingdom of God and His Messiah in a new heavens and new earth. But there are many passages of Scripture which, if taken literally, do speak of a period when Christ reigns supreme on this earth as a kind of *introduction* to His eternal kingdom. The point that I am raising is that we need to see how John in the book of Revelation *understood* this phrase which he used: one thousand years for the reign of Christ (Revelation 20:2-7). Did he intend it to mean a literal one thousand years, or did he mean an indefinite period of time?

I am insisting that the only way to indicate what John meant is to examine the *usage* of "one thousand years" in the Jewish backgrounds. After all, God does reveal Himself through the culture of a people, and this includes even the usage and understanding of language. It so happens that there are a number of passages in the so-called "outside literature" of the Jewish people, principally in the pseudepigraphical books of the first century B.C., which do use this particular phrase of "one thousand years." These passages give us the clue for understanding the meaning of the time period.

The most important passages for our consideration are found in *2 Enoch* and *Jubilees*. One of these is:

And I blessed the seventh day, which is the Sabbath, on which He rested from all His works. And I appointed the eighth day also, that the eighth day should be the first created after my work, and that the first seven revolve in the form of the seven thousand, and that at the beginning of the eighth thousand there should be a time of not counting, endless, with neither years nor months nor weeks nor days nor hours (2 Enoch 32:2—33:2).

This means that even before the first century A.D., a literal one thousand years had come to be regarded as one world day. There was the conception of a world week of seven thousand years. Six thousand years describe the period including creation and the history of man until the judgment of the nations. Then there follows a period of one thousand years of blessedness and rest.

The book of *Jubilees* also adds that those born at the period of the commencement of the Messianic kingdom will have their days lengthened to one thousand years:

And in those days the children shall begin to study the laws, and to seek the commandments, and to return to the path of righteousness. And the days shall begin to grow many and increase amongst those children of men till their days draw nigh to one thousand years, and to a greater number of years than before was the number of days (Jubilees 23:26-27).

Jubilees furthermore describes, in a different approach, the understanding of this issue of one thousand years:

Adam died . . . and . . . he lacked seventy years of one thousand years; for one thousand years are as one day in the testimony of the heavens and therefore was it written concerning the tree of knowledge; "On the day that you eat thereof you shall die." For this reason he did not complete the years of this day; for he died during it (Jubilees 4:29-30).

The point here is that while Adam lived for 930 years (Genesis 5:3,5), yet he is regarded as not living out his "world day," or one thousand years.

The apocalyptic books use this concept of the duration of the Messianic kingdom quite often, likening the thousand years to a day, so that this period is to be understood as a literal thousand years. This time usage was a part of the thinking of many Jewish people at that time and they had a familiarity with this concept of the thousand-year world day. I am saying, therefore, that John's usage in Revelation 20 merely reflected this widely-known phrase among Jewish people. He understood the thousand years in a literal sense and meant it to be so considered when talking about the length of the Messianic kingdom, particularly as the Spirit of God led the apostle to choose the material for this purpose. The second part of the day of the Lord is to be understood, therefore, as one thousand years.

Obviously we have not detailed all the great events that shall happen during the tribulation period and the Messianic reign. However, I have felt that the events cannot be properly understood and placed until we have a proper concept of the prophetic day of the Lord. In the following chapters I shall deal more at length with these prophetic events in connection with the day of the Lord. Once this key for the sequence of prophetic events is understood, the Bible student will have a good grasp of their timing.

3

GOD AT WORK IN MODERN ISRAEL

Dream and deed are not as different as many think. All
the deeds of men are dreams at first.   Herzl

In the closing days of the Yom Kippur War of October
1973, Israel was made an offer which she could not refuse. In
order to stop the fighting, the superpowers—the United
States and the Soviet Union—made possible the meeting of
Israeli and Arab leaders, a possibility that Israelis had desired
for a quarter of a century since 1948 when Israel became a
state. But there was a gloomy apprehension on the part of all
the parties in the Middle East as to whether this face-to-face
assembly could ever take place. The Arab leaders met in
Algiers in November 1973 and issued a number of statements, one of which was the assertion that they would indeed
choose security over peace rather than peace without security.
This means that unless "full national rights for the Palestinian people" be reestablished (meaning an Arab binational state in Palestine where the Jew is only one of many
people), then the Arab peoples "will not cease intensifying
the struggle."

History now records that the foreign ministers of Arab
states and Israel actually began their sessions in Geneva in
December 1973 under the sponsorship of the two superpowers. The progress of diplomacy led to disengagement of
forces of the war, and the leaders of the Middle Eastern nations started to tread gingerly the road which hopefully will
lead to peace, although there have been many setbacks.

Then in November 1977 Anwar Sadat, president of Egypt,
during the wearying process of finding proper formulas for
peace between Israel and its Arab neighbors, made a statement that he would even go to Israel to lay his burden before
the Israeli *knesset* (parliament) if it would take that step to
move the peace efforts along. Once before, in 1971, Sadat
had made such an offer when Golda Meir was prime minister

of Israel, but Israel's "mother" (as she was affectionately called by her people) didn't take the offer seriously; and neither did Sadat pursue with real interest his offer. But in 1977 Menachem Begin, then prime minister of Israel, responded with an invitation to come. In shortly under a half hour, Sadat left on a trip that had not been possible for some twenty-nine years. Israelis were dumbfounded by this turn of events which clearly signaled that there were people in the states of the Middle East who were ready to recognize the existence of the State of Israel. The world watched in amazement with this new turn in diplomacy where before there had been only harsh, abrasive words and military action. Israelis were raising the question continually, "Could there be a possibility of peace now?"

The Difficulties of Achieving Peace

I feel I need to provide some background for our reader concerning the relationship between the Israeli Jews and Palestinian Arabs (particularly those who moved during 1947-1948 from Israel because of the United Nations designated area for Israel in 1947). More Palestinian Arabs moved again from the Israeli-held territories because of the 1967 Six Day War. There is no attempt here to try to solve the difficult position of the relationship, but we can possibly set forth the problems that exist between the two peoples, Israeli concerns, and Palestinians' aspirations.

The Palestine Liberation Organization, representing some six or seven subgroups of Palestinian Arabs (both Muslim and Christian), has developed a position paper called "The Palestinian National Covenant," a document which represents their aims as a people. (See the magazine *Commentary,* January 1975, "The Palestinians and the PLO" for a discussion by Bernard Lewis, about the Palestinians as well as a copy of the covenant.) The present wording of the covenant was finally developed on July 10-17, 1968, after the Six Day War in 1967. The covenant consists of thirty-three articles and represents the specific position taken by many Arab people when Israel was founded as a state in 1948. Syria, Iraq, Libya, and South Yemen support the position of the statement by the Palestinians who make up the Palestine Liberation Organization.

Three articles which spell out some deep concerns are important for our purpose. First, Article 19 states:

The partitioning of Palestine in 1947 and the establishment of Israel are entirely illegal, regardless of the passage of time, because they were contrary to the will of the Palestinian people and to their natural right in their homeland and inconsistent with the principles embodied in the charter of the United Nations, particularly the right to self-determination.

Secondly, Article 20 says:

The Balfour Declaration, the Mandate for Palestine, and everything that has been based upon them, are deemed null and void. Claims of historical or religious ties of Jews with Palestine are incompatible with the facts of history and the true conception of what constitutes statehood. Judaism, being a religion, is not an independent nationality. Nor do Jews constitute a single nation with an identity of its own; they are citizens of the states to which they belong.

Thirdly, Article 6 adds:

The Jews who had normally resided in Palestine until the beginning of the Zionist invasion will be considered Palestinians.

In the last statement, the phrase ''Zionist invasion'' refers to the time of the Balfour Declaration, i.e., 1917, although some Palestinians will peg the date at 1947, the time of the partition of the land by the United Nations.

These articles of the covenant explain some of the state of conditions between Israel and the Arab states and Palestinian Arabs ever since 1948, the founding of the state. The covenant position means that its Arab supporters will not rest until the Jewish state is dismantled and in its place an Arab binational state will come into being. It is no wonder that, in the light of this position, Israel feels threatened as a state and has determined she will not yield her sovereignty. One must also recognize that for centuries Jewish people have been pressured and have suffered much. The holocaust (the death of the six million) in this century alone did something to the Jewish psyche so that Jews are understandably jittery in the face of a determined position that seeks to finish off the Jewish state once and for all. This had been the state of affairs until November 1977 when Sadat announced his intention to go to Jerusalem.

A Solution through Diplomacy. President Sadat of Egypt in 1977 articulated a moderate stance on the part of many Arabs toward the State of Israel. Until Sadat's official articulation, Arabs with moderate views had been fearful of championing a position contrary to the Palestine Liberation Organization covenant. Sadat was forthright and courageous to indicate that he for one would recognize the accomplished state of affairs: the State of Israel. As far as he was concerned, he was willing to realize the established fact that Israel is a reality and is in the Middle East to stay.

For the willingness to recognize the State of Israel, Sadat obviously wanted something in return. His position was that the Arab peoples on the West Bank and Gaza Strip be given the privilege to organize a state that will legitimately recognize the rights of the Palestinian Arabs. In the face of the requests by the president of Egypt, it seemed only fair that Israel should yield on this point. However, nothing is simplistic in the Middle East. The reality that Israel faces is the position of the covenant of the PLO.

In December 1977 Israel and Egypt began to conduct a number of consultations to effect a peace settlement between Israel and Egypt and also to bring some sort of a solution of the Palestine Arab situation. After many fluctuations, President Carter of the United States called President Sadat and Prime Minister Begin to the United States in an all-out attempt to stem the tide of a complete breakdown in the negotiations between Israel and Egypt. The Camp David Accord, signed in the Spring 1979, called for an ultimate cessation of hostilities between Israel and Egypt, the exchange of ambassadors between the two countries, and the gradual yielding of the Sinai by Israel to the established international borders between Israel and Egypt. These two states, along with the United States, were then to continue the negotiations concerning the future of the West Bank and the Gaza Strip. Depending, however, on the resultant agreements between Israel and Egypt, Israel was to enter further into negotiations with Egypt to effect a solution for the Palestinian Arabs of the West Bank and Gaza Strip.

After Camp David. It is not possible to go into the many ramifications of the Camp David Accord of 1979 and the subsequent negotiations between Israel and Egypt to effect some kind of settlement for the Palestinian Arabs. It appears that two general views have emerged within the Israeli frame of thinking.

Autonomy Plan. The first of these is held by Prime Minister Begin and others who support his position. Once the autonomy plan has been accepted by Israelis and Palestinian Arabs, then the latter for five years in the West Bank and Gaza Strip are to have full control in their areas. According to this plan, the Palestinian Arabs of these areas, represented by from eleven to fifteen ministers, can support their own school systems, maintain their own security forces, have their own parliament, and all that is involved in the control by a separate people. The only stipulation for these five years is that Israel should retain the right to ultimate security should the police force of the Arabs break down, or should there be any further difficulties in the broader picture of relationships between other states of the Middle East.

After the five-year period, according to the autonomy plan, arrangements will then be made for the Palestinian Arabs of the West Bank and the Gaza Strip, along with representatives of Israel, Egypt, and Jordan, to enter into negotiations as to what shall be the future of the areas.

Quite understandably, the Palestine Liberation Organization people outside of Israel and the West Bank, and the PLO supporters within the West Bank are unhappy with autonomy. What they wish is full statehood and a full recognition of Palestinian rights. They do not want Israelis to settle in the West Bank and create Jewish settlements. To them, autonomy is a factor which does not recognize their statehood.

In reply, however, by Israelis to the Palestinian Arab objections to autonomy is the cold, hard fact of the covenant of the PLO. Israel lives with the dangers posed by the statements of the covenant. Suppose the Israelis, as they point out, should permit the creation of a third state in the region, comprising three states: Israel, a Palestinian state, and Jordan. But as long as the covenant remains in force, Israel has indicated that it will be extremely difficult if not next to impossible to permit the existence of a third state of Palestinian Arabs. "What is to prevent," say the Israelis, "the leadership of the PLO (living mostly in Lebanon and Syria) from moving into such a third state? From then on, it would be an intensified effort on the part of those who support the covenant, with Soviet influence, to try and realize their goals of dismantling the Jewish state." So autonomy appears to be stalemated for the time being, while the PLO who support the covenant are certainly not quiet about what they want.

The Two-State Reality. The second position held by many Israelis, principally those of the Alignment, the opposition party to Begin's Coalition, is to establish a two-state reality in the region: Israel, and a *union* of the West Bank and Gaza Strip with Jordan. With minor variations, a number of Israelis in the alignment camp support a position set forth by former Prime Minister Yitzhak Rabin in his *Rabin Memoirs* (Little Brown, 1979). Rabin points out that 90 percent of all Palestine Arabs live in the West Bank, Gaza Strip, and the State of Jordan. For this reason he argues it would be most natural to create a second state besides Israel, and he feels this is the most viable approach to the solution of the problem. Rabin states that the 90 percent of Palestine Arabs comprising such a state would be a good counterbalance to the remaining 10 percent of Palestine Arabs who live in Lebanon and Syria and make up the major core of those who support the covenant. The only stipulation, according to Rabin, is that Israel's areas be secured, possibly guaranteed by other major powers, once an agreement is implemented.

The key, however, is the reality of the covenant of the PLO. No amount of persuasion by various pressure groups will change the covenant unless the PLO leadership, in writing, guarantees Israel's right to exist. Only then can an Israeli two-state view be viable. But there is another problem. The Palestinian Arab who wants an Arab secular state will not agree to be subservient to the king of Jordan in a monarchy. Monarchies can represent political regression and the Palestinian Arab does not want it. So, we are back to the PLO idea of the covenant which calls for a Palestinian state from the Jordan River to the Mediterranean (see Figure 8), and obviously Israel will not agree to its own demise. We seem to reach an impasse once again.

Egypt After the Death of Sadat. Tragically, President Anwar Sadat was killed on October 6, 1981 while reviewing a parade of Egyptian troops. Without warning, several supposedly loyal Egyptian soldiers veered off from the main parade and as they were running toward the reviewing stand they began firing, with the deadly intent to kill Sadat. These soldiers represented the view that the Camp David agreement was a mistake and, acting on behalf of many like-minded Arab peoples, they took matters in their own hands to put Sadat to death. Ironically, Sadat died on the very date of the anniversary of the beginning of the 1973 war with Israel, October 6, 1873. I shall not make any further comment except that it does appear strange that Sadat died on this very date.

What will now happen to Egypt's participation in the Camp David agreement and the continuation of the peace process with Israel, as well as the direction of the talks between Egypt and Israel concerning the West Bank? Sadat's successor, Hosni Mubarak, is certainly not a Sadat; yet he had been groomed by Sadat to succeed him in the presidency of Egypt. However, already by February 1982 it has become somewhat clear concerning the course Mubarak will take. He certainly is committed to the Camp David agreement whereby by the end of April 1982, Egypt will repossess the entire Sinai Peninsula, up to the international recognized border between her and Israel. An attempt has been made by the United States to hasten the understanding between Israel and Egypt regarding the autonomy for the West Bank and Gaza Strip but no finalization of talks has been arrived at between Egypt and Israel by spring 1982. It is, as we have already noted, very difficult for Egypt to speak for the Palestinian Arabs on the West Bank; so the matter of any understanding at this point is held in abeyance.

But in addition, other trends already appear as to Mubarak's position in the post-Sadat era. The new president clearly wants Egypt's links reestablished with the rest of the Arab world. During Sadat's regime, after the ratification of the Camp David agreement, the Egyptian press had mounted an attack on other Arab nations which refused to go along with and were so opposed to this agreement. One of Mubarak's first actions was to stop the Egyptian press from these attacks. He has also reopened the border between Egypt and Libya, which had been closed by Sadat because of the acrimonious relations between him and Qaddafi. The change at the border is a further sign that Mubarak wants some kind of understanding between himself and Qaddafi, although no further word yet has come concerning the tightening of the links between these two countries.

In addition, Mubarak also wants closer links to the Muslim world as well as the African states. It appears that the new president does not want to isolate himself by taking too much of a pro-United States stand, whereby he will have no rapport between himself and other African countries. Mubarak has also recalled Soviet technicians which Sadat had put out of the country; from this move it would appear that the new president also wants some ties with the Soviet Union. He does desire to continue the prowestern stance which Sadat opened up, but clearly from the trends observed already it appears that Mubarak wants Egypt committed to a broad relationship with many peoples. We might say that his position is a pragmatic one and that he does not want to be linked to any one major power or major cause. It would seem that Egypt has achieved what it wanted in receiving back occupied Sinai, and then in the future a course will be charted for the best national interests of the Egyptians. Hopefully, links will continue to be established between Israel and Egypt, and some evidences are already in progress regarding commerce and cultural exchanges. But the normalization process will take a long time before the two countries will feel completely at ease and comfortable with each other.

Saudi Arabia. On August 7, 1981, Saudi Arabian Crown Prince Fahd Bin Abd al Aziz granted an interview to the Saudi news agency SNA in which he proposed eight "guidelines toward a just settlement" in the Middle East. Saudi Arabia, because of its more vocally moderate stance as a contrast to the rejectionist Arab nations, has attempted to provide an alternative to the Camp David agreement whereby the Palestinian Arabs could have a state of their own. The Saudis clearly felt that the Camp David pact is a failure in solving the Israel-Arab problem. The alternative includes this eight-point peace plan:

1. The withdrawal of Israel from all Arab lands as of 1967, including Arab Jerusalem.

2. The removal of settlements established by Israel in Arab lands after 1967.

3. Security of the freedom of worship and religious rites for all

religions in the holy places.

4. Confirmation of the right for the Palestinian people to return, and compensation for those who opt not to do so.

5. The West Bank and Gaza Strip will be subject to a transitional period under the supervision of the United Nations, for a period not exceeding a few months.

6. The establishment of an independent Palestinian state with Jerusalem as its capital.

7. Confirmation of the right of the countries of the region to live in peace.

8. The United Nations or some of its members shall guarantee the implementation of these principles.

What is interesting was Sadat's analysis of the plan on August 9, 1981 in "Meet the Press" (NBC TV) when he declared: "Unfortunately, Fahd didn't add anything new. . . . I should like to have him share and contribute rather than adopting the old ways which I don't agree to at all and I reject."

What is distressing about the eight-point peace plan is that point seven does not mention Israel at all and gives the Saudis the opportunity to exclude Israel because it does not recognize Israel as an independent state. In connection with the lack of recognition, neither is there any statement regarding the United Nations resolutions 242 and 338 that imply recognition and which also call for Arab—Israel peace negotiations. What is also apparent is that points five and six do not address themselves to Israel at all; there is simply the machinery to establish the Palestinian state under the auspices of the United Nations. The fact remains that, after one studies the eight-point plan, and keeping in mind the long history of the Arab program for eliminating Israel in stages, one begins to wonder whether the Saudis have anything to say regarding the State of Israel.

The nations of Western Europe have strongly urged further discussions regarding the plan and the United States also in a hesitant way suggested some kind of discussion regarding the points among all of the nations in the Middle East region. Accordingly King Hassan II called for a summit meeting in

November 1981 in Fez, Morocco. *Time* Magazine, December 7, 1981, describes the meeting:

> It began as an unprecedented effort to forge Arab unity. . . . It ended after five and a half hours of bickering . . . which . . . undermined the prestige of the Royal House of Saud, which had striven mightily to bring the conclave to a successful outcome.

The rejectionist states were so bitter about this plan, on which they felt there was some kind of a veiled recognition of the State of Israel, that they would have nothing to do with the eight-point so-called peace plan. What is interesting is that within a day or so after the meeting in Fez, the foreign minister of Saudi Arabia denied the plan itself. But he spoke in Arabic, which obviously was designed as news for nations in the Arab world; he did not speak in English, for the benefit of the western world, and it seems that there is a double design to try and cool the passions in the Arab world while signaling to the western world, because Arabic was not understood, that the plan is still on.

What is significant is not what people say but what they do. The Saudis support the PLO in their desire for a Palestinian state. But once again, on what basis can there be a Palestinian state apart from the covenant of the PLO? No other plan has been forthcoming. The only understanding the Israelis have is that the way to have an Arab-Palestinian state is at the expense of the State of Israel. What is more, the Saudis, because of their huge oil revenues, have supported the PLO in the hopes of implementing such a state.

Is it any wonder therefore that Israel views with the greatest of alarm an implementation of this eight-point peace plan? Peace can come between Israel and its Arab neighbors only when all recognize each other, respect each other, put aside personal interests, and try to come to an agreement mutually acceptable through the democratic process. An agreement never will come when nations dictate to one another, which does not allow for any overlap of interests whereby a peace process can begin. The situation in the Middle East will never find a solution which calls for the cessation of Israel as a state.

Even though the United Nations General Assembly voted in April 1982 that the Palestinian Arabs must have a homeland, yet it cannot be at the expense of Israel's existence as a state.

The Golan Heights and Syria. I have been asked many times since December 14, 1981 why Israel annexed the Golan Heights (see Figure 11 and the short comment there regarding this area). At least, this is what the news media had reported. However, this is *not* what took place when the Israeli knesset vote affected the people living in the Golan Heights region. The Israeli vote had to do with the repeal of military law (1969—1981) and the shift to Israeli civilian law, and its administration and jurisdiction that would apply to the Israelis who are living there in their settlements, along with some twelve thousand Druze (Arabs who are not Muslims) and some three hundred Syrian Muslims. What this means is that, whereas the Palestinian Arabs on the West Bank can appeal to Jordanian law, the inhabitants on the Golan Heights will be covered by Israeli law. Citizenship was even offered to the twelve thousand Druze but this was not accepted, by and large; these people have many relatives living in other parts of Syria and it would not have gone well with their kin because of Syrian repercussion and reprisal for Druze who would become Israeli citizens.

Some might say that this is just some play on semantics and that Israeli designs are to annex the Golan Heights. In no way is this the case, but the other Arab countries have called for a meeting of the United Nations Security Council so as either to condemn Israel or even try to vote Israel out of the United Nations for the charge of Israeli "annexation of the Golan Heights." But again, the Israeli decision was only with regard to people living in the territory and had nothing to do with the land itself. At any time in the future when it will occur, Israel is still open to negotiation with regard to the Golan Heights, even though this may be very difficult.

The Golan Heights is a very small territory, about forty-five miles long and from fifteen to twenty miles wide. Prior to the 1967 War the Syrians had heavily armed the rim overlooking the Sea of Galilee and the Huleh Valley just to the north of the sea. From that vantage point Israelis were fired upon, time and time again, and many lost their lives in the settlements and in the fields. Israel does not want to return to the pre-1967 situation where this harrassment can start all over again. However, if Syria will recognize Israel's right to exist, then an understanding can come about, even as it was done between Israel and Egypt.

The history between Syria and Israel has been a long hard excruciating one that dates back even to Old Testament times when Syria and Israel fought each other, and also to the time when Syria had actually captured Israel (198 B.C.) and Antiochus Epiphanes had desecrated the altar (167 B.C.) in Jerusalem. Syrian statements regarding Israel since 1948, and particularly since 1967, have been so bitter and so caustic that Israel takes the statements seriously and wants to guard its sovereignty with the greatest care possible until the day when negotiations are possible.

The Realities of Prophecy. Regardless of how we may discuss the political implications of the needs of Israelis and Palestinian Arabs, we must also recognize the fact that there is a divine interest in the peoples of the Middle East and particularly those of the State of Israel. My wife and I have lived in Israel every summer since 1968. We were in Israel also for almost seven months in 1973, including the period of the Yom Kippur War, and we watched at close hand the events of that war. In all this time in Israel we have had opportunity to talk with scores of people, lay as well as key people, Arabs as well as Jews. As students of the Scriptures, and in contact with the people in Israel, we have had time to think again and again of how God is very definitely at work in modern Israel.

From our reflections, I want to assert that the presence of today's Israelis compels our acknowledgment that God is engaged in a very unique movement of Jews in the modern period so as to accomplish His purpose regarding His people Israel.

Two distinctives emerge to emphasize this unique work of

God. The first one to indicate how God is at work in modern Israel points to:

The Providential Circumstances in Modern History. Some twenty-seven hundred years ago one of the eighth century B.C. prophets had declared:

> For the sons of Israel will remain for many days without king or prince, without sacrifice or sacred pillar, and without ephod or teraphim. Afterward the sons of Israel will return and seek the LORD their God and David their king; and they will come trembling to the LORD and to His goodness in the last days (Hosea 3:4-5).

By no means is this verse to be confined only to the regathering from the exile in Babylon. From our vantage point today concerning Judah, which has been without king or prince since the Babylonian exile because Jeremiah said of the kingly line of Judah in the early 500s B.C.: "No man of his descendants will prosper, sitting on the throne of David or ruling again in Judah" (Jeremiah 22:30). Judah's throne of David has officially been empty from the end of the first commonwealth of Israel in 586 B.C. until today. That is why during the second commonwealth of Israel, 536 B.C. to 70 A.D., the high priests of Israel, while serving as the priestly representatives, also served as the regal heads of the nation.

From our view today also, while Judah had a second temple with its altar during the second commonwealth, yet that temple was tragically lost in 70 A.D. and for some nineteen hundred years Jewish people have had no legitimate Levitical sacrifice on their behalf nor an altar on which to place the sacrifice. Jewish worship was restructured during the period of 70-90 A.D., to become a religion without a temple and with no sacrifices.

Hosea also made reference to the ephod and teraphim. The former refers to the peculiar garment worn by the high priest on the many occasions of his ministry, while the latter term represents some aspect of prophetic guidance. While Judah had a priestly ministry and a prophetical message after the Babylonian exile and during the first century A.D., yet the nation has not had a Levitical high priest and has not heard the fresh voice of a prophet for almost two thousand years. The prophet speaks meaningfully and descriptively concerning Israel after the flesh in the long night of her wandering experience.

But Hosea also held out *hope.* He states unequivocally (Hosea 3:5) that "afterward the sons of Israel will return." However, here we must ask ourselves an important question. Will this return be represented only by some cataclysmic deliverance, or does this return take place within the development of the providential circumstances of God? Rabbis, and even some Christians, are divided on their answers. Some rabbis insist that when Messiah will come the State of Israel will be established, all Jewish people will be miraculously drawn together, and the kingdom will be instituted. Other Jewish religious leaders insist that man must have his part in the establishment of the state, working in harmony with the purposes of God. In our position, we assert that God someday in the near future will cataclysmically bring this age to an end; by the visible demonstration of His might and power, He will institute the fullness of the kingdom over which David's greater son will reign.

But we must face up to a common failure of which we are too often guilty, and that is to think in terms of God's working only in the cataclysmic event. We therefore very easily overlook the providence of God working quietly in and through the events of human history. This is especially true concerning the establishment of modern Israel, but before we show the providential work of God for modern Israel, let us notice such an example on behalf of Israel in the past.

An Ancient Example of God's Providence. When God delivered Israel from ancient Egypt, believers for the most part think only in terms of the great exodus event when God opened the Sea of Reeds (the Red Sea) so the people could escape as on dry ground. But did not God work in time prior to the exodus to prepare for it? He certainly did, and we can point to at least three areas of divine activity.

First, over a period of time there was a miraculous population explosion of Israelites, in spite of the Egyptian edict of race genocide. Regardless of the ethical problem posed by the replies of the midwives to the Egyptian pharaoh (Exodus 1:19-21), God protected and also multiplied the numbers of the Hebrew slaves. I imagine Moses must have chuckled to himself years later when he wrote this account. God wanted a burgeoning population when Israel was ready to leave Egypt, and He used faithful women as midwives to nullify the wishes of the king of Egypt!

Secondly, in another work of God long before the exodus event, the Egyptian pharaoh of the oppression had moved his armies into Canaan to crack the defenses of the Canaanite city states, and made them subservient to and dependent upon Egypt. This happened almost a hundred years before the Israelites even entered Canaan land. When Joshua with the Israelites later took Jericho and then was poised on his military campaign to conquer Canaan, the city states in the land really needed help in the face of an impending attack. The people in Canaan feared the Israelites because they still remembered the great exodus event, forty years after it happened, and they were aware of what had occurred more recently at the Jordan River when it parted to let the Israelites cross (Joshua 2:9-11). There is actually an archeological record in the El Amarna tablets, dated at about 1400-1375 B.C., where the kings of the states in Canaan asked for help from Egypt because of the *habiru* who had entered the land.[1] The term *habiru* is generally understood as invaders, and this conceivably can be a description of the Israelites who entered to conquer the land. But the divine providence of God in the Egyptian military action in Canaan, long before Joshua and his armies ever arrived there, made the work of later conquest by Israel just that much easier.

The third area of divine activity in the past was the gracious intervention in the life of Moses. For eighty years, forty years in the education in Egypt's schools, and for another forty in the education of the "knifing of a soul" in the desert, Moses

[1]"The Amarna Letters, EA, 271, 286-89." J. B. Pritchard, ed., *Ancient Near Eastern Texts* (Princeton, New Jersey: Princeton University Press, 1955), pp. 486-489.

was readied for his task of leadership. God worked in his life to prepare him for the responsibility of leading Israel out of Egypt, guiding them to the promised land, but more importantly, molding a slave people under God's direction into the mindset of free people.

A Modern Providential Work. Can we not see through all of these circumstances that for over a hundred years, quietly and surely, God was providentially working in the many details of history which finally led to the cataclysmic event of the exodus? But God has been working likewise for over a hundred years to bring Israel to the place where she is today in the land of Israel. And the process is not over yet, by any means. Let us note only a few significant movements, dates, and circumstances in the modern sense.

1. In 1860 a few people moved out of the Old City of Jerusalem and began a very small settlement just outside the western walls. A windmill was constructed for the purpose of pumping water, but it never did work! One can see the windmill today as a symbol of a vision for the modest beginning of the modern city of new, or west Jerusalem.

2. The first agricultural school was established in 1869-1870 in the land of Israel, representing the first attempt in modern times to encourage Jewish people in a back-to-the-land movement. This concern for working the land was vision with far-reaching implications because, as Jewish people were to come from the ghetto, there would be resources that would make possible the transforming of the then arid desert and wasted homeland into a fertile productive land.

3. In the 1870s and 1880s Jewish people suffered much in the persecutions in Eastern Europe, and great numbers began their emigration to the New World. But at the same time, because of a number of essays and books written by Jewish people who sought to explore solutions concerning the desperate plight of their brethren, a new hope was expressed that called for a homeland on the ancient soil of their forefathers. As a result, with no real wide organizational backing except for regional interest groups in Eastern Europe,

these "lovers of Zion" started a trickle of Jewish immigration to the land of Israel. They took the name *Bilu* which is an acrostic of Hebrew words that stand for: "House of Jacob, come ye and let us go." This was the beginning of the first *aliya* or immigration wave in modern times. There are communities in Israel today which are almost a hundred years old, dating back to when this first movement of Jewish people returned to the land of Israel.

When the first immigrants arrived, they did not come to plush farms, developed vineyards, and productive orange orchards. Rather, most of the land bought from the Arabs was sand dunes and swamps. But these immigrants broke their backs to clear the swamps and flatten the sand dunes for farms and orchards. Many died from malaria in draining the swamps and others left because the work was so difficult. An idealism for living in Israel had to be transformed into a hard resolve that, come what may, there would be a willingness to pay the price to make the homeland a reality. Those who remained sank their stakes down deep enough, in a sense, to prepare for future immigration waves to come.

So, there began a process that would lead to a miracle. After all, what did Jewish people know about farming, coming out of the ghettos of Europe? Life in the confined quarters of ghettos was a grinding and difficult round of poverty as they tried to make a living from their menial tasks. Could these people become successful agriculturalists? History now indicates that Israelis are some of the best and most knowledgeable experts in agriculture in all the world. But what is even more important is that, as the new immigrants began to transform the land, a people also was transformed. A new breed of Jewish person was in the making: his mindset was altered in moving from the ghetto to the soil of the homeland where he once again could live in his own country.

4. The next move of great importance was the lifework of Theodor Herzl. Working as a correspondent for a Viennese newspaper, he covered the Dreyfus trial in Paris in 1894. Dreyfus was a captain in the French army, and he was ac-

cused of selling state secrets to the German government, obviously regarded as a crime against the French state. But the real problem was that he was Jewish! He was court-martialed in a court drama charged with emotion, reflecting the rise of a virulent anti-Jewishness in the country. Subsequently he was stripped of his rank and sent to Devil's Island for life. It took a number of years and the persuasive pen of Emile Zola in his *J'Accuse* (I Accuse) in 1898 before the evidence was gathered that condemned the captain's court-martial as a gross mistrial. Dreyfus was brought back, pardoned, and permitted to rejoin the French army where he served with distinction.

This whole affair, however, changed Herzl profoundly. It was clear that in a land that had championed liberty, equality, fraternity there was little or no justice for the Jew by elements in the state, and that, under the right circumstances, responsible men in high places were not averse to gross anti-Jewishness. Herzl felt that, with this expression of inhumanity in the degradation of the Jewish person in the European west in one of its best expressions of humanism, there was no more future for the Jewish person in the West. His book, *The Jewish State* (1896), and the first Zionist congress in Basel (1897) started a movement which is a very important circumstance in the providence of God. This author stood one afternoon in the square in front of the Opera Hall in Basel, Switzerland, and reflected on the idea that from this place at the first Zionist congress Herzl had declared, "In Basel, I founded the Jewish state," and "in five years, perhaps, and certainly in fifty, everyone will see it." He spoke as a prophet, for within almost fifty years there was a Jewish state!

5. In spite of the great difficulties that followed in successive meetings of Zionist congresses on making the Israel homeland a reality, the circumstances of providence became more evident. The Zionist congresses which met year after year encouraged emigration and from 1904-1914, there was a second wave of emigrants out of Eastern Europe. These were hardy pioneers, fiercely dedicated to the rebuilding of the

land of Israel. This period before World War I marked the birth of the *kibbutzim* movement, groups of communal farms operated by dedicated Jewish immigrants.

6. In 1917 just prior to the arrival of the British in the land of Israel during World War I, Great Britain brought out the Balfour Declaration which was a promise that Palestine was to be a homeland for Jewish people who wished to emigrate there. Although some of the original aims of the promise were whittled down, especially that of the amount of land called Palestine, yet the declaration was ratified in 1922.

This was another case of the providence of God. Who but He Himself could have foreseen what was yet to come on the continent of Europe only a scant ten years after the ratification in 1922, with the advent of Hitler in 1932. God indeed prepared the circumstances for Jewish emigration out of Europe to Israel. If only Jewish people would have listened! During the 1920s and until 1936, there were three emigration movements and by mid-1930s thousands of German-speaking Jews had fled Hitler's Germany. The history of the period of Israel is quite complicated, e.g., 1, Arabs rioting in 1921, 1929, and in 1936, which was a major disturbance, all of which was directed against Jewish emigration; 2, Great Britain actually restricting emigration of Jewish people from Europe, especially with the White Paper in May 1939 which limited emigration to ten thousand a year for five years, a time when many Jewish people were desperately trying to get out from Hitler's clutches; and 3, because of the precarious position of Jewish people in Europe under Hitler an illegal emigration developed after 1939 as a consequence of the White Paper. Jewish people regarded British restrictions, particularly during the Hitler era, as a violation of the promises of the Balfour Declaration.

The end of World War II, and the deep soul-searching realization by the world community of nations of the horrible holocaust of six million Jews, made it painfully evident that Herzl was right. While for the present the Jew in the West can have his part in the cost of the rebuilding of the land of Israel, yet there is an unmistakable divine pointer that the focus of the future of the Jewish people is not to be in the West. This was true for European Jewry as it faced Hitler's final solution of Jewish liquidation. Most of the Jewish people in Europe who somehow made it through the concentration camps and were able to escape the gas ovens saw the land of Israel as the only place where they could find rest for their bodies and spirits.

In 1947 the United Nations voted to partition Palestine into two portions, one part to the Israelis, and the other to the Palestinian Arabs. The Israelis accepted the decision while the Arab nations refused; the rest is now history. One wonders however as to what could have been the consequences of a decision by Palestinian Arabs to accept the resolution of the United Nations. They could have had their state on an even larger portion of land than what the discussions center on today concerning the West Bank and the Gaza Strip.

7. In 1948 the modern state of Israel was born, but it was destined to be refined in the crucible of fire. Yet another circumstance of God's providence began to unfold. In spite of untold suffering on the part of many Arab refugees who fled from the Jewish state (although many remained to be citizens), there was also a new exodus of Jewish people. Between 1948 and the end of the 1950s, almost a million *Jewish refugees* began to stream out of the Arab countries, most of whom emigrated to the land of Israel. Many came with only the clothes on their backs. Those who had assets could not take any monies with them because funds were frozen in the countries of their origin. The Jewish people who came are Sephardim Jews from Mediterranean countries and Oriental Jews from Arab states in the Middle East; today they comprise one-third to one-half of the modern State of Israel. (A pointed sidelight is that while attempts are made to settle the rights today of the Palestinian Arabs who left their homes, yet a parallel concern exists where the rights of lost and impounded monies and properties also have to be considered for Jewish people who fled from Arab countries.)

8. Then came the lightning Six Day War. But beyond the

military battles of that conflict, there is again the circumstances of providence. From 1948 until 1967 hardly any Jewish people came from the Soviet Union or North America, but in these two areas live the bulk of Jewry, almost five-and-a-half million in the United States, and about three million in the Soviet Union, totaling eight-and-a-half million. What would be the catalyst to fire their desire to emigrate from these countries? It was the Six Day War that made painfully evident again that the finger of God was pointing to the place of destiny for Jewish people. Accordingly, emigration picked up from the Soviet Union and the North American continent. In the six years from 1967 to 1973, about one-hundred thousand Jews came from the Soviet Union and almost half that number from North America, totaling almost one-hundred-fifty thousand Jewish people.

9. The Yom Kippur War in 1973 also had its effect upon world Jewry. It united Jewry as never before. It is unfortunate that it has to take this kind of pressure to bring Jewish people together. Nevertheless, God permits these seeming tragedies to keep the eyes of Jewish people ever on the homeland where He has His purposes yet to be enacted.

Even the Yom Kippur War demonstrated to us the circumstances of providence. Israel was hit hard on Yom Kippur. The Israelis had been lulled into complacency and had not expected this war to begin as it did. But in spite of the pain of twenty-six hundred fallen in battle, most of whom fell in the first few days, God said, "Just so far, and no more." In an ancient parallel in the Assyrian invasion of Israel, the Lord had declared then, "I will put a spirit in him so that he shall hear a rumor and return to his own land" (Isaiah 37:7). Just a little spirit and a rumor and the invasion of that time was over, and the Assyrian army hurriedly retreated back to its own land after suffering the loss of one-hundred-eighty-five thousand troops (Isaiah 37:36).

God worked in much the same way in 1973, except that this time He providentially used the spirit of fear. Syria hit

Israel hard and instead of taking a scheduled thirty-six hours for her advance units to get near a strategic bridge, *gesher ya'akov,* north of the Sea of Galilee, they made it in only a few hours. Then they stopped. The Syrians were afraid to proceed further because of the fear of a trap. One shudders to think of the consequences if they had pushed on. Syrian officers were executed because they failed to take advantage of the situation, and this hesitancy was enough for Israel to mobilize her reserves and have them on the line in the north so that the Syrians were consequently pushed back. This was another evidence of the providence of God as He protected Israel.

A similar miracle also took place in the south at the Suez Canal. Israel sustained losses at the Suez and Sinai and many Israeli soldiers were taken prisoner when Egypt managed to cross the canal in the first few hours of the war. A record number of Israeli planes were also shot down. Then, in the beginning of the second week of the war, Israel's "Patton tank commander" General Ariel Sharon asked for permission to take a task force of Israeli troops across the Suez Canal at a juncture between Egypt's second and third armies. Israel's leaders were understandably very concerned about this venture and hesitated. Eventually Sharon had his permission. Within a matter of days, Israel's defense forces were in Egypt and had pinned down the Egyptian second army at the north end of the canal, and had defeated the Egyptian third army which sustained great numbers of losses at the south end of the canal and in Suez City. Only the God of Israel could have turned a stunning defeat, when everything seemed against Israel, into a tactical victory and thereby protected Israel.

One consideration must be kept in mind. I am not counting up Israel's victories over that of Egyptian and Syrian losses which amounted to about twenty-five thousand men in the last Arab-Israeli war. War is just as painful to Egyptian and Syrian families as it is to those in Israel. Yet God did protect Israel in a miraculous way, and for the first time for many young Israelis, they were praying and asking basic questions about life.

Since 1973 the immigration into Israel has dropped. Perhaps this might be good while Israel catches its breath to take care of its own internal needs in providing for its citizens. But with the past one hundred years as a divine indicator, and if the Lord tarries, we can look for future immigrations as God works in history to bring His people Israel home under any circumstance.

In summary then, Hosea had said that "afterward the sons of Israel will return." We are living in the days of the return! We are compelled to acknowledge, from the perspective of history of over a hundred years, that God is at work, and I don't believe that Israel will ever be put out of the land, in view of what we have just seen. It is a marvelous demonstration of the providential circumstances of God in the modern history of Israel that will ultimately lead to a cataclysmic deliverance. God is at work in modern Israel!

The second distinction that God is at work in modern Israel is:

The Spiritual Preparation of a People. Hosea declared:

They will seek the Lord their God . . . and will come trembling to the LORD and to His goodness in the latter days (Hosea 3:5).

Reading these words most Christians usually think only in terms of the cataclysmic conversion of the nation, that is, the experience when Israel will be born again as in a day. But how much thought is given to the spiritual preparation of the people Israel over a longer period of time?

Long before there is a harvest a farmer will toil hours in his fields, breaking up the soil, sowing good seed, and then caring for the crops in cultivation or using insecticides, etc. He is dependent upon God for the moisture to water his crops and for the sun to help them grow. Only after weeks or even months is there a harvest, if the farmer has worked hard and if he is fortunate.

In the same way there is a spiritual parallel. Long before

Israel will greet Messiah her king, the nation will be purified and spiritually prepared for that auspicious occasion. There is a great harvest yet to come but *only* after a period of intense preparation that will be difficult and painful. Even religious Jewish thinking teaches that in the days of the "foot of the Messiah," that is to say, just before the Messianic kingdom is instituted, the pressure experiences of the nation will cause many to say that they actually hear footsteps of the coming of the Messiah in the midst of their trying times.

Now what are the means that God is using in this distinctive of spiritual preparation? Again, we enumerate as follows:

1. Old Testament study in the schools is a required subject in the curriculum. In every grade, as long as the Israeli child or young person is in school, from the first to the twelfth grade, there is a systematic study of this portion of the Word of God. In their early years the children study the heroes of Scripture: Abraham, Isaac, Jacob, Moses, Joshua, David, etc.

Then in the junior high years the young person studies geography and history. It isn't a dry textbook situation because many times the young folk are taken out to the countryside and they stand at the very places they read about. Think of studying the Bible in this way! If they read about Jericho, they can take the bus down to Jericho and stand at the site. They can actually see the various levels of many Jerichos and particularly the level of Joshua's day. If they read about Elijah on Mount Carmel, they can take a bus to Haifa, which is perched on the sea end of the Carmel hills; and a city bus can take these young people further inland on the hills near the approximate site where Elijah stood. They can relive the drama which the prophet enacted when he said to the prophets of Baal, "Is your god on a jet and has he gone away on a long trip? Yell louder so he can hear." We need to realize that God is taking His people Israel around the land so that His Word is seeded into their hearts.

The young people in high school study the lives and messages of the prophets as well as morals as taught in the

Old Testament. The lessons of righteousness, justice, and equity are derived from the prophets and students learn how to derive a moral from the prophets and apply these lessons for everyday living.

Now I know that most of the time the Old Testament is studied for its history and background for the modern State of Israel. Most of the time the students are imbued with a critical approach to the miracle element of the Word of God, and very little attempt is made to inculcate the dimension of faith. But we also have the assurance of what Isaiah once said, that the Word of God will never return empty; it will accomplish what God desires and it will succeed in the matter for which He sends it (Isaiah 55:11).

2. As for the New Testament, many students take courses in the university and these studies are very popular. There is genuine interest in the background and figures of the New Testament as well as an intense curiosity in the person of Jesus. For centuries the study of the life of Jesus was a forbidden subject, the penalty being excommunication from the community. Times have indeed changed.

New Testament studies may come as a surprise to Christians. Many times I am asked, "If Jewish people do not believe in Jesus, then why are Israelis in particular so interested in Jesus?"

Yet why should Israelis not be vitally aware of the teachings of Jesus, and even Paul, but especially the former? Israel is such a small country. When Israelis travel south from Jerusalem, they will pass Bethlehem and be reminded that Jesus was born there. There are times when Israelis will drive to the Kinneret Lake (Sea of Galilee) and will pass Nazareth and realize that Jesus grew up there. On certain occasions Israelis visit in the Old City of Jerusalem and see the sites associated with the gospel backgrounds, e.g., Calvary, the empty tomb, the temple mount, etc. Associated with these sites in the hands of traditional churches are the basics of the testimony of Jesus's ministry: His death, His burial, and His resurrection. The point is that no matter where the Israeli turns in his land, he comes face to face with Jesus. And the average Israeli is not like the proverbial ostrich who sticks his head in the sand and pretends that he is all alone. Since Jesus is such an important part of the scene in Israel, the Israelis cannot help but be interested in Him and try to understand His life and ministry. Therefore the New Testament has a profound interest for Israelis who are very involved with New Testament studies. This is bound to have some deeply significant long-range implications.

An even more exciting development is the pilot project of teaching the synoptic Gospels (Matthew, Mark, and Luke) in the junior high schools. In one of many key interviews in Israel, I had opportunity to spend an evening with a professor of New Testament in Israel's schools of higher learning who was involved in this project of Gospel studies. I was interested in the objectives of this program, and my friend stated that Israelis are interested in the study of Jesus as a Jew at the end of the second-temple period, the first century. The need, he emphasized emphatically, was to demonstrate that Jesus was a Jew among Jews of that period, and a teacher of the first rank who sought for a spiritual revitalization of the people in His day. Of course, in the conversation of the evening we had our differences of opinion as to the fullness of the person and ministry of Jesus. While the resurrection of Jesus did not prove to be a great difficulty, since traditional Jews do believe in the resurrection, yet a lively discussion ensued over Jesus's unique relationship with God when He answered Caiaphas before the Sanhedrin (Matthew 26:63-65).

But I must add a note of caution to Christians; there is a need to realize that we can learn from the way Israelis approach the life of Jesus as a man among men. When I came away from our meeting with the professor, I wrote a letter of thanks to him for having me in his home. I expressed my satisfaction primarily in that we seem to have an increasing area of the New Testament upon which *we can agree.* The professor himself had admitted that there could not have been any program of Gospel studies in the years prior to the short span of Israel's existence; and he questioned how much interest in the life of Jesus there would have been among Jesus's own people in general as much as fifty years ago. Do we not see the spiritual preparation of a people in the area of Bible study in the schools?

But I find many times that Christians are too impatient. A good lesson can be learned as to what is taking place in Israel today by examining closely John's description of the blind man (John 9). As we progress through this chapter, this man born blind first knew Jesus as a man, then as a teacher, then as a great prophet, and finally as a person with a divine nature. In the same way with respect to the nation, God can be seen as patiently marking time as the Word of God is intellectually grasped by the Israelis, and then the day will come when there will be the spiritual harvest of the whole nation. We too need to be patient with the Jewish people in general, patient with Israelis in particular, and walk in step with God's work among His people.

3. In the spiritual preparation, we also see a number of Jewish believers in the land, organized in their local fellowships, as a presence witness. There is a revival again of a situation which existed in the first century when Paul visited the apostles in Jerusalem. He declared on that occasion that he was still unknown by sight to the congregations that be in Judea (Galatians 1:22). There is a renewal of this situation today because once again we see indigenous fellowships of believers around the land. These fellowships have their way of sharing the message of the Word of God with their fellow countrymen, not from outside the country as foreigners and not acceptable to the average Israeli, but from within, demonstrating that one can be loyal to the community of Israel and still acknowledge that Jesus is the Messiah and Redeemer.

Remember, the Jewish believer is not speaking, as a rule,

with a younger generation who does not know the Word. Rather, the witness is with an Old Testament based on the New Covenant fulfillment. Here and there Israelis do make decisions for Jesus the Messiah and Redeemer. The rest, while not now making a decision, nevertheless hear the Word, and it is a Word that will never be forgotten. This intense encounter with the Scriptures is also going to have a profound effect in the future situation of Israel as we shall see in chapter seven.

Israel's religious situation, molded by the political and economic context and brooded upon by the Holy Spirit, has within itself the implications that will eventually speak to the hearts of the people. I shall never forget a conversation my wife and I had with a woman in a kibbutz. For two hours we exchanged our views concerning the Bible, the Messiah, and personal relationship with the Lord. Finally she said to me, "You see, everything is just as it was at the beginning of our conversation. You have your views and I have mine."

I answered her, "I have listened to your ideas and have really taken them to heart. But you will never be the same again with what I have shared with you. No one ever listens to the Scriptures and remains the same, for the Word of God never returns void." With that, she fell silent for several moments, and then she said softly, "I know I will never be the same!"

4. Israel's pressuring of five wars since 1948 (the war of independence in 1948-1949, the 1956 Sinai campaign, the Six Day War in 1967, the war of attrition in 1968-1970, and the Yom Kippur War in 1973), also have had their part in spiritual preparation. War always has a way of making people test their values and beliefs. When one is reduced to the issues of life and death, a lot of false ideologies and philosophies melt away. At no time in modern Israel's experience has there been such a challenge to think on spiritual things as during the Yom Kippur War and afterward.

I have an Israeli friend, a wonderful believer, who is a commando in the defense forces. He belongs to a unit that was sent down to the Jordan River on the first day of the October 1973 war. Israel was expecting an attack from Jordan. By the third day, in the morning, when the attack did not come, my friend happened to have a number of the men in the outfit around him. He took the occasion to open his Bible and by referring to Israel's history in the past, he showed that previously Israel usually had been attacked by nations from the north or from the south. Then he voiced his feelings that the outfit would be sent to the south and that eventually they would end up crossing the Suez Canal into Egypt. He didn't have any pipeline to the Israeli staff headquarters, but he certainly did have a pipeline to the staff of the Captain of the Lord's hosts. That afternoon, the unit was ordered to the canal, and a few days later the company crossed it and was in Egypt. By that time my friend was considered a prophet and he found many fellows interested in the Word of God.

This Israeli believer also shared an experience of when he was standing guard duty in Egypt where the area around him was extremely dangerous. There were Egyptian snipers, and many Israeli soldiers had been hit. On that particular night it was all so quiet, so still. All of a sudden, he heard rustling in the bushes and he was instantly on the alert, his gun ready to fire. The noise became louder, and just when my friend was ready to pull the trigger to fire in the direction of the sound, he heard a whisper from out of the dark from an Israeli comrade, "A [name omitted to protect identity], tell me more of what it says in Ezekiel 38—39." Indeed that was a welcome word and an opportunity to share from the Word of God to give life, rather than let go a blast from a gun that would kill.

Let me conclude my observations on these two divine distinctives. God is working in a definite manner with His people who are in the land of Israel today. The process to the ultimate goal of world peace, when Israel will recognize her Messiah, will be a trying experience. Of necessity some aspect of a progress of fulfillment of the Hosea prophecy involves the people who are in the land now, and we shall develop this further in chapter seven when we consider Israel's experiences in ''the day of Jacob's trouble.'' The refining of a Jewish remnant to the point of ultimately accepting the Biblical concept of Messiah Son of David will not be exactly as the Jewish religious leaders envision it. Neither will the preparation of Israel for spiritual redemption take quite the path as charted by some Christians. God will have His own sovereign way with Israelis to refine them, and our God-given mandate is to pray for them and seek as much as possible to share the Scriptures with them. Living as we are in the midst of the flow of history and fulfillment of prophecy, it can come as a surprise to see how God is working in the providential circumstances of Israel today, as well as with her spiritual preparation. But to understand this divine movement, we will need to keep in step with what the Lord is doing as He aims for the target of the fulfillment of His Word concerning the coming Messianic kingdom.

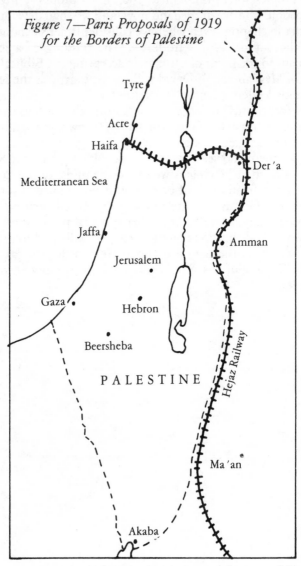

Figure 7—Paris Proposals of 1919 for the Borders of Palestine

Note: Palestine includes the areas east and west of Jordan River (both east and west banks).

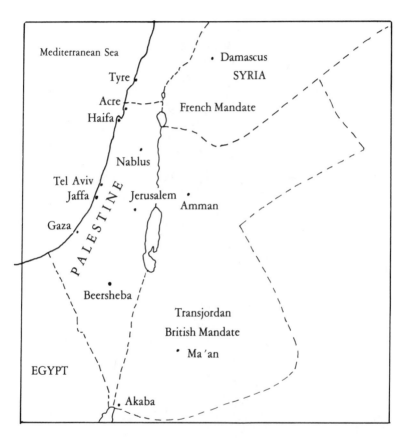

Figure 8—British Partition of 1922
Creating two countries, Palestine (west of Jordan River)
and Transjordan (east of Jordan River)

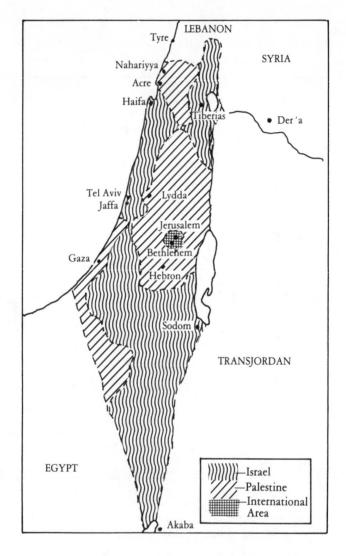

*Figure 9—United Nations Partition in 1947
Creating Arab Palestine and Jewish Israel*

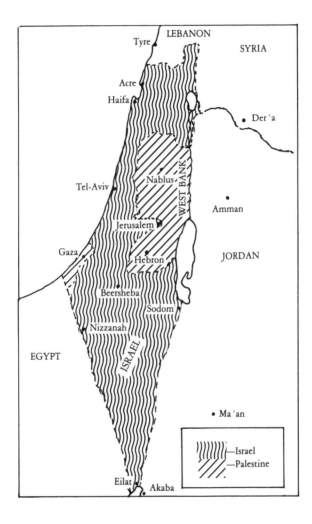

*Figure 10—1949 Armistice Lines
After Israel's War of Independence*

Note: What is marked as West Bank was annexed by Jordan during the war of 1948-1949. The Gaza Strip was occupied by Egypt. Jerusalem was divided.

After the Six Day War in 1967, Israel held as territories the Golan Heights (east and northeast of the Sea of Galilee), the West Bank, the Gaza Strip, and the Sinai.

After the 1973 war, after an almost disastrous start for the Israelis, they were able to hold the territories, and then even push into Egypt, and also push to within forty kilometers of Damascus.

In the Camp David agreement of 1979, the Sinai is eventually to be ceded back in steps to the international border between the two countries by April 1982. In any future agreement concerning the Palestinian Arabs on the West Bank, either linked to Jordan or as a separate state, the West Bank borders need to be negotiated; the distance from the West Bank to the Mediterranean Sea just north of Tel Aviv is only about seven miles.

Jerusalem is the most knotty of all the problems. Israelis do not want a divided city again as was the case before 1967.

An agreement still needs to be reached with Syria as to the Golan Heights. Israel does not want a recurrence of what happened before the Six Day War when people were fired on in the valley north of the Sea of Galilee.

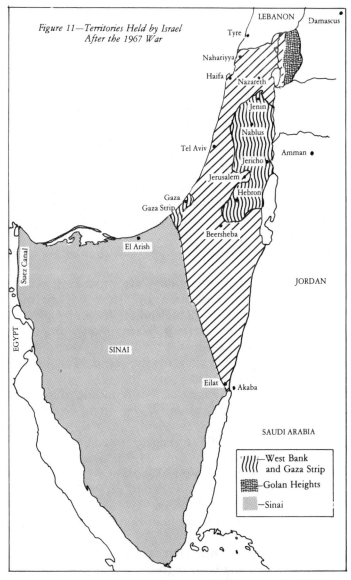

Figure 11—Territories Held by Israel
After the 1967 War

LEBANON
Damascus

Tyre

Nahariyya

Haifa

Nazareth

Jenin

Nablus

Tel Aviv

Jericho

Amman

Jerusalem

Hebron

Gaza

Gaza Strip

Beersheba

El Arish

Suez Canal

EGYPT

SINAI

JORDAN

Eilat • Akaba

SAUDI ARABIA

||||—West Bank
and Gaza Strip

—Golan Heights

—Sinai

*Figure 11—Territories Held by Israel
After the 1967 War*

Figure 12—Facts at a Glance
Concerning Israel

1857	Essay, Judah Alkalai, A Lot for the Lord
1860	First quarter of New Jerusalem, outside of Old Jerusalem's Walls
1862	Essay, Moses Hess, *Rome and Jerusalem*
1862	Essay, Zvi Kalischer, *Seeking Zion*
1870	First Jewish Agricultural College, Mikveh Israel
1881	Start of First Immigration Wave, from Eastern Europe
1882	Essay, Leo Pinsker, *Auto—Emancipation*
1896	Essay, Theodor Herzl, *The Jewish State*
1887	Call for First Zionist Congress, in Basel, Switzerland
1898	Ahad HaAm, *The Transvaluation of Values*
1904-1914	Second Immigration Wave, from Eastern Europe
1917	Balfour Declaration by Great Britain, making Palestine a homeland for Jewish people
1919-1923	Third Immigration Wave, mostly from Russia and Poland
1922	British Partition of the Land, Palestine, and Trans-Jordan
1924-1928	Fourth Immigration Wave, mostly from Poland
1929-1936	Fifth Immigration Wave, from Germany and Poland
1939	Britain's White Paper, severely limiting immigration to only 75,000 over five years, on the eve of World War II
1947	United Nations Partition of Palestine, in Israel and Arab Palestine
1948	Israel accepts the partition and declares her independence
1949	Armistice after Israel's War of Independence
1956	The Sinai Campaign
1967	Israel's Six Day War

1968-1970 Israel's War of Attrition, with Egypt primarily
1973   Israel's Yom Kippur War
1977   Sadat's declaration that Israel is a political fact
1979   Camp David, end of hostilities between Israel and Egypt; also, the call for negotiations between the two countries to solve the needs of those living on the West Bank and the Gaza Strip
1982   The return of the Sinai to Egypt completes what was outlined in the Camp David agreement
           The United Nations General Assembly votes for a homeland for the Palestinian Arab peoples

4

EXCURSUS:
GOD AND THE ARAB PEOPLES

Above all, we must talk to each other. Our hostility has
been autistic. We have not even reached the most basic
level of human communication. We haven't even found
a way to explain to each other our aggravation, our rage.
If we could only achieve that much communication, then
there would be some ground for hope.

Sana Hassan to Amos Elon
in *Between Enemies—A Compassionate Dialogue*

To this point, we have already discussed the major
covenants God has with Israel, how history revolves around
these covenants, the way God has been working in the
modern period to make possible the State of Israel, and also
the process whereby Israel will eventually be prepared to meet
its Messiah when He comes.

Often overlooked by Christians, however, is the place God
also assigns to the Arab peoples as we come to the end of this
age and their preparation for the coming kingdom. We have
already noted in chapter one some of the promises which concern *all* of Abraham's seed, which has a much wider connota-
tion than the people Israel. Involved are peoples across the
Middle East who are descendants of Abraham but we also
have to recognize other Semites who trace their ancestry back
to Shem. The history, geography, and politics of the peoples
of the whole Middle East are vast and complex and we cannot
in the confines of this chapter deal with every one of them.
However, for the purposes of our study we shall consider what
God has to say concerning selected Semitic peoples related
directly to the people of Israel, those either of the descendants of Abraham on the other line, or, Semitic peoples at
large. Involved also however, are non-Semitic peoples in the
Middle East who have embraced Islam as their religion and
culture.

One devastating word of divine prophecy was aimed at the

sons of Esau, the Edomites in the ancient world. God never forgot their attitude to the Israelis as the latter were on their way from Egypt to the promised land, The easiest route would have been through the territory of Edom but the reigning king of Edom would not permit Israel to pass through on this route (Numbers 20:14ff). Centuries later, with the fall of Jerusalem and the loss of the first temple, God abhorred what the Edomites, actually close brethren of the Israelis, did to Israel at the time when Nebuchadnezzar came up to attack Jerusalem in 586 B.C. These "brothers" aided Nebuchadnezzar and took glee in the destruction of Jerusalem while denouncing Israel, and then sought to appropriate the land of Israel for themselves. God had no recourse but to issue a curse on Edom (Ezekiel 35:3ff; 36:5). While it took time for the curse to take effect, nevertheless over the centuries the Word was ultimately fulfilled.

A few remaining Edomites in the first century B.C. were known as Idumeans and, in the political situation of that period, the latter plotted and schemed to control Judea and eventually obtained the approval of the Romans to do so. Herod the Great became the king over Judea in 37 B.C. While this Idumean (Edomite) had nothing to commend him concerning his morals, killing many members of his family, wives, and children, yet he appeased the people of Judea by diverting their attention from his personal life as he engaged himself in a tremendous building activity in Judea. His most crowning achievement was the refurbishing of the second temple, making it a most beautiful place indeed (Matthew 24:1-2).

Israel: The Land Bridge

The land of Israel has always served as a land bridge between the three continents of Asia, Africa, and Europe. One could hardly in the ancient world go from one continent to the next without having to pass through an area of the Middle East and some part of the land of Israel.

Ancient World. Time and time again the land of Israel has been subjected to the policies of expansionism and aggression by its neighbors. When the countries of the Middle East sought to expand their borders, Israel became the land bridge. When Assyria engaged in conquest it had to go through Israel, taking a good bit of the land, and even extended its influence into Egypt in Africa. After Assyria, when Babylon became the world power, they also conquered Judea, and continued to expand their conquest into Egypt.

Still later on, when Persia succeeded Babylon as the dominant force in the Middle East, Persia also controlled Israel and the latter again became the springboard for expansionism into both Egypt and Africa. Persia in the ancient world was able to have an empire that stretched from the borders of India to as far as the borders of Greece, while at the same time extending their influence into Africa by way of Israel.

The tide turned again and once more Israel became the land bridge, but this time the invading forces came from the northwest. Alexander the Great of Greece came to Jerusalem to take the land of Judea as a province of the Greek Empire. This in turn became the pathway to Egypt when the latter was also added to Alexander's conquest. Greece was able also to extend its empire eastward to include Babylon as well as Persia.

Still another force from the northwest was Rome, which was dominant in the Middle East beginning with the first century B.C. The land of Israel also was the land bridge for Rome to enter the rest of the Middle East, and the Romans used the overland road connections between Egypt (Africa) and Israel. We can therefore see that whoever controlled the land of Israel also was able to control most of the travel routes between Asia, Europe, and Africa.

The Byzantine. Pagan Rome's influence lasted until the early 300s A.D. when Constantine accepted Christianity and for all practical purposes it became the main religion of the Roman Empire. What this meant insofar as the land of Israel was concerned was that religious leaders particularly in Greece and Asia Minor, came to build church buildings, places of worship, and shrines on Biblical sites. While in one sense this activity may be questioned because the actual sites are unknown, yet the building activity did serve to spur an interest in the Bible and places associated with the Biblical message. The growth of the Byzantine (Greek Orthodox) presence became quite prominent by 451 A.D. Jerusalem was made a patriarchate. This meant that the land of Israel included the presence of a number of theological schools, a place where Christian art was developed, and also where monks and monasteries, nuns and convents, and many basilicas were in abundance. Today we see the ruins of the churches of the Byzantine but at one time there were as many as some fifty thriving churches.

This period came to an end in the early 600s. In 614 the Persians conquered this land from the Byzantines, but Emperor Heraclius reconquered it in 629. However, a new threat then was rising on the horizon which would bring the Byzantine control of the land of Israel to an end.

Arab Conquest

Once again the land of Israel as well as the rest of the Middle East was to feel a new source of aggression and conquest from a totally unexpected source. A new major religion was now to be spawned but which would extend beyond mere religious observances and actually become a strong political power.

In the early 600s, this new belief sprang up in Arabia. Muhammad proclaimed his religious ideas, similar to what he felt concerning Judaism, and he thought that Jewish people in Arabia would join and recognize in him the prophet as the consummation of their hopes. However when Jewish people did not merge with the followers of Muhammad, he moved farther and farther away from Judaism. The two religions, Islam and Judaism, eventually became separate and distinct.

Muhammad died in 632 and the religion which he started began to spread. During the 630s the entire Middle East was forcibly arabized as the outreach of the religion was carried on by means of the *Jihad* or holy war. Subsequently, in a few decades, by the 700s the authority of Islam covered the entire Arabian Peninsula spreading northward to the gates of Constantinople, spreading eastward to the borders of India, and stretching westward to the shores of the Atlantic. By 711 A.D., the Spanish Peninsula was under Islamic control and if it had not been for Charles Martel in the battle of Pontiers in 732, who stopped the Arab advance in France, one wonders how far Islam could have spread. Islam now became a new political and religious power structure, and guided by Muslim jurist-scholars.

Particularly the land of Israel which had been controlled by the eastern branch of the church, the Byzantine, now came under the control of Islam. Arabic became the official language and most of the people in Israel became for all practical purposes as Arab peoples. Christians prior to Arab control became Arab Christians. There is even evidence that Jewish believers in the land of Israel, because of the Arab conquest, dropped their ethnic Jewish identity and became Arab Christians. Most of those in the land with no religious affiliation then adopted Islam as their new religion. However, there were religious Jewish people who continued to live in the land even during the period of Arab control.

Contributions by Arab Peoples. After the initial conquests opportunity then came for Arab scholars to make their contributions, first in the Middle East, then to Jewish people as the intermediaries, and eventually to Europe in general. Most Christians have only a dim awareness of the tremendous contributions Arab peoples have made to the pursuit of scholarship in the European west.

Not too long after the Arab conquest of the Middle East, there began a feverish translation into Arabic of the Greek classics of science and philosophy. It was an effort that lasted for about two hundred years, into the 800s. Translations were made mostly from Syriac versions of the Greek philosophers and the work invariably was done by Arab Christians. From this effort Arab scholars were able to develop a technical philosophical language which expressed the theological beliefs of the Arab Muslim. Arab theologians therefore grounded their religious beliefs, using the philosophies of Plato and Aristotle, much like the Church had done following 300-400 A.D. This distinct Muslim development became a boon for scholarship in Europe, particularly in the Middle Ages of the 1200s, when what little learning existed was confined to the monasteries. Arab poetry was also developed, which became a dimension of beauty as well as the vehicle by which one could express his feelings within a religious and cultural context. Many of the sciences developed by Arab scholars were to be a contribution to Europe, including the Arabic numerals for doing mathematics.

In Babylon in the 800-900s as well as in Spain (800-1300), particularly the latter, Arab scholarship had a profound effect upon Jewish thinkers. In Babylon Saadyah, 882-942, besides producing an introduction to the Talmud and writing a Hebrew grammar, also became in a sense the father of Jewish philosophy who made the effort to present the mass of Jewish learning in accordance with the categories of philosophy. It was, however, the Arab philosophers using Greek philosophy which enabled Saadyah to produce this accomplishment on behalf of the Jewish people. Another distinct contribution by Saadyah, because of Arab influence, was the translation of the Hebrew Scriptures (Old Testament) into Arabic. Saadyah's work in this respect was an important link along the way in producing at least the Old Testament for the classical rendering of the Arabic Bible.

By far the greatest contribution of Arab thought to Jewish

scholars was in Spain where Jewish people enjoyed a golden age of literature. In wedding Arab scholarship with Jewish tradition, Jewish scholars made quite a formidable contribution in a philosophy which expressed Judaism, and also was instrumental in producing Bible dictionaries and Hebrew grammars. The Arab influence also made possible the production of some of the best poetry in Hebrew, still used in the synagogues. By 1492 the last vestige of the Muslims was driven from Spain by the Spanish Christians when the latter finally had control of the Spanish peninsula. Jewish people were also expelled from Spain in that year, but by that time the contributions by Arab and Jewish scholars had already passed into the Church to men like Thomas Aquinas and other Roman Catholic theologians.

Crusaders. Once more, in the providential circumstances of God, the land of Israel became subject to a mass invasion. This time it was because of a curious combination of political and miliary power of professing Christendom which sought to wrest the Holy Land from the ''infidel.'' This movement was actually a series of military attempts by the warriors of western Europe, fighting under the sign of the cross, to conquer the land of Israel and establish a kingdom, the kingdom of Jerusalem. These efforts lasted from just before 1100 A.D. until nearly 1300 A.D. Although the Crusaders tried repeatedly to maintain their hold in the land, gradually the Muslims (Mamelukes of Egypt) pushed the crusader presence from the land and in a series of battles the Muslims were able finally to oust the knight warriors from western Europe.

The European invasion of Israel had more important overtones, however. The Europeans took a renewed interest in the Bible sites and their significance. The Crusaders engaged in tremendous activity, building churches and defense fortifications. Also of importance, the events of the Crusades opened up many other opportunities for Europe. Interest in travel and exploration quickened as men learned to make better maps, and Europeans journeyed to the lands of the Middle East and even further east. One well-known effort to explore and learn were the trips Marco Polo and his family made to the Far East at the end of the 1200s; the land of Israel again served as the land bridge to the Far East from Europe. Of even greater importance was the contact of Europe with Islamic learning in the Middle East, in addition to the contacts with Spain in the west, that broadened European intellectual life in philosophy, science, and mathematics.

The Middle East in the Doldrums

A new turn of events was to take place which would temporarily decrease and remove interest in the Middle East. With the discovery of the New World by Columbus, and the round-the-world trips by Sir Francis Drake of England and Magellan of Portugal in the 1500s, the focus on the Middle East ceased, and it eventually sank into the doldrums and became the backwash of the nations. The Turks took control of the land of Israel in 1517 and, under the reign of Suleiman, the walls which today enclose the Old City of Jerusalem were built between 1539 and 1542. But after Suleiman passed off the scene in 1556, except for some French influence in trade and consul representation in Israel, the land slipped into despair, and the Turkish regime was characterized by heavy taxation, negligent and unjust administration, and an absence of industry and safety for the inhabitants until the end of the 1700s.

Modern Revival of Interest in the Middle East

The early 1800s saw a revival of interest in the holy places in Israel, particularly in Jerusalem. Russia and France vied with each other for representation of holy-land sites, and they fought for the privileges to be wrested from the Turks. Eventually both had legitimate representation. The British also entered the scene and opened their first consulate in

Jerusalem; they took on the cause of Jewish elements in Syria and in the land of Israel. In the 1800s also, missionaries from Britain and the United States entered the Middle East. Scholars from Britain, the United States, and France launched into studies of archeology in this period. All of this activity meant greater travel between Europe and the land of Israel. In 1868 the first postal and telegraphic connection was instituted and the first good road was constructed between Joppa (Jaffa) and Jerusalem. The greatest impetus for development of the entire region came with the opening of the Suez Canal in 1869. The Middle East was beginning to revive and western nations realized that the area was a pivotal interest and a land bridge for control. Once again, whoever controlled the Middle East had, in a sense, his hand on the lifeline among the nations.

Already near the end of the 1800s and in the first decade of this century, England, France, and Germany were carving out their spheres of influence in this region by the building of railroads: the Germans with their rail line to Bagdad, the British railroads from what was Mesopotamia to Palestine (Israel) and Egypt, and the French in Syria. World War I accelerated the concern for this area. The Turkish Empire was in alliance with Germany and these two countries wanted to retain their influence in the Middle East. But the Allies, particularly Britain and France, wanted Turkey out of the area. To enlist Jewish support for the land of Israel, the Balfour Declaration made of Palestine a homeland for Jewish people. But T. E. Lawrence, a British officer with the support of the military, sought also to enlist Arab support in a revolt against Turkey. For this effort there was to be an understanding concerning Arab interests in Palestine. The efforts by Lawrence aided the British in their entry into Palestine to defeat the Turkish forces and oust them from Palestine, and also helped the Arabs to enter Damascus, capital of Syria, and defeat the Turks. However, by enlisting both Jewish and Arab support for the same land, Palestine (Israel), serious repercussions were to follow, consequences with which we live to this very day.

After World War I, the Middle East was carved into countries with specific nationalisms for the purpose of western interests. France became dominant in the political structure of Syria and also the area which was eventually to become Lebanon after World War II. Great Britain's sphere was in Palestine (Israel), Iraq, and Egypt. The development of oil in the Persian Gulf area also marked specific interests with leaders of territories which are today small countries in this region. The Middle East has finally come into its own today, and the wealth of the world in the modern era flows in this part of the world where Middle East nations have vast oil reserves.

While the carve-up of the Middle East was for the interests of the western world and particular powers in western Europe, yet today, with money from oil for development in every sphere of modern life, the Arab peoples of the region are able to enter into and take their place in the economic and political picture of the world. There is no doubt that the providential hand of God is in this region and the modern development serves His purposes that all the people of the Middle East will be prepared for the prophetic geo-political and economic interests in the events yet to come.

The Prophetic Future

While it is difficult to speculate on what the prophetic message has to say concerning every part of the region of the Middle East, yet the Bible does offer some guidance on the future of some of the nations and specific areas of the Middle East.

Egypt. The Prophet Isaiah, amidst his oracles concerning the ancient nations of the Middle East, had something very specific to say regarding Egypt (Isaiah 19). From the view of his day the content of verses 1-15 was future, but from our vantage point in history the events mentioned in these verses are already past.

Beginning with Isaiah 19:16 however, with the phrase, "in that day," to the end of the chapter, the prophet describes some of the fortunes of Egypt which are intertwined with some of the great events of prophecy. The phrase, "in that day," as well as the simple designation, "the day," are references to "the day of the Lord" which was already considered in chapter two. Isaiah's future message actually describes the events which will yet take place in Egypt, events which spell out disaster and also those which describe great blessings. The prophet describes the catastrophic experiences which happen just before the coming of the Messiah, the darkness events of the day, but Israel's prince of the prophets also gives us a glimpse of the blessings yet to be given to Egypt in the day of world peace associated with the brightness of the day.

We can select only some of the descriptions which refer to Egypt's future. One observation must be noted: Isaiah is not speaking chronologically in verses 16-22; rather, he moves back and forth between events associated with the darkness and the brightness of the day of the Lord. We in the West might question why Isaiah, and other prophets as well, don't think chronologically but rather deal specifically with topics regardless of time sequences. In the West we tend to think chronologically but in the Orient, and we have to consider the Middle East as a part of the Orient, the thinking is more topical and this also includes Old Testament descriptions of prophetic events. It is our task to establish the chronology of what will yet happen to Egypt.

We note in verse 17 that the "land of Judah will become a terror to Egypt." I think we have to relate events which occur in Israel and to Jewish people that will have an adverse effect upon the future of Egypt. We know that Israel will be pressured in its darkness, but I think that this pressuring will also extend to the misfortunes of Egyptians. I shall discuss further some of these reasons in chapter seven, but one can very well see that if a political antichrist demands worship, not only will Israel refuse to do so, but Egypt will do likewise. These decisions will have disastrous consequences. The antichrist will be so enraged with Israel that he will begin to pressure her, but at the same time this will also be true of Egypt, who will never worship a man because of the similarity between Islam and Judaism to worship only the divine being.

In verses 18-19 of Isaiah 19, we observe some peculiar and startling information. Cities in Egypt will be speaking the language of Canaan and we would have to assume that this is Hebrew. This means that there will be a link, in the experiences of the brightness of the day, when Egypt will communicate with Israelis in the latter's language. But the information is even more startling because the people of Egypt will give their allegiance to the Lord of Hosts, who can only be the God of Israel. This message must mean that in the events of the brightness of the day, the Egyptians will acknowledge the God of Israel as their Lord.

What is even more startling is the description of an altar to the Lord in the midst of the land of Egypt. We know that in the Messianic period Israel will yet have a temple and priesthood (Ezekiel 40—46), but actually to recognize an extension of the Israel altar also in the midst of Egypt is a reality that is difficult to comprehend. Yet Isaiah does state it as such and we have to recognize, therefore, some specific privilege Egypt will have that other nations will not enjoy.

The time sequence changes in Isaiah 19:20, and once more the prophet refers back to the darkness experiences when Egypt cries to the Lord because of oppressors. My suggestion is that in the time frame when Israel will be pressured in its darkest hour and cry to God for divine intervention, so Egypt will do likewise. And as God sends the Redeemer to end the pressuring of Israel by the antichrist, so the same set of experiences will also be true for Egypt.

This is extremely interesting from our point of view today.

It is my feeling that the present linking of Egypt and Israel is not some accident or fluke of history. One can very well recognize that as Egypt's leaders have sought a state of peace with Israel, and have recognized her legitimate existence in the Middle East, so God will acknowledge this statement of policy on the part of Egypt and in the end will provide her with special privileges.

Jordan. Jordan today is land that was once occupied by the Ammonites and the Moabites in ancient days. The background of these people goes back to the sordid and deplorable situation of what happened between Lot and his two daughters (Genesis 19:30-38). Their sons were Ammon and Moab, and in turn they fathered the nations known by these names.

The prophets in their oracles concerning the future of nations and regions of the Middle East had a word regarding the Ammonites and the Moabites. Because of the idolatry and other sins of the two nations, divine judgment was predicted for them (Isaiah 15—16; Jeremiah 48—49; Ezekiel 25:1-11). However, Jeremiah the prophet adds two phrases about these peoples that suggest a reprieve; his information describes them along with others who will have a place in the Messianic kingdom. God will restore Moab in the latter days (Jeremiah 48:47) as well as the fortunes of the sons of Ammon (Jeremiah 49:6). It is difficult from today's point of view to single out any one specific people living on the east bank of the Jordan River in what is the country of Jordan: Palestinian Arabs, or the Arab bedouins who support King Hussein. Nevertheless, I would take it to mean that we are talking about territory east of Israel and the peoples living on this land will also have their part in the Messianic kingdom.

Iran. While we shall be discussing Iran further in chapters five and six, yet it is interesting to see how this non-Arab people will also have a prominent place, particularly during the tribulation period. Iran is the ancient Persia, which at one time had a significant glory and a might which controlled a great empire. Although Alexander the Great conquered her by 330 B.C., it did not mean the end totally of the power of this people. Greece was able to control Iran for some eighty years, when the Parthians then captured the country from Greek control in about 250 B.C., and ruled until 266 A.D. The Persian people were able to recover their strength under the Sassanid dynasty and conquered the Parthians and asserted their control again. The Romans were defeated by the Persians in 260 A.D. when the former tried to invade and capture Persia. The Sassanid dynasty was a strong one and ruled Iran and part of what is now Iraq until the 600s.

With the rise, however, of Islam, an Arabian army invaded Iran in 641, and subjected the Iranian peoples to the new religion. Over the next several hundred years Iran was prey to invaders from many quarters, including the Mongols in the 1400s. In the 1700s the Persians were able again to drive out their conquerors and even expand their empire eastward to conquer Afghanistan, and have troops in the city of Delhi in northern India. After this show of strength, however, and the passing of the particular dynasty that gave Iran its power, the country became poor once more.

During the 1800s Iran came under British and Russian influence, but after World War I Britain's presence prevailed, once Germany and Russia were out of the picture. We cannot provide the entire picture of Iran across the centuries, but we need to recognize that we are looking at a country that has alternated between tremendous show of strength and weakness and poverty. This can explain some of the strengths and shortcomings Iran has demonstrated of late.

What the future indicates, however, is that Iran will eventually link itself with the Soviet Union (Ezekiel 38:5). As to how this will take place, it is difficult to conjecture from our limited viewpoint today. Oil experts estimate that at some time in the decade of the 1980s, Russia's known available oil supplies will have peaked and then begin to diminish. This means that the Soviet Union will not have oil for export to eastern Europe or anywhere else. It is quite probable that, given the long border between the Soviet Union and Iran, the Soviets will somehow arrange an alliance with Iran to the latter's interests and therefore there will be a link-up between the two countries. It will not be the first time that Russia has had influence and even control of Iranian territory, but in the end times Iran will be completely in the Soviet orbit.

To contemplate this turn of events is most painful for those who planned the policy of the United States whereby Iran should be the guardian of the Persian Gulf area to protect oil interests, and also to act as a counterbalance with Iraq and other extremist Arab nations who are set against Israel's existence. American policy has collapsed, however, and modern Iran takes little stock in the United States.

Iraq. The country of today's Iraq has in the ancient world included Sumerian, old Babylonian, Assyrian, and the Neo-Babylonian peoples. Judah was sent into exile in the 500s B.C. to those mentioned last.

What appears to be prominent today is the struggle for power by Iraq in its conflict with Iran.

From a Biblical point of view, as we contemplate the tribulation period, Babylon becomes prominent in the prophetic future. John devoted two chapters in the book of Revelation to Babylon, and this was intended to signify the importance of this area in the end times just prior to the kingdom of peace. While there are various interpretations of Revelation 17—18, it is my feeling that when we examine chapter 17 we are viewing the religious context during the tribulation period. In the ancient world, from the Jewish point of view, Babylon was a city with some seven to eight thousand gods and goddesses. It was here that Jewish people learned firsthand the horrors of idolatry and when they returned to the land of Israel, never again were they caught up in this heinous practice. John's use, therefore, of Babylon in chapter 17 is symbolic and is intended to portray the ultimate course of idolatry in the tribulation period when Satan will have his men, the political and religious antichrists, establish a hideous worship system in which the nations will be involved. The Apostle John could not have used a more pertinent illustration than that of Babylon to describe the satanic system of worship.

When we come to Revelation 18, however, we are actually dealing with a specific city or some economic mart somewhere at the head of the Persian Gulf. In the ancient world Babylon was a great city which had one of the seven wonders of the world, the famous hanging gardens. The ancient site of Babylon is located today about sixty miles south of Bagdad, the modern capital of Iraq. John's point of reference was to Babylon as a literal city, and while probably not to the actual site of the Babylon of ancient times, yet I feel that the apostle used the reference as a way to talk about a specific city.

From today's point of view, we know that the wealth of the world is flowing into the Persian Gulf area. It is quite conceivable that one of the richest cities of the world will be situated there, and it will be a mart in which the nations will invest and trade with one another. Every available material means for gain will be located there. Yet somehow, as we come to the end of the tribulation period, this mart is destroyed and great distress takes hold of the merchants of the world. So aggravated are these princes of commerce that they will throw dust on their heads and cry and weep bitterly concerning the great city that was laid waste in only one hour (Revelation 18:19). While I do not want to go into the many ramifications of this chapter, it is enough to point out that we are talking about a city designated Babylon. Its exact location is uncertain because this center does not have to be situated on the ancient Babylon site. Rather, the future world mart could be closer to the Persian Gulf in Iraq, or some other country in this region, such as Kuwait or one of the emirates.

It can very well be that Iraq will be the dominant force in the Persian Gulf area in the tribulation period and the leadership of the country will somehow have their link with the political and religious antichrists.

I think it is quite significant today that Iraq is struggling for the control of this area and if this is so, then we can already see some of the future unfolding before our very eyes. The power struggle between Iraq and Iran can also suggest one reason: as Iraq becomes important enough to control the Persian Gulf region, thereby effecting a link-up with the European West because of the latter's need for its oil, then Iran will seek for its support and supplies from the Soviet Union. At any rate, we begin to see some of the shadows of great events yet to unfold in the Middle East that will have prophetic significance.

Ultimate Peace in the Middle East

The Prophet Isaiah, in outlining foreign policy for the period of the kingdom of peace, indicates that there will come a day when all the nations of the Middle East will be living at peace with one another. We shall be discussing more of this in chapter nine, but we can see how the prophecy of Isaiah is interesting as he describes the peace arrangement of the nations of the Middle East:

> In that day there will be a highway from Egypt to Assyria, and the Assyrians will come into Egypt and the Egyptians into Assyria, and the Egyptians will worship with the Assyrians. In that day Israel will be the *third party* with Egypt and Assyria, a blessing in the midst of the earth, whom the LORD of hosts has blessed, saying, "Blessed is Egypt My people, and Assyria the work of My hands, and Israel My inheritance" (Isaiah 19:23-25).

The prophet describes the great highway running across the Middle East, from Egypt to Assyria with Israel in the middle, and from his point of view Egypt represented the country to the southeast of Israel, while ancient Assyria was in northern Iraq including perhaps parts of eastern Syria. At any rate, from today's picture it is a general designation whereby the countries of the Middle East will one day enjoy peace and where all these nations will together worship the Lord. It is a beautiful prophecy of hope when we consider the situation of the region today where nations fight each other for their own specific interests while Israel seeks to maintain its existence in the area. God, however, will one day carry His promise into fruition, signifying that He alone can bring peace into this region. In His providence He is at work even today with all of the nations of the Middle East, the land bridge between three continents, to bring to pass His purposes within history.

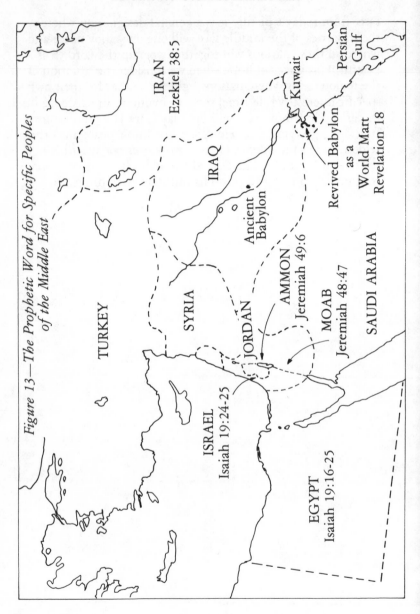

Figure 13—The Prophetic Word for Specific Peoples of the Middle East

5

THE UNITED NATIONS AND FUTURE WORLD POWERS

> The Providence of God remarkably prepared the world for the first advent . . . when Rome combined the various nations under the unity and common polity and language of an almost universal empire. . . . Just so, now, not merely most of Europe and Western Asia, but the regions of all the earth, near and far off, are being united into one whole. Asia and Europe are brought close together by the Suez Canal. . . . The Pacific and Atlantic Oceans are to be joined by the projected Panama Canal. The interior of Africa, Japan, China, and Tibet are being opened to the world. . . . Space and distance are being almost annihilated by the railway, electric telegraph, and kindred appliances in modern science.
>
> Canon Fausset, in *Signs of the Times* (1881)

Since the turn of the century, there has been a movement among the nations toward a centralized world power. While this was not so apparent prior to World War I, where so many nations of the western world jealously guarded their national sovereignties, nevertheless there was a desire by peace-loving people to have a world court, which was established in the Hague, Netherlands. Representatives of all nations were to meet there to settle international quarrels and prevent war. However, the influence of this court was limited, and today all that is left there is the Permanent Court of Arbitration.

After World War I the need was again felt for a world body that would act as a moral sounding board for the aspirations and activities of nations. It was thought that representatives of various national bodies, meeting as a League of Nations in Geneva, would be able to control disputes between the national interests. It was actually a court of world opinion, and by moral force it attempted to keep the "cooperative" nations in line. When nationals were divergent with world

111

opinion, the League tried to impose sanctions of various kinds so as to deter actions that were counter to the League's majority decisions.

In the 1930s, when Mussolini marched into Ethiopia, when Japan entered Manchuria, and with the rise of Hitler in Germany and his annexation of Austria, the League was helpless to control the rising military tide of axis powers. The League was not able to control the situation any longer and subsequent events in Europe led to World War II. Clearly, moral force alone was not able to deter national interests that were self-serving and nationals who were ready to assault their neighbors in war.

After World War II, the idea was advanced that a centralized world power was now to be embodied in a United Nations which would also have a police force to enforce its decisions. The United Nations army, comprised of troops from member nations under a centralized command, was to act against nations unwilling to cooperate with, and who actually opposed, the world body's objectives and decisions.

After more than three decades of the existence of the world body, everyone knows the scorecard of achievements of the United Nations. The smaller nations which cannot offer too much resistance are the ones against which force is imposed when there are problems. Then the smaller nations learned that, by uniting as a special interest group, they can even outvote the superpowers on many occasions. There even have been specific instances when the larger nations carry on their business and problems outside of the world body. How is it possible for the United Nations to tell the superpowers what to do and then enforce it? Nevertheless, there is a central power with the potential of a power control of the world body of nations. Even though the nations are each jealous for their own sovereignties, they are linked to the world body which will one day be a real force on this planet.

The United Nations

When we look at the basic composition of the United Nations today, what do we see? There is a European western bloc of nations with basic common interests. The creation of NATO, the calling into existence of the European Common Market, and the desire in many quarters that there be a United States of Europe, all point to the very real potential of a unified body of the nations of western Europe and the Mediterranean world. The ministers of the European Common Market and the leaders of NATO, when in special emergencies, have also had to make political and military decisions, e.g., establish a unified front when the Soviet Union invaded Czechoslovakia in 1968, and limit or even stop arms shipments to Israel during the Yom Kippur War in 1973.

At the same time we note the high profile presence of the Soviet Union and her allies. Prior to World War I, czarist Russia was a weak nation where most of her citizens were uneducated and underprivileged serfs, and the ruling family served only themselves. With the revolution in Russia in 1917, and the subsequent seizure of power by the Bolsheviks, the Soviet Union emerged after World War II to become a powerful nation which seemingly controls the balance of power in the world today.

The third powerful bloc in the United Nations is the People's Republic of China. Prior to World War I China was anything but a unified power; actually the country was controlled by powerful warlords who managed their own territories as they saw fit. It was only with the nationalization interests of Sun Yat-sen and the Kuomintang Party, starting in 1911, and the crucible experiences of invasion and occupation by Japan, and then the struggle for power between the nationalists and the communists, that eventually the People's Republic of China has emerged as the power that she is today. This colossus of power has the control of most of the population of the earth.

The question now is: Is there any significance to this line up of powers? Particularly, are there any Biblical implications to the presence of these superpowers? For one thing, we have never before seen such an arrangement of superpowers in history. I think that, as we examine the Word of God concerning the power blocs of nations at the end of this age, we shall notice a remarkable resemblance with what we see in the structure of the United Nations today.

The European Western Power Bloc

The Book of Daniel. We begin first with the bloc of nations of western Europe and the Mediterranean world, and it is the Prophet Daniel who has much to say concerning this concentration. Daniel 2 presents the well-known image of which Nebuchadnezzar had his dream. We will date the occasion at about 600 B.C.; the prophecy pictures the progress of world empires to the day when Messiah will come to institute God's empire, the Messianic kingdom over which Jesus will reign.

Daniel started with his own day amidst the Babylonian Empire over which Nebuchadnezzar ruled for many years. In succession, the prophet described the empires that followed: the Persian, the Grecian, and then finally the Roman. Daniel's interpretation of the legs of the image, representing what was the Roman Empire, is given.

> Then there will be a fourth kingdom as strong as iron; inasmuch as iron crushes and shatters all things, so, like iron that breaks in pieces, it will crush and break all these in pieces (Daniel 2:40).

From the prophet's point of view, concerning this empire he was already speaking of events six hundred years removed from his day, a situation which could only be possible because God does reveal to his chosen ones some of the interrelating events of history. The omniscience of God makes it possible for Him to know all the interrelated details in history even before they take place; part of this is then communicated to His prophets.

But this description of Rome does not end the matter, for Daniel continues:

> And in that you saw the feet and toes, partly of *potter's clay* and

partly of iron, it will be a divided kingdom; but it will have in it the toughness of iron, inasmuch as you saw the iron mixed with common clay (Daniel 2:41).

In the new arrangement of the elements there is the iron of the Roman Empire, but there is also the presence of common clay that would suggest a new political makeup of the empire. Since the iron remains, we must conclude that there is still the presence of the Roman Empire, but the mixture with clay suggests a new power representation of the fourth kingdom.

Chapter 2 of Daniel is, in reality, according to Daniel's sketch, an outline of the prophetic material which Daniel will expand in the rest of the book. For further information as to the relationship between Rome and its rearrangements subsequent in history, we shall have to go to Daniel 7. The prophet mentions again the four kingdoms he had pictured in chapter 2, but now he describes them as ferocious beasts. In chapter 2 kingdoms were described by various metals: gold, silver, brass, and iron, perhaps a feature to depict the outward glory of the nations. In chapter 7 the figure of beasts can only depict the inner character of nations in their relationships with other nations. Daniel quickly mentions Babylon, Persia, and Greece (7:4-6) but most of his descriptions in this chapter have to do with Rome and its subsequent rearrangement. Therefore the fourth kingdom is pictured:

After this I kept looking in the night visions, and behold, a fourth beast, dreadful and terrifying and extremely strong; and it had large iron teeth. It devoured and crushed, and trampled down the remainder with its feet; and it was different from all the beasts that were before it (Daniel 7:7).

In the interpretation provided by Daniel:

The fourth beast will be a fourth kingdom on the earth, which will be different from all the other kingdoms (Daniel 7:23).

Again the fourth kingdom, from Daniel's vantage point is that of the Roman Empire. But this very same fourth empire will be politically restructured. Daniel adds an important phrase to verse 7 which must be considered:

And it [the fourth beast] had ten horns (Daniel 7:7).

The further interpretation to the meaning of the horns is indicated:

As for the ten horns, out of this kingdom ten kings will arise (Daniel 7:24).

Note carefully that the ten horns, that is, the ten kings arising out of "this kingdom," is actually a reference to the Roman Empire. In other words, the Roman Empire is not superseded by a fifth empire, but rather its power wanes, and after a period of time, its makeup will consist of ten kingdoms over which ten kings, or rulers, will appear. Whatever the circumstances of the Roman Empire, it will last for a considerable period, but in the end there will be a confederation that will generally include the territory of the Roman Empire. As we see it today, this is the territory of western Europe and most of the nations surrounding the Mediterranean Sea. In the following chapters, I will try to be more specific as to which are the nations around the Mediterranean.

From our vantage point today, Rome existed until it fell in 476. Does this mean that this is the end of Roman influence and culture? By no means! Even though the territory of the Roman Empire no longer existed after 476, yet the nations of western Europe continued to be influenced by the heritage of Rome consisting of the culture, much of the governmental structure, the mindset, etc. The Hellenistic-Roman influence of Rome is the basic political, cultural, and educational trappings of the western world. Even in the dominant role of the church of Rome, and in the Hellenistic expression of Christianity, we see the lasting influence of the Roman Empire on the countries of the West to this day. The ancient Roman Empire is not a political force in the modern world; yet we cannot say that the influence of this empire has vanished.

A logical question now follows. What will be the many processes involved in the revitalization of the Roman Empire, which will cause it to become such a political force? We need to consider Daniel's further information:

> While I was contemplating the horns, behold, another horn, a little one, came up among them, and three of the first horns were pulled out by the roots before it; and behold, this horn possessed eyes like the eyes of a man, and a mouth uttering great boasts (Daniel 7:8).

The interpretation follows further in the chapter:

> And another will arise after them [the ten kings], and he will be different from the previous ones and will subdue three kings (Daniel 7:24).

In the kingdom of the ten kings will arise a power leader, a man with charisma, who will actually have people, armies, and every means at hand by which to launch his bid for control of the bloc of the ten kingdoms. A violent struggle will ensue, no doubt a great battle among the nations of western Europe and the Mediterranean world. In the outcome of this bitter conflict many will perish, including three main leaders of this bloc. It sounds incredible today, remembering the carnage of the loss in human life in Europe after two world wars. Today the leaders of Europe try desperately to work together so as to avoid what has already happened in previous wars, yet the Scriptures describe another such conflict in Europe's future.

Daniel also provides us an insight to the character of this power-hungry person who will seek control of the European bloc:

> And he will speak out against the Most High and wear down the saints of the Highest One, and he will intend to make alterations in times and in law (Daniel 7:25).

This description is a follow-up of what has already been indicated in verse 8. This "little horn" is really a man with a mouth full of boasts. So pugnacious is this evil character that, after conquering the territory of the old Roman Empire, he will even blaspheme God. While this earth has seen evil dictators before, they will be outrivaled by this wicked monster. His special object of attack will be believers who seek to live for the Lord and to give testimony of the Word of God and of salvation. This future dictator will see in the Lord's witnesses a rival to his power and for this reason he will seek to destroy them. With total domination he will turn previous political processes, customs, cultures, economics, etc., topsy turvy, so that his reputation as unique ruler will be unrivaled.

Is there a possibility, from Daniel's point of view, to determine more precisely when he will appear in history? The prophet states:

And they will be given into his hand [the little horn, or this world dictator] for a time, times, and half a time (Daniel 7:25).

This designation of "time, times, and half a time," already has a familiar ring. In Revelation 12 we have already noted that Satan will bring pressure to bear on Israel in a period designated by the "times," and that this is the very period when Satan's man will have his ultimate authority. But this is also the time slot described as the darkness of the day of the Lord in the second half of the tribulation period. Accordingly, we can equate John's designation and Daniel's reference to the "times" and that the latter is a period of three-and-a-half years. Both John and Daniel refer to the very same person who will be Satan's man in this particular time slot. Both prophets indicate that this dictator comes out of the European bloc of nations, that he will blaspheme God, and that he will eventually have the ultimate in power. This man can operate only in one time period, designated "time, times, and half a time."

We are now prepared to describe generally the sequence of events of which Daniel speaks:

1. The appearance of ten kings and the ten kingdoms in a bloc of nations soon after the body of Christ is caught away.

2. The little horn, a powerful individual who comes forth in the European western bloc of nations almost simultaneously with the appearance of the ten kings and kingdoms.

3. The struggle for power of this bloc where this powerful dictator obtains the control of a revived Roman Empire.

4. A time designation that is related to the second part of the tribulation period of total power by this ruler.

We have illustrated Daniel's time description in Figure 14.

Accordingly, we have some idea as to the occurrence of this revival of the Roman Empire. While Rome fell in 476, and while the Roman influence has continued through the centuries, so that no other empire has taken control and displaced this influence, yet the revival of this empire is still future from our point of view. It is important to realize, from all the time sequences already mentioned both here and in chapter two, that all of the events to which we referred are still yet to come.

It has been said that great events do not occur without their foretelling shadows, and the revival of the Roman Empire appears already to have these shadows of significant importance. We have hinted at the progress of the centralization of power in Europe, starting even before World War I. Today, in NATO and the Common Market, there is the potential of machinery that could mean the unification of territories of the Roman Empire under a single ruler. The ever-present threat of the Soviet Union is also a significant factor that keeps the nations of the European West in a loose form of alignment and might figure prominently as to the need for a more centralized control. At any rate, all we need is the proper catalyst that will bring about what Daniel spoke of some twenty-six-hundred years ago: the structuring of a new representation of the Roman Empire.

Like so many dictators in the past, this world ruler will also have a sudden end:

> Then I kept looking because of the sound of the boastful words which the horn was speaking; I kept looking until the beast was slain, and its body was destroyed and given to the burning fire (Daniel 7:11).

The interpretation follows, and it comes with no surprise that while God had a purpose for this tyrant's short-lived ex-

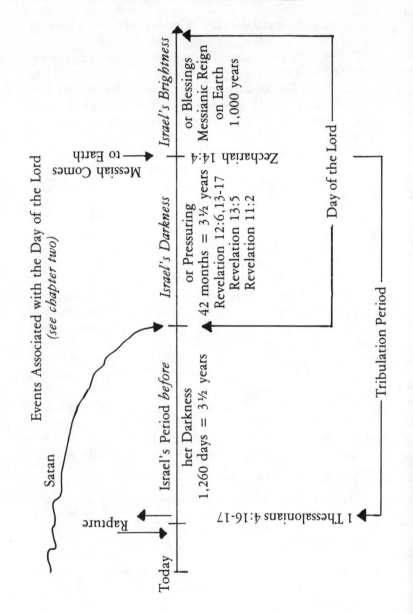

Events Associated with the Day of the Lord
(see chapter two)

Satan

Today

Rapture

1 Thessalonians 4:16-17

Israel's Period *before*
her Darkness
1,260 days = 3½ years

Israel's Darkness
or Pressuring
42 months = 3½ years
Revelation 12:6,13-17
Revelation 13:5
Revelation 11:2

Messiah Comes to Earth

Zechariah 14:4

Israel's Brightness
or Blessings
Messianic Reign
on Earth
1,000 years

Tribulation Period

Day of the Lord

Daniel's Time Description

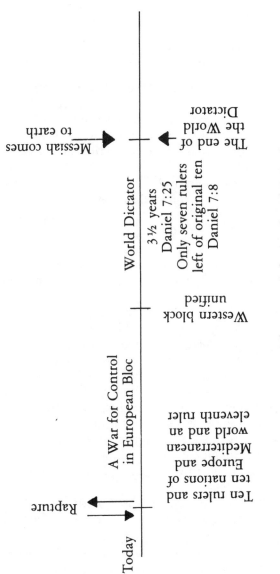

Figure 14—The Day of the Lord and Daniel's Reconstituted Roman Empire

istence, yet the sovereignty of this world will be returned to the Lord:

But the court will sit for judgment, and his dominion will be taken away, annihilated and destroyed forever (Daniel 7:26).

While his body is destroyed, yet this dictator's soul and spirit are not annihilated; forever separated from God, he will continue to exist, tortured in his conscience for the horrible deeds he perpetrated on the nations and the servants of the Most High. The point of departure from this earth is also indicated in Figure 14.

The only kingdom that will follow the restructured Roman Empire is one not dominated by man; it will be the Messianic kingdom:

The sovereignty, the dominion, and the greatness of all the kingdoms under the whole heaven will be given to the people of the saints of the Highest One; His kingdom will be an everlasting kingdom, and all the dominions will serve and obey Him (Daniel 7:27).

The second part of the day of the Lord is in view when the Messiah will reign over a world kingdom instituted by God. No kingdom of mere man, or any ideology of human invention will be permitted once God has intervened after the final fall of the restructured Roman Empire. This is the reason why in modern times, to take an example, the Nationalist Socialist regime of Germany under Hitler failed in the bid to conquer the western bloc of nations; furthermore, any move that Russia might take to conquer or drastically change the ideological alignment of the European western bloc of nations is also doomed to failure.

The Book of Revelation. The Apostle John also describes the restructuring of the Roman Empire in the book of Revelation:

And I stood on the sand of the seashore. And I saw a beast coming up out of the sea, having ten horns and seven heads, and on his horns were ten diadems, and on his heads were blasphemous names (Revelation 13:1).

Generally a reference to ''the sea'' (and this is the word in this verse) is a description of the Mediterranean Sea. The bloc of nations of which John speaks borders the Mediterranean and consists of ten horns and seven heads. The ten horns refer to a bloc of nations, and John actually uses the same kind of language which Daniel had used to depict the rearrangement of a ten-nation Roman Empire. Just as Daniel indicated that the ten leaders are reduced to seven in a terrific battle in the struggle for power, so John also indicates that this same western bloc of nations will only have seven national leaders remaining to rule within this alignment of power.

While John confirms this battle for control, he also adds additional interesting information as to what happens to the challenger:

And I saw one of his heads as if it had been slain, and his fatal wound was healed. And the whole earth was amazed and followed after the beast (Revelation 13:3).

The Scriptures are not too clear as to whether we have a conglomerate of nations in mind under the term of beast (verse 1), or whether the word is to refer to a person (verse 3). In verse 4, the whole earth will worship the beast and praise him, leading us to believe that in this verse beast refers to a person. I am suggesting that there will ultimately be such a perfect control over the western conglomerate of nations by this ruler that John uses the same term ''beast'' interchangeably in verses 1 and 3, so that it can refer to both the revitalized Roman Empire as well as the victorious ruler who comes out of the bloc.

Furthermore, when John speaks of ''one of the heads'' of the beast, i.e., of the power bloc, as almost slain (verse 3), we might wonder if he is referring to any of the heads of the nations of verse 1, or if he has in mind the word ''head'' to mean something entirely different from any of the heads of

Events Associated with the Day of the Lord
(see chapter two)

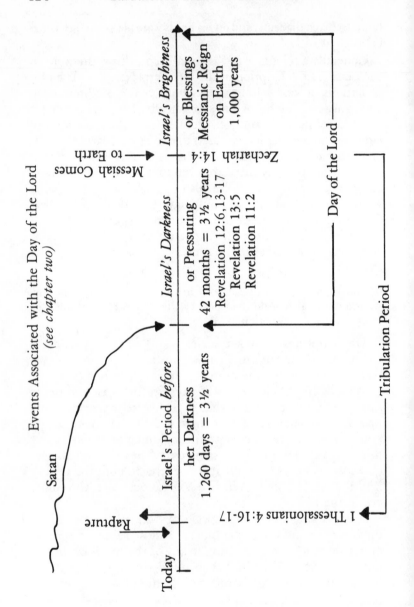

Satan

Today

Rapture

Israel's Period *before*
her Darkness
1,260 days = 3 ½ years

Israel's Darkness

or Pressuring
42 months = 3 ½ years
Revelation 12:6,13-17
Revelation 13:5
Revelation 11:2

Messiah Comes
to Earth

Israel's Brightness

or Blessings
Messianic Reign
on Earth
1,000 years

Zechariah 14:4

Day of the Lord

Tribulation Period

1 Thessalonians 4:16-17

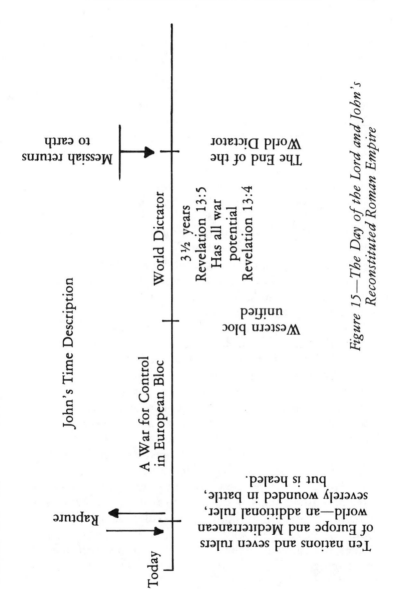

Figure 15—The Day of the Lord and John's Reconstituted Roman Empire

verse 1. Our clue for understanding this usage is probably given us by Daniel when he already contrasted for us the ten horns as leaders of ten nations, and that there is *another* little horn which is entirely different from the ten horns. If this can be applied in Revelation 13:1,3, the ten horns (kingdoms) and seven heads (rulers) are different from the additional one head of the beast as indicated in verse 3. In other words, a ruler entirely different from the original ten arises out of the restructuring of the Roman Empire to challenge the ten leaders.

This would further substantiate what we have already said of the word beast in verse 3 that refers to the actual dictator who will rule the bloc. Beast and head in verse 3 actually depict the individual who will contend for control of the European western bloc of nations.

John only hints at the battle that ensues among this group of nations while Daniel actually indicates that this challenging ruler is responsible for the death of three of the leaders. John does state that, in the battle that takes place in the bid for power, the contender for control of this bloc of nations is wounded to the point of death. There are some teachers who say that this one is actually killed on the field of battle, but a close examination of the Scriptures indicates otherwise. The phrase "*as if* it had been slain," is a simile, a figure of speech, that says he *appears* as if slain. There is no actual statement that he will be killed. So it will only *seem* that he is killed, but he will be healed and then go on to claim his victory in controlling the newly rearranged Roman Empire.

We also see the sinister character of this individual. While Daniel only reveals that power will be given to this one for the three-and-a-half years, John informs us that it is Satan who actually will give his authority to this ruler. Satan will be the source of power and wickedness for this dictator. And as Daniel had already described him as a boastful person, challenging the Most High, and persecuting the believers, John also describes him similarly:

And there was given to him a mouth speaking arrogant words and blasphemies. . . . And he opened his mouth in blasphemies against God, to blaspheme His name and His tabernacle, that is, those who dwell in heaven. And it was given to him to make war with the saints and to overcome them (Revelation 13:5-7).

The only way to comprehend Satan's man is in terms of Hitler and Stalin many times over. But while Hitler and Stalin had their authority over their respective peoples, this individual described by John will ultimately have control over all the power blocs on this earth.

John also provides for us the time period in which this ruler will have complete power.

And authority to act for forty-two months was given to him (Revelation 13:5).

This is the time period of the second half of the tribulation, also the first part of the day of the Lord. This is the political antichrist who will wreak havoc on the earth once he is under Satan's complete control.

There is a lot more that we can say about the career of the man of sin, but it is better to wait so as to see his functions in relation to the wars he wages, the influence he will wield among the nations, and his further activity with regard to Israel. Subsequent chapters will reveal more information.

John, similarly to Daniel, unfolds some of the sequence of events in connection with the revitalization of the Roman Empire:

1. Ten horns (nations) and seven heads (leaders), suggesting already some power struggle which deposes three of the ten leaders.

2. A separate head (a powerful leader), described as the beast (considered as an individual), who appears within the bloc of nations that border the Mediterranean, and no doubt includes the rest of the western nations.

3. Implied is the struggle for power where this powerful challenger is almost killed, but is healed from his near-fatal wound.

4. This leader now controls the European western bloc of nations, and will ultimately control the other power blocs.

5. A time period related to the second part of the tribulation when the political antichrist will have the ultimate power.

We compare the time sequence of prophetic events from chapter two and John's descriptions of events in Figure 15.

So far we have seen the great amount of Scripture that appears to emphasize the place of the revival of the Roman Empire in the days before the coming of the Messiah to institute the fullness of the kingdom. And as we see the prominence of the European western bloc of nations today, and their place in the United Nations, we see the possibility of what can come about under the right circumstances. Once the rapture of the Church occurs, the events within the bloc of nations of western Europe and the Mediterranean world will move very quickly to fulfill what both Daniel and John describe. Given the proper catalyst, and the right kind of leader with great charisma and powerful personality, it is entirely possible to visualize the circumstances indicated by both prophets.

The Northern Power Bloc

As we turn our attention in another direction, the Scriptures also describe another bloc of nations which will figure prominently in the last days (Ezekiel 38—39). Ezekiel was a part of the second deportation which was taken from Jerusalem to captivity in 597 B.C. by the Babylonian armies. This priest, as he preached to the Jewish captives, also functioned as a prophet, and was able to look down the corridors of time. He had a vision of the end time that included the period prior to the coming of the Messiah and the institution of the Messianic kingdom. In connection with the future of Israel at that time, the prophet saw the presence of a bloc of nations governed by Gog, prince of Rosh, Meshech, and Tubal (Ezekiel 38:2; 39:1).

In attempting to identify this leader and whomever he is

associated with, it is best not to take an ancient name and try to make it fit some current designation. For example, we must never identify Rosh with Russia, Meshech and Moscow, and Tubal with Tubalsk unless we have very good reason to do so. It is an archeological fact that what Ezekiel describes as Meshech is actually a reference to the Mushki tribes who, in Assyrian and Persian times, lived somewhere in the vicinity of eastern Turkey or Armenia. Tubal could refer to the area of Cappadocia or eastern Turkey. The prophet's reference to these tribes and areas does provide the clue as to the general area to which he is referring. This will become important for us when attempting to fix the general location of the power bloc under consideration.

Ezekiel does not leave us to wonder as to how he identifies the area occupied by this power bloc, for he declares:

> And you will come from your place out of the remote parts of the north, you and many peoples with you, all of them riding on horses, a great assembly and a mighty army (Ezekiel 38:15).

Now, geographical notations are always made with respect to the land of Israel. The prophet speaks of an area, "the remote parts of the north," and the picture before us is a land mass today known as the Soviet Union. Rosh, Meschech, and Tubal were only pointers as Ezekiel described the remote parts of the north in his day. But as we move to the end of the age, it is the Soviet Union area which the prophet is describing. In fact, if we look at a map of the Middle East and the Soviet Union, we will find that Moscow is just about directly north of Jerusalem.

But what is it that makes the Soviet Union, the remote parts of the north of Israel, so important from our day? Ezekiel would have no way of knowing what would happen in the modern period; yet God knew from His perspective! Figure 16 describes exactly how this power bloc to the north of Israel has come into being. Beginning in the 1400s the Russians have practiced a policy of expansionism until World

War I in 1914. Under the Russian brand of Marxism, and stimulated by World War II, the Soviet Union is a force in the modern period.

Note where this power bloc moves for a specific military strike in the future:

"And you will come up against My people Israel like a cloud to cover the land. It will come about in the last days that I shall bring you against My land, in order that the nations may know Me when I shall be sanctified through you before their eyes, O Gog" (Ezekiel 38:16).

God is going to bring this power bloc down into the land of Israel. As to the reasons for the attack and the battle that ensues in the land of Israel, we will discuss these in chapter six when dealing with the great world wars to come. It is enough to know that in the last days there will be a bloc of nations (the Soviet Union and some of its allies) to the north of Israel who will have evil intentions toward her. As one of the objectives in a military move, the Soviet Union will not hesitate to attack that tiny land and do harm to the people of Israel.

Can we, from today's point of view, try to point to the time when the Soviet Union will mount this attack? The prophet does provide us with a clue:

And you will say, I will go up against the land of unwalled villages. I will go against those who are at rest, that live securely, all of them living without walls, and having no bars or gates (Ezekiel 38:11).

In Ezekiel's day it was unthinkable that a city should be without fortified walls or gates that were not barred shut at night. A city's first line of defense was the strength of its walls and gates and their fortification in the event of attack by hostile invaders. For the prophet to describe a set of conditions where walls were missing in the villages and cities in Israel, and where there were no gates or bars on the gates, was his way of saying that the people will be living in peace and security. It seems Israelis will have no fear of the danger of attack and, in fact, the people will never expect to be attacked.

Figure 16—The Expansionism of Czarist Russia in Siberia (European expansionism not shown)

Beginning in 1462 around Moscow, all of the land mass indicated, as well as Manchuria, was acquired by 1914. Note the area north of Afghanistan, a portion of the area taken in 1860-1870. An attempt was made for Afghanistan, more than one hundred years ago, but the Russians were not successful then. It was no wonder that this colossus of power, the Soviet Union today, figures so prominently at the end of the age.

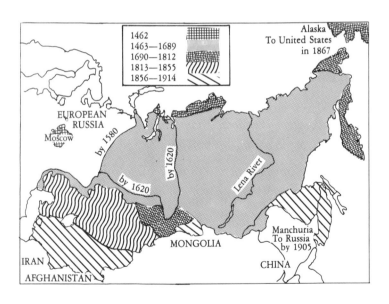

As we project these sets of conditions into the future, we realize that this is certainly not the condition today in Israel. Ever since the 1973 war, Israel has vowed that she will never be taken by surprise again. The Israel defense forces stand ready, and the reserves can be called up with very short notice. Most of Israel's economy is on a defense basis so as to insure her safety. While Israel's neighbors have enough manpower to sustain a number of defeats, Israel cannot afford to lose even once. Hence she stands ready for her defense.

But what will it be like in the future for Israel? There will come the day when Israel will live in peace, albeit a false kind of tranquility. Ever since 1948-1949 Israel has searched for the right formula by which she can live at peace with her neighbors. The recent venture with Sadat and Begin is a case in point. But we are talking about the day when, under specific circumstances which the Scriptures describe (which we will discuss subsequently in chapter seven), Israel will find that agreement to relieve her of the crushing economic load required for defense and when her people will think that they finally have achieved their objective. That will happen during the first three-and-a-half year period when the political antichrist of Revelation 13:1-10 will give her her guarantee for peace and secure borders. Israel will finally lay down her arms, trusting in the pact arranged between the political antichrist and one of her own great religious leaders.

But it is during this period of peace that the power bloc of nations from the remote parts of the north will move into the land of Israel. They will bring about untold havoc and destruction in Israel and other countries as they seek to dominate the Middle East for their own purposes. However, in chapter six, we shall continue this discussion when considering the reasons for this all-out attack in the deployment of troops for the great world wars to come. In that chapter we shall also provide a diagram indicating the time when the Soviet Union will attack Israel.

It is interesting to note that the professors of political

science at the Hebrew University today are investigating the peculiar political power axis through the Middle East. In centuries gone by, Israel has been conquered many times, but always the thrust has been from the northeast (Assyria, Babylon, and Persia), from the southwest (Egypt), and from the northwest (Greece and Rome). Never before has there been a north-south axis of power with regard to Israel. This is the first time in history that this has happened, and it is significant that Ezekiel spoke of this arrangement twenty-five-hundred years ago. This is one of the features of prophecy in which God can provide some of the details, known only to His omniscience, to specially selected men so that this information can be confirmed when the specific circumstances come to pass.

The allies of this northern bloc, from today's point of view are timely.

Persia, Ethiopia, and Put with them, all of them with shield and helmet (Ezekiel 38:5).

Persia is today the modern Iran, which significantly is much in the news. While United States policy had designed Iran to be the dominant power in the Persian Gulf for its protection, yet American plans went to pieces when the extremist Muslims revolted against the Shah and repudiated any American involvement in Iran. Someday, according to Ezekiel, Iran will actually be aligned with the Soviet Union, either because of Soviet design and the need for oil by the Russians, or a combination of other reasons. The circumstances of history make strange allies, and this state of affairs will yet be to the dismay of those who draw up United States foreign policy.

Put is the land to the west of Egypt and it is difficult to pin down which country is in the prophet's mind. However, directly to the west of Egypt is Libya with a policy which is very much anti-Egypt. While Qaddafi, as ruler of Libya, is an ardent Muslim, yet he has not hesitated to use Soviet help to embarrass his neighbor to the east. Libya's ire with Egypt will only increase if Egypt continues to foster its own ties with the West, that is, Europe and the United States. Therefore it is not inconceivable that with the right circumstances, and the desire to gain its own political and economic ends, Libya will yet join itself with the Soviet Union in the latter's military purposes. Put could also include other nations to the west of Libya, e.g., Algeria.

Ethiopia, or Cush, also provides us in the modern period with a clue as to her future designs. Given the present state of affairs the country's ruling class, after deposing Haile Selassie, continues to manifest more and more of its socialist interest and desire to link its ends with the aims and goals of the Soviet Union. Missionaries are finding it increasingly difficult to maintain their witness in that nation and are systematically being forced out. The time will come when Ethiopia will openly align itself with the military thrust of the Soviet Union in the Middle East, according to Ezekiel.

What is even more significant is the lineup of nations as we look at a map of the countries which Ezekiel mentioned (see Figure 17). Iran represents the easternmost limits of the Middle East while Put can describe the westernmost limits. Ezekiel could also be suggesting that *some* of the peoples between these limits will be linked with the Soviet Union in the day when she finally makes her move. The peoples for the most part are, between the limits indicated, what we know today as Arabs of different nationalisms. While we do not see all Arab nations linked with the Soviet Union, yet certain key ones will become its allies, and they will do so for their own purposes. One overriding aim will be to eradicate the Jewish state, a desire of the more extremist of the Arabs ever since the proclamation of the Balfour Declaration which sought to make a part of Palestine a homeland for the Jewish people.

Once more we note a very interesting aspect of prophecy where there is a description of the lineup of a northern power bloc, to the north of Israel. It is a phenomenon that will occur

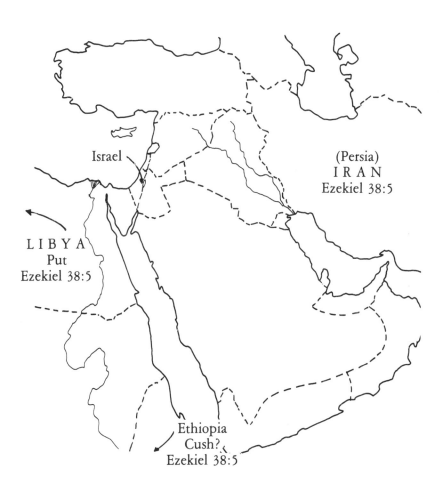

*Figure 17—Ezekiel's World of Outer Limits
of the Middle East*

in the last days when this power bloc will move into the land of Israel during a time of peace. At the same time, however, we see the prominence of this very same power bloc in the United Nations wielding enormous power and influence. It is my feeling that this is not coincidental, but that the very hand of God is operating today to bring about His purposes in this bloc.

The Eastern Power Bloc

The Bible also mentions still another bloc of nations, although not too much is said about this bloc. But the fact that the Scriptures do make some reference to it underscores its importance. The Apostle John states:

> And the sixth angel poured out his bowl upon the great river, the Euphrates; and its water was dried up, that the way might be prepared for the kings from the east (Revelation 16:12).

The geographical notation with respect to the land of Israel is toward the east. When we move eastward from Israel, we are soon confronted by a power colossus: the People's Republic of China. While we will still have to discuss the reason as to why China is drawn into some conflict in the Middle East, it is enough to recognize the prominence of this power center to the east of the land of Israel. Here again is a reference to the prominence of a power bloc which also has its place in the United Nations today. We actually live in the days when China has been finally united as a single people who will yet seek to make its imprint upon the destiny of the world community of nations.

Is it not, therefore, significant that when the Bible describes the power alignment of the end time, just before the coming of the Messiah to set up His kingdom, there is actually the description of three vital blocs of power? There is a revitalized Roman Empire, today the European western bloc of nations with some of the Mediterranean nations as a part of this bloc. The Soviet Union, the power to the north of Israel, is also one of these blocs of power with many nations on her side. The People's Republic of China, the power to the east of Israel, is also present. Now as we look at the lineup in the United Nations, these very same power blocs are very much evident, their presence being felt all the time when issues arise that affect their interests. The point is that we have never seen such a lineup in history as we see it today. We would have to be very blind not to see its significance in the United Nations, exactly as the Bible describes it. Such a lineup in the United Nations is the preparation for the confrontations between the power blocs and the ultimate takeover by the political antichrist. We are living in the shadows already, on the threshold in a sense, of great and significant events that will precede the coming of the Messiah to rule on this earth.

Diagrams which will describe the position and timing of the northern power bloc (the Soviet Union and allies) and the eastern power bloc (China) will be provided in chapters six and seven. Figure 18 sets out the three superpowers as described by Scripture.

Reconstituted Roman Empire	Power to the North of Israel Soviet Union	Power to East of Israel China
Daniel 7:7,19,23 Beast without description—Rome	Ezekiel 38:15 Location, north of Israel	Revelation 16:12 Hordes to east of Israel (China) enter into the Middle East
Daniel 7:7,8,24 Ten horns of Roman Area; The reconstituted Roman Empire	Ezekiel 38:3; 39:1 God has a controversy with this people	Daniel 11:44 Power bloc to east of Israel comes for battle
Daniel 7:8,20,24 Little Horn—Political Antichrist	Ezekiel 38:5-6 Soviets have many allies in Middle East and North Africa	
Daniel 7:8,20,24 Little Horn—Political Antichrist takes control	Ezekiel 38:8,11 Soviets move in a time of peace in Israel	
Daniel 7:11,22,26 God judges Political Antichrist	Ezekiel 39:4 Soviets are ruined and nevermore a threat to peace	
Revelation 13:1 Reconstituted Roman Empire Three of ten kings already defeated		
Revelation 13:3 Political Antichrist, wounded but recovered		
Revelation 13:4 Political Antichrist worshiped		
Revelation 13:5-8 Political Antichrist's hellish rule		

Figure 18—The Superpowers of the End of the Age

6

THE GREAT WORLD WARS TO COME

Cannon to right of them,
Cannon to left of them,
Cannon behind them
    Volleyed and thundered;
Stormed at with shot and shell,
While horse and hero fell,
They that had fought so well
Came thro' the jaws of Death,
Back from the mouth of Hell,
All that we left of them,
    Left of six hundred.
                Alfred Tennyson

War is an emotion-laden term, and it has a special meaning to different people. To the mother of a strapping young son, it can strike terror because of possible involvement with danger and even death. To the father the prospect of war might bring a touch of pride to his heart when he sees his son in uniform, or it just might provoke an underlying fear as to whether his son will make it through combat. War can mean the opportunity to don an attractive uniform so as to attract the attention of girls, or the fellow could wear the uniform with resignation and grit his teeth until his term of service is over. And to the fellow going into battle there is a time of seeking after God. War can mean a waiting period to a girl for her hero until he returns home—if he does—but for the fellow and girl who are engaged it represents wasted time before their marriage.

No one likes war unless that person has a twisted sense of values. Many have been the efforts of man to control it. When visiting the grounds and buildings of the United Nations in New York City one sees many paintings, murals, pictures, and sculptures in various motifs depicting the intense desire by men to have and live in peace among themselves. Those who designed the machinery of the United Nations attempted to devise every strategy in a centralized world body to achieve peace among the nations.

The Vietnam War was covered so thoroughly by reporters that we actually had all the worst possible scenes of bloody war brought into our living rooms. It created such a revulsion in the thinking of many in the United States and in western Europe that there was a clamor to stop this particular war. In fact, the war coverage so conditioned American minds to the horrors of war that there is very little stomach for engaging in another one, except for one that would involve the territory of the United States.

Yet in spite of all this concerning the control of war, conflict is a part of the history of mankind. The slogan of World War I, "the war to end all wars," is hollow mockery to the millions who have been killed since then. The events today in the trouble spots of the world can only mean that war is still a fact of life among nations, and there is every prospect of further bloodshed in the future. I am not given to a pessimistic frame of mind, but I must also insist that as long as man does not avail himself of the new life possible in Jesus, he will continue to spawn his wars. Man has that kind of nature where he cannot live at peace with himself or his fellowman for very long.

It is important for the believer to remember that the Lord Jesus Himself never promised a period of ultimate peace among men as they bend their own efforts for it. It was with the greatest concern that He warned:

And you will be hearing of wars and rumors of wars; see that you are not frightened. For those things must take place, but that is not yet the end. For nation will rise against nation, and kingdom against kingdom, and in various places there will be famines and earthquakes. But all these things are merely the beginning of birth pangs (Matthew 24:6-8).

While this may be the height of gloom and doom, yet Jesus had a realistic way of looking at the very heart of man, from which springs all the misunderstandings, hatred, murder, and even national leaders finally dragging their countries into war with one another.

One must also recognize that in the providential rule of God, war is permitted so that wicked nations can be judged and cast down, and other nations can be lifted up, for "the Most High is ruler over the realm of mankind" (Daniel 4:17). Man is given a certain amount of freedom to make his own choices, and this is also true for national leaders who guide the destinies of nations. But no leader is so completely free that he can pursue a rule of wickedness unchecked and break every moral law. Sooner or later God will intervene and cause other nations, through war, to bring down ungodly rulers who mislead nations. We can also see God's action in using nations with regard to His people Israel. Habakkuk struggled with this providential rule of God when it was revealed to the prophet that the fierce Chaldeans were going to attack and dominate Judah for the purpose of discipline and purification (Habukkuk 1).

So as this age draws to a close, there will no doubt be a number of conflicts and wars. But it is our concern that as we come to the strategic time periods, the two three-and-a-half-year periods just prior to the coming of Jesus to earth, there will be some specific battles which the Scriptures indicate. The point is that as well intentioned as some national leaders are about peace, and with all their efforts for it, real peace will remain as elusive as ever until the day Messiah comes to enforce it.

We shall examine these battles, and note the leaders on each side in the conflicts, the compositions of the armies, the objectives of the contenders, and then the final results in connection with the conflicts. Only in this way can we determine the specific differences in the battles and not be confused as to their identity.

The Battle in the European Western Bloc

This is a battle to which we have referred in describing the restructuring of the Roman Empire. I have already pointed out that there exists the potential in Europe right now for the establishment of such a bloc, and all we need to have are just the right catalysts to bring about a power bloc strong enough to challenge other poles of power. But for the purposes of this chapter this battle will be formally defined.

The Arena of Conflict. Ten nations make up this bloc. The Prophet Daniel in his interpretation of Nebuchadnezzar's dream of the image announced that the ten toes represent a ten-nation bloc in a new form of the Roman Empire (Daniel 2:41-43). He expanded his views in his description of the ten horns representing ten kings of ten nations that would arise in a revitalization of the Roman Empire (7:23-24). The Apostle John also saw a ten-nation kingdom bordering the Mediterranean, resembling the Roman Empire of his day, but because of the context which he outlines, there are decided differences. The only way to understand John's interpretation is to project forward in time this new view of the Roman Empire (Revelation 13:1-3) in the future.

Many try and speculate which ten nations will comprise this old-new power bloc. The empire of John's day stretched from England to the Middle East, and included England, France, the lowlands of today's Netherlands and Belgium, a portion of West Germany, Spain, Italy, Yugoslavia, Rumania, Bulgaria, Greece, Turkey, a portion of Iraq, Syria, Judea, Egypt, and a stretch of North Africa to the Atlantic Ocean. It was a formidable bloc, to say the least. But it is sheer speculation today to say with certainty which nations are to be the ten kingdoms in the revitalization of the Roman Empire. We can say that there will be some of the nations of western Europe, possibly some of the Mediterranean nations, including Egypt, and some of the presently-known moderate Arab nations. But it is difficult to discern specifically which nations it will be.

Some have sought to make a case for deciding on the ten nations based on the current common market European nations (since this is subject to change). No doubt the ten kingdoms in the future will be a tight economic unit eventually under the control of the political antichrist; but to insist on common market nations of today to be that future bloc is only a guess because there just might be a change in the member nations as they are now and others not currently included could become the mainstay of such a future political and economic unit.

The Contender, Opposition, and Results. Without question the greatest figure of this bloc is the one who eventually will be the political antichrist. Daniel had described him as the little horn among ten horns or leaders (Daniel 7:7-8, 24-25). John referred to him as the beast and head (regarded as an individual from our discussion in the previous chapter when dealing with this European power bloc, Revelation 13:3). I am stressing the point that this man is associated with this bloc and should not be confused with the great religious leader who will come forth from Israel. I shall make further distinctions between these men later on in chapter seven, but it is enough to say that both men do not have the same functions and they operate in different spheres.

I don't feel that this man arrives on the scene as the full-blown antichrist and archenemy of God. His first appearance is that of a man with charisma and appeal. This is the man who will be able to negotiate the peace which Israel will be desperate to possess. To be able to accomplish such a feat will command the respect and admiration of nations. No one will, at the point when the pact is made, be able to detect the ultimate design of power which this man will crave, and it is just possible that he himself will not realize the potential for evil of which he is capable. I am thinking of Saul who was awed by Samuel and considered himself as no one when Samuel was about to anoint Saul the Benjamite as king (1 Samuel 9:21). Even later when Samuel called for the leaders of Israel to come to Mizpah officially to anoint Saul, when the Benjamites presented themselves Saul was hidden amidst the baggage (1 Samuel 10:22). But it did not take long to reveal the basic hidden man in Saul. Given the proper circumstances, and the decisions made in these situations by Saul, it became apparent that Israel's first king could and did defy the wishes of Samuel and of God Himself. With the political antichrist there will be an even worse disposition for wickedness.

As soon as the pact with Israel is concluded, this leader will be an internationally recognized leader. This set of circumstances always becomes a crucial moment in the lives of statesmen and leaders; they can retain a humble attitude, or they can reach for additional honors and power. Given the opportune moment, this European leader makes a choice and it is possible that he does not even stop to think of alternate options to the lust and drive for additional power. Once this die is cast the basic evil nature of this leader will begin to be revealed.

It is not possible to chart the progress of the confrontation that will occur in the power bloc. Not all ten nations need to be involved when this leader challenges to take control. The possibility is that the fight need only entail three of the prominent countries and their leaders and a battle is joined between their governmental forces and the followers of the challenger. The other seven nations might stand by helplessly and watch anxiously for the outcome.

Or it could be that when this leader in question has become an internationally recognized figure in the agreement with Israel, all or certain of the countries of the European West will challenge him as a responsible leader. A military confrontation will ensue between the heads of states and their countries, with this leader and his allies as opposition forces.

Possibly because of the way Daniel described this bloc of nations, partly of iron and partly of clay (Daniel 2:41-43), this could mean that some of the nations are strong while others are weak. It might be that the weak nations will stay out of the fracas and watch the power struggle among the strong nations. The point to make here is that it is highly improbable to identify which nations are in the struggle based on the present lineup in Europe. And neither is it a fruitful exercise to try and identify the challenger from today's leadership personalities.

One fact is certain. There will be a battle in the European West and Mediterranean countries, and both Daniel and John reveal that whatever the lineup, the battle takes place, and three leaders of the ten will die in the conflict (Daniel 7:24; Revelation 13:1). All of this discussion is a sad commentary on the peace efforts in the world and in Europe in particular. In two world wars in this century millions of people have been killed in western Europe, and her fields and cities have been drenched with blood. Yet we now speak of another terrible battle there! If this isn't a testimony to the potential for evil in the hearts of men, I don't know what else could be. No wonder there will ultimately have to be a force exerted from outside the realm of men to bring about peace in the world. I am referring to the time when Jesus will invade this earth to institute His sovereign rule over the nations of this earth.

The Timing of This Challenge for Battle. Two points in history become important: the time when the political antichrist makes his appearance and the point when he has the control of the revitalized Roman Empire and is ready to take world leadership for himself. In chapter two we have already indicated that it is by the midpoint of the tribulation period that this leader is undisputed in his bid for power, and from that point forward in time antichrist's career will last for another three-and-a-half years as Satan's man (Daniel 7:25; Revelation 13:5).

What is important is to try to find the point when he makes his appearance as a world figure. Once again it is useless to point to any world leader today and say that he is the potential antichrist. Many have attempted this in the past and have been proven wrong, with the result that prophetic preaching gets "a black eye," and no one wants to listen to prophecy anymore. In the modern period we have heard preachers identify Hitler as a good candidate, and obviously he functioned as a little antichrist (1 John 4:3), but he certainly was not the real one. When Henry Kissinger was the secretary of state of the United States and was able to capture the world's attention because of the Middle East situation after the October 1973 war, there were those who confidently asserted that he was the antichrist. Where however, is he today? Once again, we must pay careful attention to what the Scriptures say so as to avoid embarrassing errors.

One major clue of timing is found in 2 Thessalonians. The people of the Thessalonian church had their problems ascertaining the end of this age. They felt that since the coming of Christ was so imminent, they just simply wanted to wait for Him, and set aside their daily round of life, confidently expecting His return at any moment. Paul exhorted them to be gainfully employed, carry on their usual round of life, and not be weary of continual well doing (1 Thessalonians 3:10-14). The point is that while the coming of Jesus in the rapture is considered imminent, yet we continue to carry on as if His coming will not be in our generation.

But Paul does specify a significant point.

Let no one in any way deceive you, for it will not come unless the apostasy [a falling away in faith] comes first, and [then] the man of lawlessness is revealed, the son of destruction (2 Thessalonians 2:3).

This means that there will come a day when there will be a great apostasy in Christendom, and then I understand that there will be the rapture of true believers in Christ. *After* the rapture this leader with the potential for great evil will then be revealed.

On the other hand, some confidently assert that the word translated "apostasy" in the New American Standard Version should really be "a catching away," and therefore this is a distinct reference to the rapture of the true believers in Jesus Christ. Whichever way the translation is provided, there is a cut-off point in history when the body of Christ is removed from this earth's scene for awhile. However, I am asserting at this point in the discussion that the rapture occurs prior to the tribulation period.

This particular battle where a European leader seeks control is diagramed in chapter five.

The Battle of Armageddon

This is a battle that is well known. Across the years it has acquired such a reputation that when anyone wants to describe the horrors of war, there is usually a reference to Armageddon.

The Armies of Heaven. One set of armies involved in this conflict is a most unusual grouping of forces:

And I saw heaven opened: and behold, a white horse, and He who sat upon it is called Faithful and True; and in righteousness He judges and wages war. . . . And the armies which are in heaven, clothed in fine linen, white and clean, were following Him on white horses (Revelation 19:11,14).

On one side of this great battle are the armies of Heaven, the hosts who do the bidding of the Lord. Girded for battle are the many ranks of angels and perhaps even archangels; it is a formidable lineup of power that describes the hosts of the Lord who do His will (Psalm 103:21). As to the specific reason why these hosts appear, we shall discuss this further when dealing with the plight of Israel in the day of the Lord. Suffice it to say that this is the greatest display of force ever to be hurled against any opposing army that would even dare to challenge the sovereignty of the Lord.

As to the leader of this awesome army, we are not left in doubt. But John also provides further information so that his identity is never in question:

And He is clothed with a robe dipped in blood; and His name is called the Word of God. . . . And on His robe and on His thigh He has a name written, "KING OF KINGS, AND LORD OF LORDS" (Revelation 19:13,16).

The specific references, Faithful and True, Word of God, KING OF KINGS AND LORD OF LORDS, all refer to Jesus the Messiah. While here on earth the first time, He appeared and lived as a Jew among Jewish people. For the first part of His life on earth, except for isolated instances, no one would have thought of Him as different from His fellows in Nazareth as He worked at the carpenter's bench. So startling was the inception of His public ministry in Nazareth that people asked, "Is this not the carpenter?" (Mark 6:3) But in Jesus's return to earth another picture is presented, that of a mighty leader of heavenly hosts. He indeed is sovereign, and who would dare to oppose Him as He leads an invincible army in battle array? We need to remember what He said on one occasion, "Do you think that I cannot appeal to My Father, and He will at once put at My disposal more than twelve legions [each legion contains about 6,000 troops] of angels?" (Matthew 26:53) The coming of Christ and His hosts is in actuality an invasion by God upon this earth.

The Opposing Armies. Who would be brash enough to be involved in a fight against the heavenly hosts? But again the Scriptures declare:

And I saw the beast and the kings of the earth and their armies, assembled to make war against Him who sat upon the horse, and against His army (Revelation 19:19).

While we shall explain this further, it should be remembered that the political antichrist and his armies will be pressuring Israel in the darkness of the day of the Lord and Israel's plight will be intense. Later on in the chapter also we shall see that as the battle is waged against Israel, this bestial ruler will also be in total control of most of the nations of this world. As we come to the end of the tribulation period and also the end of the darkness of the day of the Lord, when Israel will be almost "done in," Jesus will appear with His armies and the battle will commence. We are amazed at the sheer audacity of this political antichrist who will attempt to fight against Jesus and the armies of Heaven in order to preserve his control of power.

The armies under the control of the beast will be the power blocs already considered in chapter five. By the midpoint of the tribulation period, antichrist will have his control over the European western bloc of nations, including the Mediterranean nations that go along with this bloc. But the rest of the blocs will also come under the domination of antichrist as we shall see. In other words, in the very place to which Jesus returns, the land of Israel, representative troops of the power blocs as well as other nations will already be there, pressuring Israel. In the time of Jesus's return, these very troops will follow the lead of antichrist in his bid for power. It will be a situation as David described it:

> Why are the nations in an uproar,
> And the peoples devising a vain thing?
> The kings of the earth take their stand,
> And the rulers take counsel together
> Against the LORD and His Anointed [Messiah]:
> Let us tear their fetters apart,
> And cast away their cords from us! (Psalm 2:1-3)

There is a long battle line along which troops are deployed, from Megiddo in the north of Israel to as far as the deserts southeast of Jerusalem, the Aravah (in the Edom districts). We shall point this out further when describing Israel's experiences of her darkness. We need to realize that this is no minor skirmish, but a full-scale battle with devastating results.

The name for the battle comes from the word Megiddo, a prominent hill at the south side of the plains of Esdraelon, which is a very fertile valley in the northern part of the country. The hill overlooks what was once the great sea highway which ran along the Mediterranean coast from Egypt, but which turned inland, just north of the present Haifa. From there, the road ran approximately southeastward through the Zebulon valley, then the Esdraelon and Jezreel valleys, and then turned northeastward to Damascus. Therefore this hill of Megiddo was a strategic point, guarding the route, seeking to protect the country from any invading countries from the north. The Canaanites had fortified this place, and later Solomon had his massive fortifications there which included space for many chariots and horses. Subsequent to Solomon, Israel's invasions always came from the north, by the Assyrians, Babylonians, Persians, Greeks, and then the Romans. Therefore Megiddo becomes the figure of what will yet happen to Israel in the future when she will be invaded by various power blocs, marking the prelude to her day of darkness.

We must recognize the part that Satan plays in the final assault of antichrist upon Jesus and His armies. All during the darkness of the day of the Lord, Satan as the archenemy of God will seek to obliterate Israel and will have his man involved in the carnage. Satan knows the prominent part that the Scriptures attach to Israel in the brightness of the day of the Lord, and the consequence of blessing for all the nations of the world. It is his plan to do away with Israel and attempt to make God into a liar when Israel is finally gone from the face of the earth.

But God will not permit the plans of Satan to be realized and will intervene at the proper moment on behalf of His people Israel. One can only imagine Satan's fury which will be communicated to his man the antichrist who, while involved with his military campaign of genocide regarding Israel, will actually end up fighting against Jesus and the hosts of Heaven when challenged by the latter. It is a situation where the purposes of antichrist and Satan run parallel.

The Outcome. Obviously, the battle does not last long between antichrist and Jesus. One might even wonder why the antichrist will even make an attempt to get involved in this phase of the battle. For one thing, Satan will have so blinded antichrist that the latter will fight whoever the devil considers an enemy as a matter of course. But in addition, as we have already indicated, this world figure is so enamored with power and the position he has that he will fight like a wounded tiger. A modern example is Hitler in the last days of World War II in Europe. From his bunker he continued to issue his battle orders thinking that there would somehow be a way to defeat Germany's encircling enemies. He was defiant to the very end.

The hosts of Heaven make short shrift of any who would dare even to lift a finger against Jesus as King of kings.

And the beast was seized, and with him the false prophet who performed the signs in his presence, by which he deceived those who had received the mark of the beast and those who worshiped his image; these two were thrown alive into the lake of fire which burns with brimstone (Revelation 19:20).

Now we see that not only will the political antichrist be involved as one of the leaders, but the religious antichrist will be aligned with him as well. We can very well say that there is an unholy trinity of power: Satan, a political figure as the political antichrist, and a great religious figure as the religious antichrist. This force operates together all through the days of the pressuring of Israel, and then finally is involved in the battle for control of the nations against Jesus. Both of these antichrists are thrown alive into the lake of fire, indicating that Jesus and the hosts of Heaven have the total control, even over any conglomerate which Satan can devise. When discussing Israel's plight in chapter seven, I shall consider the roles of these antichrists and indicate how these two men will find an affinity to work together.

The lake of fire is the final destiny for all unrepentant sinners, and they go there because their names were never written in the book of life (Revelation 20:11-15). There is a great white throne judgment where the unrepentant will stand someday to be judged from the books in which are recorded all their deeds. Note, however, that after the short-lived battle of Armageddon, the two antichrists will not even be given the benefit of any final say at a judgment; they are seized without ceremony and are contemptuously tossed into the final place of retribution, where they will be in torment forever and ever for the horrible deeds they perpetrated against humanity in general and against Israel in particular (Revelation 19:20). There is no doubt that these two have never received Christ. As we have already said, men make decisions to serve themselves, and both antichrists do likewise; they lunge for power, making a mockery of every decent moral standard, and in the end become God's archenemies.

As for the troop commanders and soldiers who will be allied with the schemes and designs of the antichrists, their end is also swift and sure:

And the rest were killed with the sword which came from the mouth of Him who sat upon the horse, and all the birds were filled with their flesh (Revelation 19:21).

The carnage will be awful. One can imagine the thousands of bodies that will litter the countryside of Israel and which will attract the buzzards and vultures. The stench will be beyond description. In the slaughter of these troops, their blood will reach to the horses' bridles for a distance of two hundred miles, which incidentally is the battle line from Megiddo in the north, to the city of Jerusalem (Revelation 14:20), down to the south (Aravah). It is no wonder that the smell of blood will attract the carrion birds who will gorge themselves on the flesh of the dead bodies.

The battle gear will be strewn all over the country of Israel. It seems hard to conceive of the mountain of materiel but it is very possible. It was my privilege to travel into the Sinai in 1970 and to enter the Mitla Pass. This was a point where Egyptian troops were caught with their tanks, trucks, and other materiel when Israeli planes pounded them in 1967 in the first days of the Six Day War. When coming through in 1970, I looked out the window of the bus and saw how the landscape was still strewn with burnt-out tanks, broken-down trucks, and thousands upon thousands of pieces of smaller equipment. The guide, seeing my quizzical glance at what happened during the war, said, "Would you believe that we picked up 90 percent of the equipment left here by the Egyptians within one year after the war?" It didn't appear so as I looked again at the landscape. What came to mind was the equipment that would be left behind after the battle of Armageddon, and it wasn't too hard to visualize that it would take a long while to clear out the army materiel.

As for the troops who will die in this battle, there is one difference between them and the antichrists. While the latter are thrown directly into the lake of fire, the souls of others who die are held in Hades or Sheol. They are incarcerated until the resurrection of unsaved to stand before the great white throne judgment. Then they will join their leaders in the place of never-ending torment. It is a frightful situation to realize that men's wrong moral decisions, ultimately to reject Jesus as Saviour, will condemn them, even as in the case of national leaders and troops who join with the antichrists against Israel and Jesus in this battle.

Satan. As horrible as the deeds of Satan will be in perpetrating the pressuring of Israel and the battle of Armageddon, this is still not the end of his usefulness to God. God is not yet finished with His greatest archenemy:

And I saw an angel coming down from heaven, having the key of the abyss and a great chain in his hand. And he laid hold of the dragon, the serpent of old, who is the Devil and Satan, and bound him for a thousand years, and threw him into the abyss, and shut it and sealed it over him, so that he should not deceive the nations any longer, until the thousand years were completed; after these things he must be released for a short time (Revelation 20:1-3).

So, during the thousand years of the brightness of the

kingdom, the day of God's utopia on earth, Satan will not be able to bring disruption and confusion on this earth. He will be confined, but this is not his final place in the lake of fire. We shall discuss these implications further when treating Israel's Messianic constitution in chapter ten.

Figure 19 lays out the events of this battle and its final outcome.

The Battle of the "Little Season"

There is mention in Scripture of another great battle which will take place within a specific historical context. I have called the name of the battle after a phrase which John uses concerning when Satan will be released from the prison of the abyss for "a little season" (Revelation 20:3 AV). Now once again, we need to pay attention to the leaders of troops, the composition of the armies, and the result of the battle. John describes this battle:

> And when the thousand years are completed, Satan will be released from his prison, and will come out to deceive the nations which are in the four corners of the earth, Gog and Magog, to gather them together for the war; the number of them is like the sand of the seashore. And they came up on the broad plain of the earth and surrounded the camp of the saints and the beloved city, and fire came down from heaven and devoured them. And the devil who deceived them was thrown into the lake of fire and brimstone, where the beast and the false prophet are also: and they will be tormented day and night forever and ever (Revelation 20:7-10).

Timing of the Battle. It is very important to understand the timing and occasion of this battle in relation to the battle of Armageddon. We have already seen, as one of the results of the Armageddon conflict, that Satan is bound for a thousand years. The point in history at which he is placed in the abyss is exactly when the tribulation period is closed, or when the darkness of the day of the Lord ceases, and when the brightness of the day of the Lord begins. A thousand years elapse, and it is toward the close of the fullness of the Messianic kingdom that Satan is released for a short time. God will for the last time permit Satan, within the divine providential rule, to have his way among the nations.

Those Who Oppose God. One might wonder at such an arrangement. Why should Satan be permitted to work his havoc of ruin again after a perfect reign by a perfect king in a utopian kingdom? The point, however, is that while the brightness of the day of the Lord starts with a generation who truly know the Lord, this will not be the case in succeeding generations. It will be necessary to preach the message of the grace of God, and there will be an intensive world evangelization program to reach the masses of people in every generation of the Messianic kingdom. But like any age, as the message of grace is preached, whether in Old Testament days, the age in which we live, and even in the age of the fullness of the kingdom, while many receive this message yet many do not accept it and even despise it. Sad but true is the stark truth; even in the best conditions for the hearing of the gospel in the brightness of the day of the Lord, there will be an increasing number of people who will reject the message and deny the personal claims of Jesus as Messiah. As one comes to the end of that age, innumerable people, as many as the sand on the seashore, will be resistant to the grace of God. Even in the best of conditions on earth, God will never force Himself on those who make decisions to reject Him.

Will these unregenerate people rebel openly during the fullness of the kingdom? The answer is no. No possibility will be given to practice any wrong religion, as we shall see in chapter ten. But the political, economic, social, ecological, etc., factors of that age will be the optimum. There will be no parallel to it in all of history. Given this set of conditions, who would want to rebel? For what cause will there have to be a demonstration? In a kingdom where everything is handled judiciously and where every person's dignity will be respected, why turn against the authorities? But a spiritual

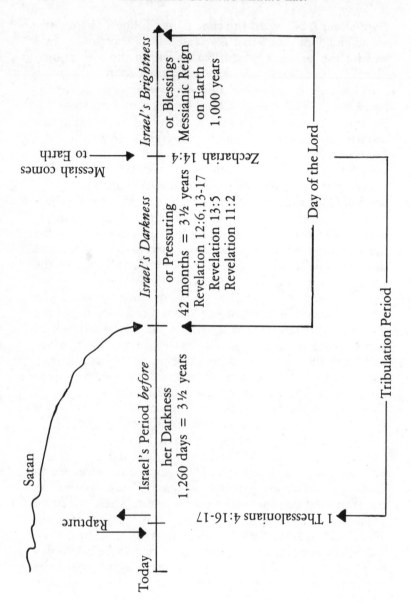

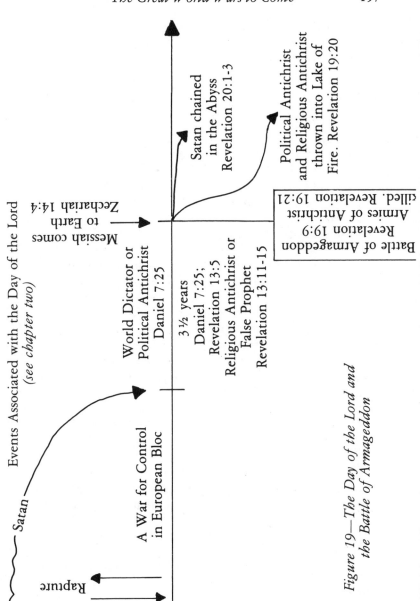

Events Associated with the Day of the Lord
(see chapter two)

Satan

Rapture

A War for Control
in European Bloc

World Dictator or
Political Antichrist
Daniel 7:25

3½ years
Daniel 7:25;
Revelation 13:5
Religious Antichrist or
False Prophet
Revelation 13:11-15

Messiah comes
to Earth
Zechariah 14:4

Satan chained
in the Abyss
Revelation 20:1-3

Political Antichrist
and Religious Antichrist
thrown into Lake of
Fire. Revelation 19:20

Battle of Armageddon
Revelation 19:9
Armies of Antichrist
killed. Revelation 19:21

*Figure 19—The Day of the Lord and
the Battle of Armageddon*

belief will not be enforced upon anyone. The acceptance of the message of grace is always on a voluntary basis; people will be given opportunity in that day to make personal deci-· sions to receive atonement for sin exactly as anyone does today.

There will come a time, however, when God will separate believers from those who have resisted His grace, and Satan becomes the means by which it will be done. He will gather them together in ranks under the leadership of individuals known as Gog and Magog. The use of these names seems to be a puzzle. Does this mean a link with leaders and armies who attack Israel from the north, that is, the Soviet Union? Names, however, can be repeated on many occasions and within many circumstances. John could very well be referring to rebel nations and peoples under the name that Ezekiel used when describing another group of men who will be God haters and who become involved in still another battle (Ezekiel 38:2-3; 39:1).

There are some interpretations which will try to relate this battle of the Little Season to what was described by Ezekiel where the same names of Gog and Magog appear. I think, however, that we shall hold our conclusions in abeyance until we have examined the entire context of this and Ezekiel's descriptions of battles, leaders, armies, timing, and results. It should be pointed out that those who oppose God in the Little Season battle *after* the thousand-year reign of Messiah will come from the *four corners* of the earth. The point of congregation of the ungodly is the camp of the saints and the beloved city, metaphors which describe the Jerusalem of the fullness of the Messianic kingdom. Satan will see to it, as he did in the battle of Armageddon, to mount an assault against the very place where the Lord will reside as if he will get the upper hand against the King of kings.

The Armies of God. There is no mention of any armies or

ranks of heavenly hosts as in the earlier battle. It might be that God will use His angels to execute His orders for destruction, but the Scriptures only indicate here the direct intervention of the Lord.

The Results. Fearful is the judgment meted out to Satan, and to the ingrates who have tasted and experienced the goodness of God in the best possible kingdom on earth. The fire of God comes from Heaven to destroy all the armies who would even dare to think that they could throw off the yoke of God which was meant for the best of man's experiences. Thousands and perhaps millions will be instantly killed, and then resurrected to stand before the judgment throne for unbelievers. Some might feel that God is unjust in the way He destroys sinners. But it is a rightful penalty. What else should God do to those who will be disobedient to the message of grace and the established order of the kingdom in that day and, after having enjoyed the optimum of utopia, then to march against the very throne of David upon which Jesus sits?

Satan is thrown finally into the lake of fire where the antichrists already were placed a thousand years previously. There is no benefit of final judgment for this archenemy of God for all his deeds through the many millennia since he took it into his head to oppose God (Isaiah 14:12-14). Satan had already been judged when he was displaced from his exalted position as Lucifer. There is no mercy for him for the way he has caused untold suffering for multitudes of people, especially Israel. In the last battle of human history, before the new heavens and a new earth, God's final use of him has been accomplished, and he is hurled into the lake of fire to be tormented day and night forever. It will be a just retribution for all the harm he ever caused.

Figure 20 places this Little Season battle at its point in history.

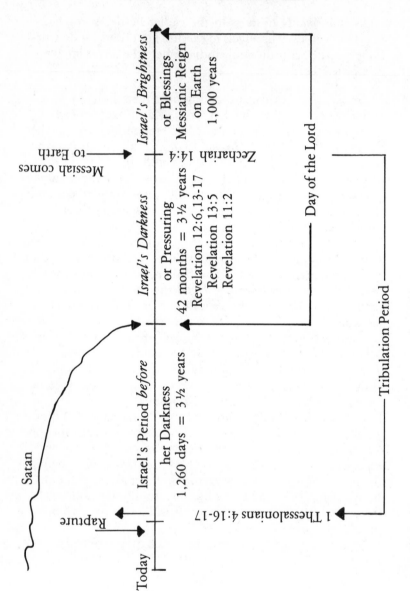

Events Associated with the Day of the Lord
(see chapter two)

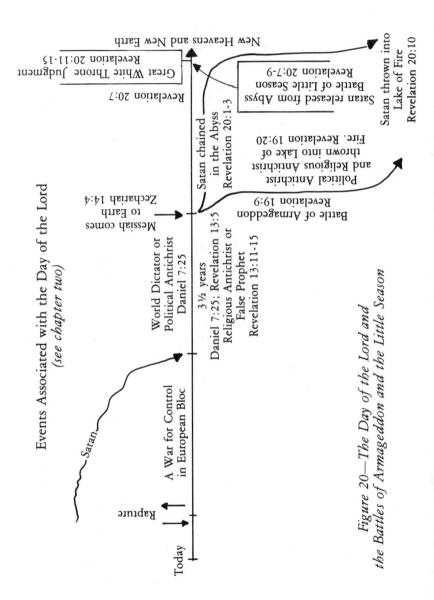

Figure 20—The Day of the Lord and
the Battles of Armageddon and the Little Season

The Soviet Invasion of the Middle East

Three great battles have now been described that will be frightful in human destruction. But there is still another battle of which the Scriptures speak, and it is one battle that is most difficult to describe, find the reason for, and decide when it occurs. But again we shall keep in mind the historical context of the conflict, the leaders, the constituency of the armies, and results.

The Soviet Alignment. Once again we remember the leader of this bloc of nations to the north of Israel:

Son of man, set your face toward Gog of the land of Magog (Ezekiel 38:2-3).

We have already discussed this formidable power bloc of nations to the north of Israel. The leader is a person known as Gog, who is prince of Rosh, Meshech, and Tubal, and whose name is repeated in Ezekiel 39:1. We shall wait for the identification of Gog, which is the very same name in Revelation 20:8, until we have all the information before us concerning the background of the battle of the Soviet invasion.

Among the many allies this bloc has, we note again the nations of Persia (Iran), Ethiopia, and the lands to the west of Egypt (Ezekiel 38:5). But in addition there are:

Gomer with all its troops; Beth-togarmah from the remote parts of the north with all its troops—many peoples with you (Ezekiel 38:6).

Once more we have to resist the temptation to identify Gomer with Germany and Togarmah with Turkey. Rather, we need to see these designations as Ezekiel saw them in his day as he referred to peoples who were familiar to him. Gomer might be a reference to the Assyrian designation of Gimarrai, who were situated in either Turkey or Armenia. On the other hand, Gomer is the son of Japheth (Genesis 10:2-3) who could have migrated to the eastern or central parts of Europe, but it is difficult to identify specific nations today. Similarly, there is nothing definite for Beth-Togarmah and it is best not to speculate further. Generally the area of the Soviet Union is in mind along with allies in the Middle East. The bloc is formidable and once aroused it will move with deadly intent.

Reason for and Object of Attack. Who is the object of attack? The Prophet Ezekiel has some definite information to convey:

After many days you [that is, Gog] will be summoned; in the latter years you will come into the land that is restored from the sword, whose inhabitants have been gathered from many nations to the mountains of Israel which had been a continual waste; but its people were brought out from the nations, and they are living securely, all of them . . . to capture spoil and to seize plunder, to turn your hand against the waste places which are now inhabited, and against the people who are gathered from the nations, who have acquired cattle and goods, who live at the center of the world . . . and you will come up against My people Israel like a cloud to cover the land. It will come about in the last days that I shall bring you against My land, in order that the nations may know Me when I shall be sanctified through you before their eyes, O Gog (Ezekiel 38:8,12,16).

In the last verse we are not left in doubt as to which people Ezekiel has in mind: Israel. In the distant day of which the prophet predicts, the people will be settled in a land that is developed. The people of Israel are described as gathered from many nations, from a worldwide dispersion, but in the last days many of Israel will be gathered into their land. The military status of Israel is described as almost nonexistent and the people of Israel will be living in peace. At some time in the future the Israelis will have an unprecedented opportunity to channel all their efforts and resources for the further development of the land. But with the Soviet attack upon Israel and its capture, the Arab nations (possibly Syria and Libya) and Iran (a non-Arab country) who have linked their fortunes with this colossus will finally feel that they have achieved their own purposes and aims in the destruction of the Jewish state.

But it appears that there is a further underlying reason for the invasion of the Middle East by the Soviet Union and her allies. Actually, Israel itself will be only a small part of the dimension as to why the Soviet Union will make a drastic military power drive. After all, why should the mighty Soviet Union take on a tiny country of about three million people? Daniel provides us with some clues of the objectives of the Soviets:

He will also enter the Beautiful Land, and many countries will fall; but these will be rescued out of his hand: Edom, Moab, and the foremost of the sons of Ammon (Daniel 11:41).

The prophet indicates that some military power will enter the beautiful land, which to him could only mean his beloved land of Israel. Sitting in Babylon as a refugee when he wrote these words, it would be natural for him to cast longing eyes on his homeland and refer to it by this description.

Our problem, of course, is to identify the "he" of Daniel 11:41 but in turn we need to understand verse 40, a very complex portion of Scripture to exegete:

And at the end time the king of the South will collide with him, and the king of the North will storm against him with chariots, with horsemen, and with many ships; and he will enter countries, overflow them, and pass through (Daniel 11:40).

The difficulty with verse 40 is to find out how many people the prophet had in mind and to identify: "the king of the South," "the king of the North," and "him." It is not my purpose to be involved in a full exegetical study of this passage, but perhaps we can begin by looking at the grammar of the passage:

The king of the South will collide   with him
    and the king of the North will storm   against him

Two possibilities suggest themselves for an interpretation:
    1. The king of the North is identical with the "him" where

the latter refers to Daniel 11:36-39.[1] Verse 40 then becomes:

| | (North: willful king) |
| The king of the South will collide | with him |

| | (king of the South) |
| and the king of the North will storm | against him |

Most conservative scholars identify verses 36-39 of Daniel 11 as the antichrist, the final great world ruler. In fact, the end of verse 35, "the end time," introduces what follows as a ruler distinct from the historical Antiochus Epiphanes (verses (21-35) of the second century B.C. It is enough to indicate however that verses 36-39 are a part of the events which unfold in verses 40-45 where, also in verse 40, there is the identical phrase, "the end time," which speaks of the events of this period.

The problem with the layout of the grammar of the first possibility is that "him" refers to two persons, the first one, "with him" and the "king of the North" as the final world ruler, and the second, "against him" as "the king of the South." It would seem to be a grammatical problem when the same pronoun in a verse should refer to two different people.

Another difficulty, a major one from my view, is to identify the king of the north with the willful king of Daniel 11:36-39. The designation "north" is usually with respect to Israel, and following the information Daniel supplied about the kings of the north (verses 5-35), this was always in connection with the Seleucid (Syrian) kings of Damascus, of which Antiochus Epiphanes was one of them. In the end time however, there will be a wider perspective of a national source than Syria: the Soviet Union, also north of Israel. But the antichrist, the political one, is identified with the "little horn"

[1]Edward J. Young, *The Prophecy of Daniel* (Grand Rapids, Eerdmans, 1949) page 251.

of Daniel 7:8,20, "one of the heads of the beast" (Revelation 13:3), and is hardly of the north. It is best to set aside this way to understand Daniel 11:40, from the grammatical as well as the identification points of view.

2. The second possibility for the interpretation of the verse is:

	willful king
The king of the South will collide	with him
	willful king
and the king of the North will storm	against him

From a grammatical point of view, it is more proper for the pronoun "against him" to agree with the pronoun immediately preceding it (that is, "with him") and not as in the first view where the pronouns "him" refer to two different people.

I would say then that the king of the north is the Soviet Union and her allies; the king of the south is Egypt who will attempt to oppose any dominance; and the "him" is the political antichrist with the troops of the newly structured Roman Empire.

Movement and Timing of Soviet Troops. It remains now to try and establish a sequence of the movements of the northern power bloc. There is a distinct possibility that, near the midpoint of the tribulation period, when the "little horn," the political antichrist, finally achieves his goal of control of the western bloc of nations, then a formidable economic, political, and military power, the Soviets will view this build-up with alarm. (Certainly this would be true today!) To the Russians, the European leader of the western European power will be seen as a threat and a danger. In addition, it is just possible that by this time the People's Republic of China will also have become a giant power bloc, and if there is any country which the Soviets fear, it is China. We can well imagine that the Russians will assess any build-up of power in China as a grave danger to her security and existence.

It is for these reasons that the Soviets, near the midpoint of the tribulation, will consider it expeditious to make a desperate move to protect their interests, and they will mount a power drive through the Middle East. The strategy will be to divide the two superpowers, Europe and China, and also then to continue the drive on to North Africa in the attempt to contain Europe and its leader of the newly revived Roman Empire. For this reason, I feel that Daniel's description in chapter 11:40b is to the point: the king of the north will storm against him (the European leader) (see above), and he (the north) will enter countries in an all-out attack.

But which countries will this northern bloc enter? Daniel 11:41 describes the beautiful land which we have already identified as Israel, and the "he" seems to carry forward the designs of the Soviets from verse 40. However, there are scholars[1] who will want to identify this "he" of verse 41 as the antichrist as well as the "he" of the last phrase of verse 40. By so doing, antichrist becomes the sole subject of Daniel 11:41-45. However, as we shall see in the next chapter concerning Israel's great crisis to come, antichrist does *not* initially enter Israel to attack her. Rather, he will enter Israel to come to her aid and also to stop this wild lunge for power control by the Soviets, who attempt to endanger Europe's existence. It will be only after the defeat of the Russians that antichrist will be at the pinnacle of his power, and only for a very definite reason, when he demands worship, will he use his might as described in Daniel 11:36-39. I think that the identity of the power bloc with the Soviets north of Israel is what Daniel had in mind in verse 40. They are the ones who have the abundance of armaments and, from this point forward in the verse, it appears that they move their troops to invade countries, beginning with Israel.

---

[1]Leon Wood, *A Commentary on Daniel* (Grand Rapids: Zondervan, 1973), p. 310, and John Walvoord, *Daniel* (Chicago: Moody Press, 1971), p. 279.

This will mean that the Soviet Union has a very definite battle plan in mind. It makes its move, as we already indicated in the last chapter and earlier in this chapter, when Israel is at peace (Ezekiel 38:8, 11). In the move, it appears that the old regions of Edom (possibly the southern area of today's Jordan, or even part of northwest Arabia), and Moab and Ammon (probably peoples on the east bank of the Jordan River, referring to modern Jordan) who do not become involved in the Russian invasion (Daniel 11:41).

But which other countries do the Soviets invade? And who are their friends? Daniel adds further:

> But he will gain control over the hidden treasures of gold and silver, and over all the precious things of Eygpt; and Libyans and Ethiopians will follow at his heels (Daniel 11:43).

In their onward march the Soviets will gain control of much plunder in Israel, but we observe that they move into Egypt to take its precious things, the control over the Suez Canal, its oil, its iron ore deposits only recently discovered, and whatever else Egypt will be able to develop from now until the time that the Soviets move. This means that Egypt's fortunes will no longer be linked with the Soviet Union, or else why should they attack Egypt in this way and take its sovereignty and wealth? The only answer is that Egypt is linked with the European bloc of nations.

All this indicates that the Soviet Union will regard Egypt as one who cannot be trusted fully. Sadat had established links with the western nations of Europe and the United States and preferred to deal with them. Sadat's successors, Mubarak and others, prefer a more evenhanded approach to all nations, but very definitely want strong links with other African nations to the south of them, particularly with those who are Muslim. Couple this also with the hard economic facts that Egypt owes billions of dollars to the Russians for previous military ventures with Israel and, considering the present economic situation in Egypt, she does not have the resources to repay the debt. At any rate, the Soviets have a very definite battle plan in mind to make such a move through the Middle

East, and will get as far as Egypt. In the wake of their move there will be destruction and death in Israel and Egypt. There seems little doubt that Egypt, as the king of the south along with her friends, will join with antichrist in this battle to fight against the Soviets (Daniel 11:40b-45).

The friends of the Soviets in Africa are already indicated by Daniel: Put (peoples to the west of Egypt and the Ethiopians who follow in the footsteps of the Russians, allies already described in chapter five. The Soviets therefore have some kind of an alignment in North Africa, in the Middle East— Iran and possibly Syria (Ezekiel 38:5), and others in eastern Europe (Ezekiel 38:6), by which they try to contain the leader of the European bloc.

Now if we try and take the alternative interpretation that the leader of Daniel 11:43 is the antichrist, then in what sense do the peoples west of Egypt and the Ethiopians follow in *his* footsteps? There will certainly be the time (darkness of the day of the Lord) when antichrist will fight Egypt, those west of Egypt, and Ethiopians as well, but this will be only after the defeat of the king of the north. Therefore, again, I would identify the personality of Daniel 11:43 as the king of the north, who has his allies arrayed against Europe, just before the midpoint of the tribulation period.

Further clarification will be needed, however, as to the timing of Daniel 11:40a, when "the king of the South will collide with him." It appears, then, when considering the sequence of action of Daniel 11:40a and b, that 11:40b-45 occurs *first* because of the invasion of Egypt by the Soviets, when Egypt will oppose the king of the north. *After* the Soviet movement, Egypt will oppose the antichrist (Daniel 11:40a). Once more, as we saw in chapter four, the events of Scripture are not necessarily chronological but are handled topically. Daniel chose to discuss primarily the king of the north (Soviets, 11:40b-45) in this passage. As to why the timing occurs as it does, we shall discover the context for it, the pressuring of Israel and even of Egypt by the political antichrist, in chapter seven.

Those Who Oppose the Soviets. Who will be the power blocs to try and stop the Soviet Union in its move through the land of Israel? Or do they try to stop them? But the Soviets definitely will be stopped and even defeated in their greatest fiasco and blunder in history. Ezekiel describes one factor which will contribute to Soviet losses:

And with pestilence and with blood I shall enter into judgment with him; and I shall rain on him, and on his troops, and on the many peoples who are with him, a torrential rain, with hailstones, fire, and brimstone (Ezekiel 38:22).

In the invasion of Israel God will engage the elements of nature to wreak untold damage on the armies of this northern power bloc. The torrential rains will make it difficult for any heavy military equipment to operate. The hail will be of such a devastating quantity and size that it also will be responsible for the death of many. The elements of nature were able to hinder the movement of armies many times in the past and this will be no exception; God will design it as a harassment to the movement of this bloc and the armies associated with it until Israel will also receive other substantial help.

There is an even more ominous factor in view which will prove devastating to the invading armies:

"And I shall call for a sword against him on all My mountains," declares the Lord GOD. "Every man's sword will be against his brother" (Ezekiel 38:21).

It seems to be a situation where God calls for other nations to deploy their armies to foil the designs of the northern power bloc's troops. God is pictured many times pursuing this very action. When He wanted to discipline His people Israel, He used Assyria and its troops to attack and invade the land of Israel and push the battle forward to where advance units were even at the gates of Jerusalem. In this instance, Assyria is regarded as the club of the Lord, who accomplished His purpose (Isaiah 10:5). So when the Soviets will try to execute their military adventures, God will also use human means to stop them.

Now which power blocs would be able to stop the Soviets? The other two poles of power are the revitalized Roman Empire and the eastern (with respect to Israel) bloc, the People's Republic of China. What will it take to bring one or both of these blocs into the Middle East? While we have not as yet discussed the kind of pact Israel will have with the political antichrist, yet one of the features will be a guarantee of Israel's security so that if she should ever be threatened by any force, the nations of the European West bloc will come to her aid. The day that the Soviets move through the Middle East, including Israel, will be the signal for a confrontation leading to battle. Israel will call for help in the face of the Soviet advance, and shortly European troops under the political antichrist will enter the land of Israel. Tragically, it will be in the land of Israel that the major portion of the battle will be fought.

The Prophet Daniel and John add further pertinent information to this great battle:

> But rumors from the East and from the North will disturb him [the king of the North], and he will go forth with great wrath to destroy and annihilate many. And he will pitch the tents of his royal pavilion between the seas and the beautiful Holy Mountain; yet he will come to his end, and no one will help him (Daniel 11:44-45).

> And the sixth angel poured out his bowl upon the great river, the Euphrates; and its water was dried up, that the way might be prepared for the kings from the east (Revelation 16:12).

While these are difficult passages to understand, yet I am suggesting that by the time the Soviets get to Egypt and are poised to move on further to link up with friendly countries in North Africa, intelligence information describes the landing of European troops in Israel to engage in battle. With the advance Soviet troops in Egypt, this would mean that the news of an impending battle pinpoints the danger to *their north*. But the intelligence messages concerning troop movements from the east (with respect to the position of Soviet units in Egypt) are even more disturbing. This could

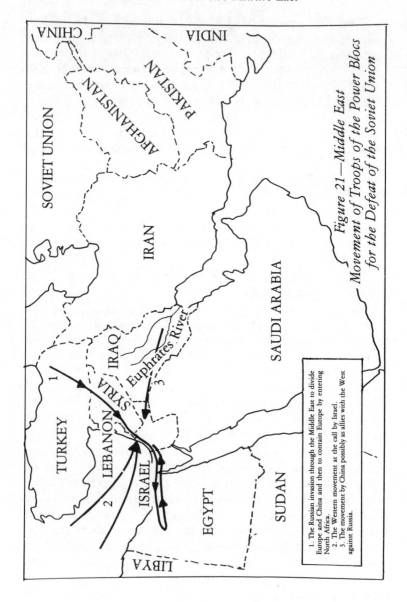

Figure 21—Middle East
Movement of Troops of the Power Blocs
for the Defeat of the Soviet Union

1. The Russian invasion through the Middle East to divide Europe and China and then to contain Europe by entering North Africa.
2. The Western movement at the call by Israel.
3. The movement by China possibly as allies with the West against Russia.

very well mean that China will seek to engage the Soviet Union because of an alliance with the political antichrist of the European West. Wars can make strange bedfellows, but it is not inconceivable that China could get involved in a war with the Soviet Union, given the right circumstances. It is this grand Soviet movement to divide Europe and China which provides the context for China's entrance into the Middle East to engage Russia in battle. The map of the Middle East in Figure 21 describes these possible military movements.

Daniel also describes the place of the battle as "between the seas." From the perspective of Israel, this puts the battle between the Mediterranean Sea and the Dead Sea. A further point of reference, "the Holy Mountain," is obviously the mountains in which Jerusalem nestles, primarily Mount Zion. The conflict is in Israel; the horrors of war again pervade a land already drenched with Jewish blood across the centuries.

There are those who pinpoint the Soviet invasion just before the rapture of the Church. I personally have my problems with this view. Can Europe become a strong pole of power without a strong-arm leader to accomplish it? While there are one or two western European nations now which are strong, yet the western bloc in Europe as an aggregate is weak and divided, and apparently will remain this way for the present. But this strong leader we are talking about will play out his role in history only *after* the rapture of the Church.

The timing of the Soviet invasion is at a time when Israel will be at peace, and furthermore will be lulled into such a frame of mind that her defenses will be nil and she will trust a European power to protect her. It is my considered opinion that Israel will not be able to conclude such a peace treaty that will be lasting with any of the existing power structures in the Middle East. While there may be some moments of respite, yet the differences run so deep between Israel and, let us say, the PLO covenant position that the Jewish state assuredly will not let its guard down. It can be only within the context of a radically different historical situation that we can envision Ezekiel's description of peace: 1, a leader who is strong, with diplomatic finesse, and completely acceptable to the Israelis; 2, Israel's strong desire for security and protection resulting in a link-up with certain nations in Europe and moderate Arabs in the framework of the new form of the Roman Empire; and 3, this empire as a strong economic unit appealing to Israel in her economic woes. All of these and more the Israeli government will want as terms for peace and she will accept them readily. We shall discuss further some of these positions in the next chapter. Admittedly, I may be accused of too much speculation when attempting to establish a time schedule of the Soviets, but it seems to me that we are talking about a set of conditions that can be possible only in the first part of the tribulation period.

The Results of This Conflict. The battle between the Soviet Union and those who will oppose her will take place in the land of Israel.

And I shall turn you around, drive you on, take you up from the remotest parts of the north, and bring you against the mountains of Israel. And I shall strike your bow from your left hand, and dash down your arrows from your right hand. You shall fall on the mountains of Israel, you and all your troops, and the people who are with you; I shall give you as food to every kind of predatory bird and beast of the field (Ezekiel 39:2-4).

God is pictured working actively behind the scenes, causing the fall of the Soviets. But on the human level the European western and eastern blocs are more than a match for the Russians. This northern bloc of nations will be defeated finally and completely on the soil of the land of Israel. We hear of people who say that the Soviets are going to take over the world and turn it into a huge communist camp. Actually, these fears will never materialize. The Soviet system as it is structured today will never commend itself to *all* the peoples of the world, and there is no reason to believe that this situation will ever change. Even now down deep in the hearts of peoples living in eastern Europe lies always a discontent because of the lack of political and economic freedom. The Soviets are not invincible and can always be kept at bay before a strong determined front. Like any dictatorship in the long history of Russia, the Soviet system will also one day be destroyed. It is providential that it meets its final defeat in the land of Israel, at the hands of the God of Israel, the very God who is loathed by the Soviet communist leaders.

Daniel likewise stresses the defeat of the Soviet bloc. While he describes the king of the north as a great power, yet in the battle in Israel he comes to his end, and no one will help him (Daniel 11:45).

After this battle, the political antichrist will be at the height of his career. He will be the recognized titular head of his own bloc and will have sovereignty over the eastern bloc and whatever bloc is represented by the king of the south. He will finally have all that he ever wished to have, except for just one more desire. He will now desire that the nations actually worship him as god, proof now that Satan has actually entered him, after being cast down to earth. But all of this feature is another story, because it must be told in the next chapter with respect to Israel in her experience in the darkness of the day of the Lord.

Comparison of the Great World Wars

We are now in a position to compare the various factors of the three great battles (excluding the struggle for power in the revitalized Roman bloc) and see if they are separate ones or if some are to be combined.

First of all, with regard to the *leaders* of the different battles: in the conflict between the northern power bloc and the other blocs, Gog of Magog is the leader of the Soviets according to Ezekiel 38:2-3 while Daniel calls him the king of the north (Daniel 11:40). On the opposing side, we see the political antichrist as the head of the blocs that defeat the Soviet Union.

In the battle of Armageddon, the leaders of the blocs are the beast (political antichrist) and the false prophet (religious antichrist). They head the nations in a battle against Jesus as King of kings and the armies of Heaven.

In the battle of the Little Season, after a thousand-year reign of Jesus the Messiah, Satan stands again behind a leader called "Gog," while God is the one opposing this challenger.

Secondly, with regard to the *armies involved* in the three battles: in the fight with the Soviets, the northern bloc has a number of allies: Iran, Ethiopia, the peoples to the west of Egypt, Gomer, and Togarmah, to mention a few. On the side of the antichrist, there is the alliance of the western European bloc of nations and China. As for Armageddon, the political antichrist has *all* the nations, primarily the two remaining blocs of power after the defeat of the Soviet Union. The armies of Heaven engage the political antichrist and his armies. In the battle of the Little Season, there are the rebels from the whole earth (the unregenerate and unrepentant) trying to capture Jerusalem while God rains down destruction from Heaven on them.

Finally, we note the *results*. In the battle with the Soviets, it is this particular bloc that is defeated, never again to threaten mankind. As a result, the political antichrist is completely victorious and becomes the head of the remaining power blocs. In the Armageddon conflict, the beast and the false prophet are thrown into the lake of fire, their troops are defeated, Satan is bound in the abyss for a thousand years, while the King of kings will reign in the fullness of the Messianic kingdom of peace. In the battle of the Little Season, the rebels who oppose Jerusalem are destroyed forthwith, and Satan is cast into the lake of fire; from God's side this last rebellion will lead to the great white throne judgment and then finally to the eternal state.

Therefore, while some scholars try to combine the battles and confuse the details, yet by looking at the historical contexts, the various leaders, the objectives, and the results, a clear pattern emerges to make these three battles distinct and different. We are reminded again rightly to divide the word of truth when handling the specifics of the Word of God so that we can, as best as possible, interpret the living Word of God. While these battles will be devastating and will cause millions to die and be the reason for the frightful destruction of property, yet we see a definite purpose in what God permits. In the tribulation period He will purify a remnant among Israel and the nations, and at the same time purge out those who rebel against Him, first among the Soviet Union and then among the nations of the earth. The Lord will be sovereign in His kingdom in the brightness of the day of the Lord. But then in the last battle of human history as we know it, the conflict of the Little Season, the last of the rebels will be separated from the believers. Then finally, in the eternal state, there will be no more rebellion, and everyone will always desire to do the will of the Lord.

Figure 22 pictures the timing of the Soviet invasion, the battle that ensues, and the consequences.

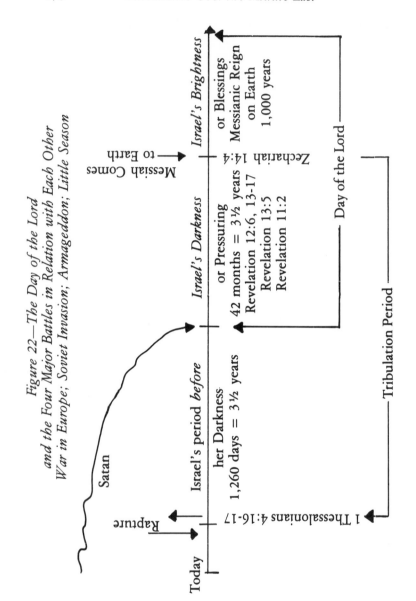

*Figure 22—The Day of the Lord
and the Four Major Battles in Relation with Each Other
War in Europe; Soviet Invasion; Armageddon; Little Season*

Events Associated with the Day of the Lord
(see chapter two)

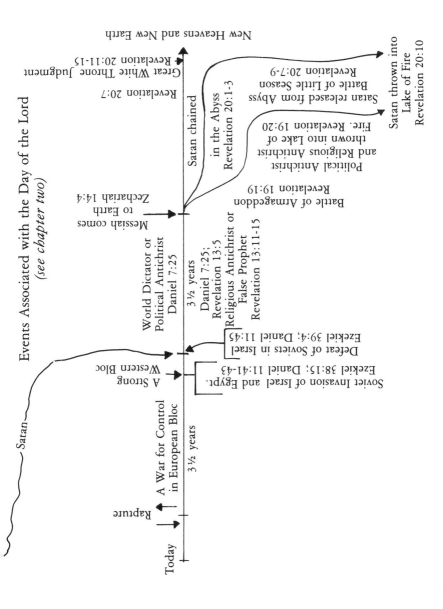

7
ISRAEL'S GREAT MIDEAST CRISIS
TO COME

What is thy business here, O son of man?
Rise, to the desert flee!
The cup of affliction thither bear with thee!
Take thou thy soul, rend it in many a shred!
With impotent rage, thy heart deform!
Thy tear upon the barren boulders shed!
And send thy bitter cry into the storm!
Hayyim Bialik in *The City of Slaughter*

It is a chilling prospect to talk about a future crisis and catastrophe for Israel in view of all that Jewish people have already experienced. In the short history of the modern State of Israel, they were involved in the 1948-1949 battle for independence when the armies of five Arab nations tried to throw Israel in the Mediterranean Sea. In that battle alone Israel lost some six thousand persons, about 1 percent of the entire population, a staggering proportion for a little country of six-hundred-fifty thousand. Since then Israel fought a 1956 war in the Sinai with Egypt, and the Six Day War in 1967 on primarily three fronts of her borders with Egypt, Jordan, and Syria. Then followed the war of attrition at the Suez Canal between Egypt and Israel for about two years (1969-1970), when Israel again lost a number of lives. In 1973 Israel was caught by surprise on the day of Yom Kippur, when many of the soldiers in the army and reserves were either home or in the synagogues. In the first few hours of that conflict Israel lost heavily, before she was able to mobilize and get troops on the battle lines. As a result of that battle, and in the subsequent sniping and skirmishing on the Israeli lines in Egypt before the agreements were signed, Israel lost some twenty-six-hundred men, and many more were wounded and maimed for life. And still there is no let-up while the heads of state in the Middle East search for the formula for peace.

But these were not all the losses that modern Israel sustained in her existence. As we have already pointed out, there was a community, in the modern sense, in the land of Israel that dates back about a hundred years to 1881-1882, when the first immigration wave in the modern period took place. From that time until 1948, when Israel became a state, Arabs attacked many of the settlements from time to time, and Israelis died in the defense of their homes and communities and in the course of just normal everyday life.

Jewish people, however, have suffered much in the longer history of their persecution, which led many times to death and destruction. The destruction of the Solomonic temple and the end of the first commonwealth in 586 B.C. was marked with loss of life and property. In the intertestamental period, when the Seleucids (Hellenized Syrians) controlled Judea, the fight for religious freedom and then for political freedom by the Jewish people also meant loss of life (167-132 B.C.). The situation in the destruction of the second temple in 70 A.D. and dispersion of Jewish people also meant that thousands died at the hands of the Romans. In the second revolt against Rome in 132-135 A.D., the Romans were so infuriated that they killed thousands more Jews and plowed under the city of Jerusalem, renaming it Aelia Capitolina. They also changed the name "Land of Judea" to Palestine, a term which has been in use to this day. Where once stood the great temple, the Romans erected their own worship center and altar to their divine emperors.

In the long history of Jewish people during their dispersion to so-called Christian countries, they also suffered. For a time, Jews were expelled from Germany and France in the 1200s and 1300s, respectively. In 1492 Spain, with its infamous edict of expulsion, expelled permanently all Jewish people who would not convert to Christianity; they were not permitted back until modern times. This meant a frightful loss to those poor souls, and many lost their lives in search of a new home until a remnant could find a country which would take them in. In 1648-1658, between one hundred thousand

and two hundred and fifty thousand Jewish people lost their lives in eastern Poland because of the uprising of the Russian Cossacks, and in the subsequent wars waged against Poland by Russia; these incidents against the Jews by the Cossacks came to be known as the Chmielnicki massacres, named after one of the Cossack leaders. The life of Jewish people in eastern Europe was filled with hardship, suffering, and pain for the most part until as late as World War I. And what can one say concerning the holocaust, the death of six million Jews during the period of the German Third Reich? Jewish history already is a ghastly tale of misery and woe. How can we talk now of a coming future plight of Israel?

Israel Before the Darkness Period

Before we speak of a plight of Israel, however, let us see what will happen in the period before the darkness of the day of the Lord, that is, the first part of the tribulation period.

From our point of view, the next great event in God's program is the rapture of the Church. This view with its blessed hope is a grand note for Christians. The dead in Christ are raised from the dead, and a living generation of Christians at the time of His return will not die, but will be translated with glorified bodies to join the ones raised from the dead. There will be a reunion of all those who have ever believed in Christ after the judgment seat of Christ (see chapter eight).

But in this chapter I am interested in the future implications for Israel from our vantage point today. We have already discussed the intense Bible study of both Old and New Testaments that goes on today in Israel. We have indicated that there is a preparation by God concerning the sowing of the seed of His Word in the hearts of Israelis. All of this involvement with the Word is going to have an effect on Israelis, and at the right moment and within the appropriate conditions some very specific events will take place in the thinking and spiritual decisions of Israeli people.

The Presence of Jewish Believers. Two movements appear to develop side by side in Israel after the rapture. The first of these is the presence of Israeli Jewish people who will become believers.

And I heard the number of those who were sealed, one hundred and forty-four thousand sealed from every tribe of the sons of Israel (Revelation 7:4).

By this point in the book of Revelation we have passed the rapture of the Church, because after chapter 4 we are discussing the things, from John's point of view, which shall *yet* take place, i.e., after the Church is caught away (Revelation 1:19). However, with the rapture of the Church, God now turns to Israel as the means to convey the message of salvation. He never leaves Himself without a witness in this world, and knowing beforehand that the Church will be gone, He is even *now* preparing those in Israel who will yet respond to His Word in order that they can initiate a new witness.

Now what is the specific catalyst that will cause thousands of Israelis, as John indicates, to turn to the Lord? It is the rapture itself that will be the means by which God is going to call certain ones to be His witnesses. In fact, the call of the body of Christ will be a shock to many in Israel! As we have already affirmed, there are many today in Israel who know the New Testament. But while they have an intellectual knowledge of it, and particularly the description of the resurrection in 1 Thessalonians 4:14-16, they have their ways of explaining away many of the assertions concerning Jesus, and certainly the New Testament statement as to the rapture.

But can you imagine what is going to happen to many knowledgeable Israelis, the one hundred forty-four thousand, when they find out that many genuine Jewish believers in Jesus will be gone after the rapture event? Imagine, for example, what will take place when these Israelis seek out their friends among the Jewish believers in Jesus, either in their services, or through a phone call? What do you think is going to be the response on the part of Israelis when they find Jewish believers gone, and their places of meeting empty? What of the worldwide report that Gentile Christians in other countries will also be gone? This is exactly the set of conditions, a testimony to the truth of the rapture, that is going to elicit a response from one hundred forty-four thousand Israelis in the land of Israel, and eventually Jewish and Gentile peoples outside of Israel. But it is the Israelis who first become believers that God will use to start the worldwide evangelism program all over again after the rapture, as was done with the disciples on the day of Pentecost when they began their ministry.

At this point, I think that I need to make two points regarding these phenomena of the shock of the rapture. First, some of my readers might question whether people can become believers after the resurrection. The question usually arises because many statements have been made that there is no more opportunity to accept Christ after the rapture; in other words, there is no second chance. Either a person accepts salvation before the rapture, or else it is too late. But such a belief is possible only if one does not accept the possibility of a tribulation period or a Messianic reign of Jesus on earth yet to come. Obviously, if in one general resurrection there is the end of the earth as we know it, and then the eternal state begins, then a decision for Christ must be made before the rapture. But in the scheme that we presented, in the understanding of the day of the Lord, then it is entirely possible for one to live from one period to the next, even as Jewish people lived in the age prior to the destruction of the second temple in 70 A.D., and on into the time when temple sacrifices were no longer possible. And just as Jewish people accepted the Lord after surviving that great crisis event, so will certain Jewish and other peoples accept the Lord right after the rapture when they realize the stark truth of it.

But some will also raise a second point regarding the identity of the one hundred forty-four thousand. There are cult adherents who proclaim that only their very pious and elected ones will be able to be among the one hundred forty-four thousand and have their place in the heavenlies, while the rest of the worthy ones will have their place here on earth when the kingdom comes. The rest of John's statement should be enough to settle such questions:

From the tribe of Judah, twelve thousand were sealed, from the tribe of Reuben twelve thousand, from the tribe of Gad twelve thousand, from the tribe of Asher twelve thousand, from the tribe of Naphtali twelve thousand, from the tribe of Manasseh twelve thousand, from the tribe of Simeon twelve thousand, from the tribe of Levi twelve thousand, from the tribe of Issachar twelve thousand, from the tribe of Zebulon twelve thousand, from the tribe of Joseph twelve thousand, from the tribe of Benjamin, twelve thousand were sealed (Revelation 7:5-8).

When some of these folk come to my door and try to make the point that they are seeking to be one of the one hundred forty-four thousand, it is my procedure to ask them to which tribe they belong! When they try to spiritualize the passage and make it apply to their cult, I ask them from which tribe they originate! You see, I am still enough of a Jewish person that when I read the Scripture that says, "Judah, Reuben, Gad, Asher," etc., to me it can *only* mean the sons of Jacob. There is no warrant to take the Scriptures other than literally at this point. Therefore, John is definitely speaking of a significant turn to the Lord by many in Israel.

The Religious Jewish Presence. Secondly, there is another movement that will take place in Israel which will ultimately have important repercussions on the state. Not too long after the rapture of the body of Christ, the political antichrist will make his appearance as a great magnetic leader in Europe. He will somehow attract the nations' attention with a proposal for the "final" settlement of the Middle East problem. The moment will be auspicious; the nations involved will consider it to their best interests to accept the proposals; and the agreement will be ratified. Israel's desperate desire for peace will become a reality and her borders will be guaranteed. She will be able then to turn her attention to her own internal needs and will become, as Ezekiel described her, as a country without walls around her cities and without bars on the gates of the cities (Ezekiel 38:8,11).

But there is another factor to be considered as well. Evidently this is the time for the appearance of the religious antichrist. In the beginning he appears as a leader representing the religious party in Israel, and perhaps, as this leader from Europe conducts the negotiations, it is with this religious leader that the negotiations are concluded. But even as the European leader achieves his notoriety for his part in concluding the pact, so the Israeli religious leader will become prominent because of his share in the negotiations.

We are provided with some description of this religious leader:

And I saw another beast coming up out of the earth; and he had two horns like a lamb, and he spoke as a dragon (Revelation 13:11).

The reference to the "earth" can also be translated "land," and therefore to any Jewish person, including John, this is a reference to the land of Israel. But no leader arrives on the scene with full capacity for evil and this religious leader is no exception. John pictures him as one who *looks like* the lamb and in the beginning he is the lamblike person whom the Israelis will accept and trust, almost as a hero. In fact, he is regarded as a kind of Messiah. This will be the one of whom Jesus had said, "I have come in My Father's name, and you do not receive Me; if another shall come in his own name, you will receive him" (John 5:43).

It is important to note that this religious leader will be a representative of a religious bloc in the nations that becomes prominent in the power structure of the country in the future. We can well ask ourselves just what are the significant signs that point to the coming to prominence of the religious groups in Israel today. But to understand the place of the religious Jew in the land of Israel today, we need to know something about the relationships between the religious and secular people in modern Israel as well as the political arrangements within the governing process.

Religious-Secular Controversy. Ever since the first immigration to Israel in 1881-1882, there has been a running series of encounters between the very religious Jews and the secular ones. Before the turn of the century the difference really heated up between what was called the old *yishuv* (the strictly orthodox Jewish people in the land) and the new *yishuv* (the newcomers, for the most part secular), but just after the start of the 1900s, the numbers of the secular Jewish people arriving in the land of Israel outnumbered the old *yishuv*.

In the attempt to insure a place and presence, religious Jewish people outside of the land of Israel then organized their own religious Zionist movement, and encouraged their adherents and religious sympathizers to emigrate to the land. This meant that the more moderate religious Jews, Zionistically inclined, also wanted their part in the formation of an Israeli society in the prestate days. These folk served as a counterbalance to the secular Israeli Jew and sought to provide a religious dimension to Zionism, but yet at the same time they were different from the old *yishuv* who resisted change. The strictly orthodox Jew of that period, and his followers through the 1900s, felt that if there was to be a state eventually, then the Messiah will have to institute it when He comes. Obviously we have a lot of differences in ideas among the religious elements of the state today. The religious elements of various shades of opinions feel that the secular Jew has desecrated the worship system of the fathers, while the secular people claim that the more strict religious folk are not relevant for the needs of the twentieth century. With the formation of the state, most religious Jews formed themselves into political parties in order to have a part in the government process. (Obviously there are extremely religious elements who will have nothing to do with the government because they feel that this is not of God.) The major religious party, the National Religious Party, which is the more moderate group, along with two more orthodox parties, will draw about 20-24 percent of the vote in the elections.

Also, since the founding of the State of Israel in 1948, there have been in addition to the religious parties from fifteen to eighteen parties which represent specific ideologies, ranging from left to middle and to the right of the political spectrum. The electorate then votes its preferences of ideological thought in the elections. Now, while some of the parties are larger than others, no one party can control a majority in the knesset, or parliament, with its one hundred twenty seats. Therefore, parties which receive most of the votes have to make arrangements with each other to insure a majority control. For example, the Labor Party-Mapam (primarily Socialist) formed an alignment in 1969 under Golda Meir to insure a majority. Then the coalition opposition was formed by Begin and other leaders, who captured the majority from the alignment of Labor Party-Mapam in 1977.

But no matter which arrangements are made among the nonreligious parties, the plurality most of the time is a slim one, and the only party which can make a decisive difference to provide for an effective government is the National Religious Party. Golda Meir in 1969 sought out this religious party to work with her alignment structure, and Menachem Begin did likewise with this same party to enable his coalition to establish a good majority in the parliament.

It is apparent that many times the religious Jewish parties become the key factor for political power. But even more important, the religious parties, moderate and strict, by their presence in the government continue to exert pressure on the ministry of education that more Bible study and Jewish values be taught to Jewish youth in the schools. They also continue to introduce legislation which attempts to give the country more religious values.

Future Religious Influence and Control. As we said already in chapter two, in the period before the darkness of the day of the Lord, there is to be a sanctuary which will be erected in the future, even from our point of view today. In these passages there is mention of an "altar and those who worship in it" (Revelation 11:1). To have an altar, however, means that sacrifices have to be placed on it; but this means a need for priests to minister on behalf of those who present sacrifices and offerings. This kind of arrangement for worship: an altar, priests to minister on behalf of those who come to worship, and worshipers present in the courtyard of the sanctuary, can only mean that a significant change will have taken place in the power structure of Israel. While not all Israelis will be involved in this worship, e.g., genuine believers preaching the gospel, yet it does mean that the religious could very well have the confidence of the electorate for the control of the country. This would mean a definite shift in the thinking of many Israelis from what is evident today, where most do not adhere to the position of the religious.

We come now to understand the place and influence some prominent religious leader will have in Israel, especially in his negotiations with the European leader, whereby peace is effected for Israel. If we can suppose an Israeli religious person with expertise and charisma, supported by the majority of his countrymen in the quest for peace, can we question the possibility that he also will be able to negotiate for the erection of a sanctuary? For not only will Israel have the peace for which she has long craved, but the religious leaders and their followers will also see, in the acquisition of the sanctuary for worship, their agelong desire to have the restoration of the Mosaic worship in an age of peace. With these ratified agreements, it would appear that Israel will, at long last, have all that she could ever hope or wish. It will also seem to the Israeli leaders that, as soon as the European leader will have the nations under his influence in the grasp for control of the European western bloc of nations, then this arrangement might be the beginning of the Messianic kingdom on earth. Any man who would be able to guarantee Israel its peace and then subdue the nations, will appear to the religious in Israel to have divine credentials.

But it is the believers who will see through this mock peace, and the error of establishing a Mosaic worship system which was superseded by the New Covenant at Calvary. Furthermore, when the true Messianic kingdom will be initiated, it will be under the New Covenant with a system of worship as described by Ezekiel, and *not* as per the Mosaic one. We shall discuss further the Ezekiel worship pattern in chapter nine. So, it appears that there will develop in Israel, after the rapture and during the first part of the tribulation period, two main movements. While Jewish believers in this period will testify to their faith in Jesus the Messiah and also point out the error of the sanctuary worship, there will also be the prominence of the religious Jewish people who will follow the Mosaic worship procedure.

We need also to point out the location of this sanctuary. Many times this writer has been asked where such a worship center could be built. When I suggest the site of Mount Moriah, where the present Dome of the Rock Mosque is located, many times the reaction is swift, "How will it be possible to erect a sanctuary on this site today?" So as to avoid the problem of denying the Muslims their place of worship, this writer has heard many suggestions by Christians, e.g., that the sanctuary will be built *alongside* the Dome of the Rock mosque; that it will be erected in the new city, associated with a building called the Great Synagogue, near the seat of modern Israeli orthodoxy, the temple of Solomon (actually nothing to do with a temple, but merely an office building); or somewhere else.

Let me say with absolute certainty that no sanctuary for Jewish worship will ever be located anywhere except where the two previous temples stood. Religious Jewish people will never hear of any other site to put a place of worship except in the proper place where Abraham once tried to sacrifice his son, but was stayed by God, and exactly where Jewish people worshiped in previous temples. The place is hallowed, even to the extent today that no religious Jewish person even goes on the temple mount for fear of walking across where once was located the area of the holy of holies; this is an indication as to what extent the holy place is revered, and where a sanctuary is to be located.

It is difficult to say, nevertheless, how it will be possible for the sanctuary to be built on this exact site. When we ask some of the pious Jewish people praying at the wall, they look up to Heaven and say, "Maybe there will be an earthquake!" Earthquakes are quite possible on that spot, since there is a fault running right through this area; as a result both mosques on the mount, the El Aqsa as well as the Dome of the Rock, have suffered extensive damage in the past. This could happen in the future at the time of negotiations between the European and Jewish leaders, and the latter along with other religious people might seize on the opportunity to press the claims for the sanctuary.

Other possibilities exist as well. It just might be that in one of these Arab-Israel wars, a surface-to-surface missile could be fired from the Syrian or Jordanian side which might unintentionally hit the mosque and destroy it. The area involved in any conflict between the Mideast countries is so small that there can be no absolute guarantee as to where a missile or rocket could land if, let us say, one were aimed at Jerusalem's Jewish west side.

Whatever the means necessary to build a sanctuary, it must be recognized that the Scriptures are the court of last appeal. If the Word of God says that there will be a sanctuary, then we must accept the truth of what the Scriptures say. And this sanctuary is one that will precede the temple of the Messianic kingdom.

Plight of Israel in the Darkness of the Day of the Lord

While Israel will enjoy her peace agreement in the first part of the tribulation period, plowing money back into education, development, etc., monies previously used for defense, the European leader is involved in his struggle for power in Europe. Finally, however, by the midpoint of the tribulation he has the control of the western bloc of nations. To the Israelis he will appear as a hero, and they will look confidently for him to gain control of all the nations.

Soviet Advance and Defeat. As we pointed out, though, it is at this point that disaster strikes Israel. The Soviet Union and her satellites, eyeing the military progress of the European leader, become alarmed at what they feel to be a threat to their security. As we explained in chapter six, this will be the time when the Soviets make their move to counter the growing menacing power they fear. Some of the Arab nations on the side of Russia will also consider it auspicious to move with Russia against Israel, although Russia has more in mind than just Israel. But when the attack is mounted against Israel by the Soviets, the Israelis, who have a pact with the European west (Daniel 9:27), now call for help from the one they feel to be their benefactor. He will bring his troops of the west (the bloc of the revived Roman Empire) into Israel so as to aid her in her distress.

This is what leads to the confrontation between the Soviets and the west, who will also have the possible help of the eastern bloc. Unfortunately the battle takes place largely in Israel, causing her untold destruction. It is indeed painful to consider such devastation when we realize the sacrificial effort that has gone into the rebuilding of the land and cities across the decades since the first immigration wave in 1881, as well as what will be accomplished in the period just prior to the day of the Lord. As we already suggested in chapter six, the defeat of the Soviets in the land of Israel occurs just about the midpoint of the tribulation period.

With the Soviets defeated, Israel will certainly feel that the great victorious European leader and her own religious leader, who has rapport with him, are the world's liberators. It is easy to see how Israel could very well regard these two as sort of messiah representatives, who have come finally to bring peace to the whole world. Even though Israel will suffer much in the Soviet invasion, she will feel that, with the defeat of the Russians, the world is on the verge of her view of the Messianic kingdom.

The Political Antichrist. But the sinister now enters into the picture. The cosmic battle occurs in the heavenlies (Revelation 12:9) and Satan is thrown down to the earth, nevermore to have opportunity to stand before God's presence. He knows that his time is short (Revelation 12:12) and looks around for the man through whom he can work to create a revolt against the Lord. The man is now ready: the European leader who has just defeated the Soviet bloc is now regarded as a world leader. He is drunk with power, and it has gone to his head. He now controls the remaining power blocs and most of the nations of the world. But this one will now become the vessel through whom Satan enters. Satan now has his man to thwart God's purposes for the Messianic kingdom. Awesome it is to contemplate that, when a person is filled with pride, he is also easy prey for manipulation by the evil one.

The Religious Antichrist. But another ominous development also takes place. The religious leader of Israel, tempted by the power the political antichrist now possesses, apparently seeks further ties with the political ruler. Even as the great European leader made his grasp for power, so this religious leader will seek power for himself as well. He perhaps sees himself as the one who can be involved with the political antichrist's plan for a kingdom. But this religious leader is unaware of the consequences of his senseless decision, which will only lead him into Satan's trap. God's archenemy actually wants to set up a counterfeit to God's plans for the Messianic kingdom, and even to duplicate a perverted trinity. Satan will engineer the plans for world control, work through the political antichrist for the military control of a kingdom, and through the Israeli leader who will become the religious antichrist. The latter will involve the nations of the world to revere the political antichrist and even worship him. Satan will really think that he has just the power structure to accomplish his purposes for world control, the destruction of Israel, and finally even to fight against God.

Even while the Israelis are rejoicing in the defeat of the Soviets and are seeking to clear the land of the war materiel left behind by the defeated invaders, the political antichrist makes his move. Drunk by his success, his heart lifted in the pride of his accomplishments, and now indwelt by Satan, he asks for the nations of the world to worship him. Most of the world leaders will do so.

And they worshiped the dragon [Satan], because he gave his authority to the beast; and they worshiped the beast, saying, "Who is like the beast, and who is able to wage war with him?" (Revelation 13:4)

Perhaps the world leaders who now revere this beast have every right to fear his power and authority, but for whatever reason they make their obeisance to him; there is the satanic touch in it all.

Leaders and peoples of the nations will be dazzled and awed by the miracles and signs which the religious antichrist will perform so as to enlist an allegiance to his copartner, the political antichrist:

And he exercises all the authority of the first beast in his presence. And he makes the earth and those who dwell in it to worship the first beast, whose fatal wound was healed. And he performs great signs, so that he even makes fire come down out of heaven to the earth in the presence of men. And he deceives those who dwell on the earth because of the signs which it was given him to perform in the presence of the beast, telling those who dwell on the earth to make an image to the beast who had the wound of the sword and has come to life. . . . And there was given to him to give breath to the image of the beast, that the image of the beast might even speak and cause as many as do not worship the image of the beast to be killed (Revelation 13:11-15).

The position and function of this religious antichrist is of one who has unwittingly sold himself to perversion so that he actually encourages people to worship a man. To gain his objectives, he becomes involved in making images of this world dictator, much like Nebuchadnezzar who completely perverted his divine revelation, and the Roman emperors who made gods of themselves and forced people to worship their images. Satan gives his power to this religious antichrist to deceive people so that the image appears actually to live and speak. If people do not worship the image, and thereby pay their homage to the political antichrist, the religious leader has the power to put to death any who refuse to honor his wishes. This will mean that the one hundred forty-four thousand and those whom they win to the Lord will suffer greatly, even becoming martyrs for their faith.

But some will raise the question as to how a religious leader from Israel can actually become involved with a political antichrist even to corrupt himself in man-worship, contrary to any expression of Judaism. How can it be possible that a so-called religious Jewish person, and a religious leader at that, can actually apostatize from basic Biblical truths which insist that only God can receive worship. Unfortunately this is not the first time in history that such a phenomenon has occurred. There have been religious leaders, even political leaders who outwardly were religious, who have at crucial points in their career turned from the basic Biblical truths which they knew and perverted themselves. This highly esteemed religious leader in Israel is no exception, and he will prove to be an apostate to the chagrin and keenest disappointment of his colleagues and kinsmen. At the critical point, tempted by the power of the political antichrist and by what it would mean for him to have total religious control, not only over his people Israel but over all the nations of the earth, he will sell himself—body, soul, and spirit—for what he will be able to obtain for his own wild ambitious schemes. In a most horrible and despicable move, he will even turn against his own people. At this point he will cease looking like the lamb of God, and will speak and act like the dragon (Satan) (Revelation 13:11). His true character will be found out.

The Reason for Israel's Suffering. Our whole focus now is what will happen to Israel. We have passed the midpoint of the tribulation and have now entered the darkness of the day of the Lord. The black day for Israel will commence when the political antichrist, present in the land already after the defeat of the Soviets, will ask that all nations reverence and worship him. Most of the nations will oblige. But one nation in particular will refuse to do so. Can you imagine the utter shock in Israel when their benefactor, who had provided peace for them, and who had come to their rescue when the Soviets attacked them, now has the audacity to act like a god?

A generation of Israelis will have firsthand experience concerning a warning that had already been given centuries before:

That you may not be quickly shaken from your composure or be disturbed either by a spirit or a message or a letter as if from us, to the effect that the day of the Lord has come. Let no one in any way deceive you, for it will not come unless the apostasy comes first, and the man of lawlessness is revealed, the son of destruction, who opposes and exalts himself above every so-called god or object of worship, so that he takes his seat in the temple of God, displaying himself as being God (2 Thessalonians 2:2-4).

Paul long ago had warned the Thessalonians that they should not look, in a sense, for the brightness of the day of the Lord, the kingdom, before there should be an apostasy first, especially in the land of Israel, leading to the darkness and blackness of the day of the Lord. The ominous occasion will come, however, when the political antichrist will ask for what no Jewish person will ever do: worship a man. In addition, the apostasy of the greatly esteemed religious leader will come down like a thunderclap on Israel. The presence of the political antichrist in the sanctuary desecrates it, and his demand for worship is the beginning of sorrows for Israel in its own land that will lead to the experience of the "day of Jacob's trouble." With the turning of Israel from the political antichrist, the latter's fury will be unleashed against the sons of Jacob for what he feels is Israel's ingratitude for all he did for the people. Israel will enter a holocaust experience in its own land.

When Israel refuses to worship the political antichrist, he breaks the agreement which he had made with them:

And he will make a firm covenant with the many for one week [unit of seven, i.e., years], but in the middle of the week he will put a stop to sacrifice and grain offering; and on the wing of abominations will come one who makes desolate, even until a complete destruction, one that is decreed, is poured out on the one who makes desolate (Daniel 9:27).

Admittedly, these passages in Daniel (9:24-27), are some of the most difficult to interpret in all of Scripture. But we cannot place the entire context merely in the first century, or stretch out verse 27 and identify it as the end of the Church. As we pointed out, and will continue to do so, this unit of seven years comes after the rapture of the Church, and should be looked upon as the period when God prepares Israel to recognize the identity of her true Messiah in order that the fullness of the Messianic kingdom can commence. But for the purposes of our discussion regarding Israel, Daniel made the point that the political antichrist will break his agreement with Israel when Israelis refuse to worship him as god in their own sanctuary. But unfortunately, the designs against Israel do not stop here; the antichrist will begin a terror campaign to make desolate the land and people of Israel, and this will continue until the moment when he himself will be desolate in the lake of fire.

Antichrist's Military Campaign. As we have seen, the political antichrist already has his troops in the Middle East (which he had used for the defeat of the Soviet Union in Israel), and he now deploys these armies against Israel to pressure the life out of her. He seeks to put an end to the evangelistic campaign of the believers emanating from Israel; therefore he and the religious antichrist will immediately put to death the two witness leaders who are responsible for the evangelism thrust in Israel and the whole world (Revelation 11:7-10). But we shall say more about this later.

A number of details of Israel's pressuring are provided:

Behold, I am going to make Jerusalem a cup that causes reeling to all the peoples around; and when the siege is against Jerusalem, it will also be against Judah. And it will come about in that day that I will make Jerusalem a heavy stone for all the peoples; all who lift it will be severely injured. And all the nations of the earth will be gathered against it (Zechariah 12:2-3).

Note carefully what the prophet emphasizes: his message cannot belong to any historical context we already know concerning Jerusalem's experience. The reference is made to "that day," which is another way of referring to the day of the Lord. The phrase depicts the period before the brightness of the day of the Lord, when Jerusalem will go through a period of intense pressuring. Furthermore, the statement that "all the nations" have surrounded Jerusalem is very important. These are a set of conditions which cannot be said to have occurred in any phase of Biblical history, including even the first century. In all situations past, only one nation at a time was involved in an attack on Jerusalem, e.g., Assyria, Babylon, Persia, Greece, Rome. Rather, Zechariah has in mind a historical context when many nations will come against Jerusalem, and this has never occurred in history as yet. (We are excluding the time when western nations attacked Jerusalem in the Middle Ages in the first Crusade, which certainly is not associated with the "last days.") To fix our historical reference points we must examine Scripture thoroughly.

But the prophet further pursues his message:

Behold, a day is coming [the day of the Lord, literally] for the LORD when the spoil taken from you will be divided among you. For I will gather all the nations against Jerusalem to battle, and the city will be captured, the houses plundered, the women ravished, and half of the city exiled, but the rest of the people will not be cut off from the city (Zechariah 14:1-2).

Once again the day of the Lord is mentioned, emphasizing the darkness or suffering of Israel. All the nations are involved in action against Jerusalem, at least representative troops from the European bloc as well as the Eastern bloc. In antichrist's attack on Israel, Jerusalem falls into his hands; once more Jerusalem will be taken away from the Israelis, not just a part of it, as was the case in the War of Independence in 1948, when the Jordanians held on to the Arab east side of Jerusalem and also captured the Old City of Jerusalem, including access to the wailing (western) wall. But this will be an all-out capture of the Jewish western side of the city. It will be a bitter pill to swallow in view of the magnificent strides Israel has made since 1948 to be a respectable member of the world community of nations, especially after waiting almost nineteen hundred years to be a free nation again. To think of Jerusalem falling into the hands of the troops of antichrist will be more than what any people can take; it will be demoralizing to Israel.

Zechariah indicates that half the population of Jerusalem will be exiled while the other half will not escape. I want to be very clear here concerning what we mean by exile and death. There are some Bible teachers who insist that the present Israelis are to be put out of the land because ''they are in unbelief'' concerning their faith in Jesus the Messiah. Therefore, the argument goes, in order to prepare for the kingdom, it will be necessary to put out the present Israelis from the land so as to prepare for the Jewish people who will believe in Jesus the Messiah. It is my considered opinion that this makes a mockery of the providence of God in caring for His people Israel in the modern context as well as in the spiritual preparation of His people in the Bible study that has gone on since 1948, as we have indicated in chapter two. The point to be made is that God is doing a work in preparing His people to identify the Messiah, and it won't be as Christians think it should be done, neither will it proceed according to the opinions of religious Jewish leaders. God will have His way in ordering the circumstances and fortunes of His people and guiding them to where He wants them to go. Therefore, to think of the present Israelis being exiled totally from the land of Israel, or everyone in it being killed to make way for other Jewish people is nonsensical.

So, when speaking of Israelis being exiled, the prophet describes what Jewish people have always done when Jerusalem was put under siege. They ran away to the wilderness of Judea, east of Jerusalem, and down to the regions of the Dead Sea where there are many caves in which to hide from their enemies. This is exactly what Jesus mentioned that Jewish people should do when the calamity of Jacob's trouble would strike them:

> Then let those who are in Judea flee to the mountains [actually the backbone running on a north-south line in the land of Israel, or into the hills of the Judean wilderness], and let those who are in the midst of the city depart, and let not those who are in the country enter the city (Luke 21:21).

The exiles are to be seen trying to find a hiding place in the *land of Israel,* and not in a worldwide dispersion again. In view of the events of the past hundred years in the regathering of Jewish people, a worldwide exile is impossible.

The Battle Line. The Scriptures also point out a battle line across the land of Israel in what is the antichrist's deployment of troops and, although this is the line-up at the time of the battle of Armageddon at the end of the darkness of the day of the Lord, yet the concentration of troops will constitute a pressure against the Israelis. Three prominent points are mentioned in Scripture:

1. And the angel swung his sickle to the earth, and gathered the clusters from the vine of the earth, and threw them into the great wine press of the wrath of God. And the wine press was trodden outside the city, and blood came out from the wine press, up to the horses' bridles, for a distance of two hundred miles (Revelation 14:19-20).

While we shall discuss later in this chapter the judgment of God upon the political antichrist and his armies, it is enough to note now that there is a contingent of troops outside of "the city," which can refer only to Jerusalem. This agrees with the Zechariah passage about the siege against Jerusalem that will cause destruction to this city.

2. There is still another point where troops are gathered:

For they are spirits of demons, performing signs, which go out to the kings of the whole world, to gather them together for the war of the great day of God, the Almighty. . . . And they gathered them together to the place which in Hebrew is called Har-Magedon (Revelation 16:14,16).

Once again there is an undeniable reference to the battle of Armageddon, but one needs to see also how the political antichrist will use his troops to thoroughly cover the land in the time of Israel's darkness, wreak havoc on all that Israel has, and then try to obliterate the people of the land. The site of Megiddo is about eighty miles northwest of Jerusalem, and if troops are concentrated on an approximate line from Jerusalem to Megiddo, this will cut right across the land where people and possessions are concentrated.

3. The third point to consider is:

> Who is this who comes from Edom,
> With garments of glowing colors from Bozrah,
> This One who is majestic in His apparel,
> Marching in the greatness of His strength?
> "It is I who speak in righteousness, mighty to save."
> Why is Your apparel red,
> And Your garments like the one who treads in the wine press?
> "I have trodden the wine trough alone,
> And from the peoples there was no man with Me.
> I also trod them in My anger,
> And trampled them in My wrath;
> And their lifeblood is sprinkled on My garments,
> And I stained all My raiment.
> For the day of vengeance was in My heart,
> And My year of redemption has come" (Isaiah 63:1-4).

This is a view from the Old Testament concerning a great battle that will take place at the time of the coming of the Messiah to initiate His kingdom. From our point of view today, this can be none other than the battle of Armageddon, but again our interest is in the concentration of troops for the terrible pressuring of Israel. The prophet talks about the day of vengeance, and this has relevance in the darkness of the day of the Lord. So as to accomplish thoroughly his purposes, antichrist will have troops not only in the center of the country around Jerusalem, and in the north of the land at Megiddo, but even as far south as the old areas of Edom and Bozrah. These are districts about one hundred twenty-five to one hundred fifty miles southeast of Jerusalem. It is interesting that when we put together the three points mentioned, we find that this will correspond quite adequately to what is indicated in Revelation 14:18-20 where a distance of two hundred miles along which troops are deployed is mentioned. All of this is initially for the purposes of destruction in Israel!

Antichrist and the Muslims. While the burden of this chapter was to do with Israel's plight in the day of the Lord, I feel I also ought to make some comment that Israel will not be the only nation that will suffer at the hands of antichrist because of the refusal to worship him. Obviously believers in many nations will refuse to acknowledge this beast and for that decision and action they will be hunted down, tortured, and many will be killed. There will also be nations as well who will disregard the call by the religious antichrist to worship the political antichrist, and principally among these nations are those which are Muslim; these peoples worship Allah and him alone.

Now, even as the people of Israel will be thoroughly shocked by antichrist's demand for worship, so the shock will register on the moderate Arab nations which will be a part of the western bloc, as well as upon Arabs sympathetic to this great European leader. But just as the political antichrist will mount an attack on Israel for its refusal to worship him, so this beast of a man will do likewise to Arab Muslims who will be violently opposed to a perverted worship of a man. Egypt in particular is singled out, where there appears to be some military action by antichrist because of the refusal to worship him.

We have already pointed out in chapter six how, *after* the Soviet invasion in Egypt fails (Daniel 11:40b-45), the Egyptians become involved in an action with antichrist: "the king of the South will collide with him" (Daniel 11:40a). I would suggest therefore that once the political antichrist defeats the Soviet Union, just prior to the midpoint of the tribulation period, he will demand worship after the midpoint of this period, in the darkness of the day of the Lord. Egypt as a Muslim country in particular is singled out for defying antichrist, and troops are therefore sent to quell any rebellion. While this nation will put up some kind of resistance, it will be powerless in the face of antichrist's armies of the world's power blocs. There follows then what we have already indicated in chapter four, that as Israel will be pressured, so Egypt will be pressured likewise (Isaiah 19:17,20b). When the day comes that Israel will be redeemed, as we shall soon see, so will Egypt be delivered along with Israel (Isaiah 19:20b).

The Frightful Loss of Life. The holocaust of Hitler's Third Reich was and is still horrible to contemplate. How does one comprehend the loss of six million people simply because they were Jewish? This figure included the death of one million children, the future generation that would have provided continuity to the Jewish community in the future. The several hundred thousand who were able to survive the concentration camps still carry within themselves in both body and spirit the scars from their horrible experiences of suffering and deprivation. But as we view the darkness in Israel yet to come, it is with a wrench in one's heart concerning what is yet to happen in the land. One plea is necessary here: we should never glibly teach or preach about Israel's future plight, but rather there should be a heartfelt compassion for those beloved of the fathers (Romans 11:28).

The Prophet Zechariah described the holocaust in the land of Israel:

> "And it will come about in all the land,"
> Declares the LORD,
> "That two parts in it [the land] will be cut off and perish;
> But the third will be left in it.
> And I will bring the third part through the fire,
> Refine them as silver is refined,
> And test them as gold is tested"
>   (Zechariah 13:8-9a).

The dire proclamation is that two-thirds of the land's population will perish. This means that of the three-million population today in Israel, should this horrible event take place now, two million will die because of the political antichrist's fury against Israel, in exact accordance with Satan's desires. It will be a day when Israel will have few friends, and those who would wish to help will be unable to come to her aid. A people who have suffered so much in the past will again have their backs to the wall as they never have had before. This is not a situation where only one nation like Rome tried to subdue Israel because of sheer military might, but instead, all the power blocs will be involved in attempting to snuff out Israel's life. As we saw in the first part of the chapter, Israel has had many attempts against her to harm her, first in one country in Europe, and then in another country, but this attack is a holocaust in the land itself. It is terrible to contemplate!

I remember talking one day with a strong, tanned, young Israeli. We had sat down for coffee in one of the shops in Jerusalem. We discussed the future of Israel in terms of immigration, industrialization, desalinization of sea water so as to cultivate more land to feed more mouths, etc. Finally, I turned to him and said, ''Hanan, you know perfectly well what Zechariah 13 says.'' This bronzed Israeli's face turned chalky white! He well knew what the prophet said because as a sabra (native born Israeli), he was educated in the Old Testament, and understood exactly what the Zechariah passage taught. Inwardly many Israelis know they are in a context that can become disastrous.

The Spiritual Battle. One must recognize that there is a spiritual battle involved when it comes to Israel. Behind all of the carnage and destruction stands Satan who has in mind to destroy Israel. The real antagonists are, therefore, God and Satan. God's promises for a better world are bound up in the covenants which He made with Israel. Some of these agreements are still to be actualized in the fullness of the Messianic kingdom, in a day when Israel will yet recognize her Messiah. Satan knows these purposes which God has in mind and therefore seeks to destroy Israel so as to make God's agreements null and void. Once this archenemy of God can try to accomplish Israel's demise, he can feel that he has made a liar out of God. Satan's tricks never change, and this is just one more evidence of his old game.

But Satan will fail again, as he always has in the past. Even though God will permit this situation regarding Israel, yet God too has a purpose in what He is doing. While the Israeli believers will understand God's coming program, it will be difficult for the rest to fathom God's designs, particularly those who will have to flee for their lives and those who will perish at the hand of the foreign invaders. The only answer God gave Job in the midst of his trials was to elicit a trust from his precious servant in that, as God knew how to run the universe and care for all the creatures He created, so He certainly would know how to care for Job. The patriarch understood this in the end as he exclaimed:

> I have heard of Thee by the hearing of the ear;
> But now my eye sees Thee;
> Therefore I retract,
> And I repent in dust and ashes (Job 42:5).

In the same way, God has also a marvelous design for Israel in this worst trying experience.

We can point to at least three objectives God will bring to pass with regard to Israel:

1. The work of evangelism by the one hundred forty-four thousand in the period before the darkness of the day of the Lord will be fruitful, and many Israelis will also become believers, in addition to multitudes in other countries. But God's work in reaching Israelis in the first part of the tribulation is preparatory to what will occur when the political antichrist begins his pressurizing of Israel. It is unfortunate that it has to take these kinds of conditions for Israelis to accept the Lord, but always in times of distress there are people who turn to the Lord. Many of us also can testify that it was in those times of distress when we turned to the Lord; likewise there is a very definite divine design in the link between Israel's pressuring and many turning to the Lord.

2. So as to enforce his system of worship on Israel, the political antichrist will see to it that the leaders involved in the strong effective witness to the Lord will also be executed: Elijah, and the other witness. The strength of a movement can be measured by the reaction to it. Both antichrists will feel threatened by these two witnesses who direct the evangelistic attempt of the Lord's believers; in particular, Satan does not want the presence of many believers because the latter will understand perfectly the designs of God's archenemy. The two witnesses are regarded as rivals by Satan and consequently he wants them out of his way. So that the two key leaders can be humiliated further, he will give orders that their bodies lie in the streets of Jerusalem as an example to the rest of the world (Revelation 11:8-9) that no one should oppose him. Everyone across the whole face of the earth will be able to view them by way of a worldwide telecommunication system. The God-haters will rejoice, including the antichrists, and they will feel that they are now the masters. The killing of the witnesses is also intended to strike fear in the hearts of any others considering placing their faith in Jesus as Messiah and Saviour.

But God again thwarts Satan with the unexpected. After three days the whole world will see these two great spiritual leaders rise to their feet, and God will translate them into Heaven (Revelation 11:7-12). Can you imagine the effect upon those in Israel and in the whole world? No doubt this overpowering witness will be the means whereby many more Israelis, and people all over the earth, will become believers. Most who take the step to acknowledge God's sovereignty and receive salvation in Jesus will die for their faith as they become particular targets of Satan and the antichrists (Revelation 13:7).

3. The desecration of the sanctuary by the political antichrist will mean that the religious Jewish people and leaders will be utterly dismayed; they will be horrified when along with the cruel desecration of the worship center there is the

subsequent frightful loss of life in Israel. But the circumstances are designed and permitted to have deeper meaning. With the enforcement of the religious system designed by the religious antichrist, and with no rival beliefs permitted to exist, there will occur a wide sweep of mixed feelings: anger, frustration, determination to hold on to the Mosaic faith, but very likely also a collapse of faith in religious Judaism.

When the second temple was destroyed in 70 A.D., a group of scholars and rabbis met as a council in a small village called Yavne, a few miles inland from Jaffa. Their task was to accommodate Judaism to be a traditional belief and practice without the temple, until the time when Israel could again have her sanctuary.

God, however, in the darkness of the day of the Lord, will not permit any time whatsoever to restructure Judaism as religious Jewish leaders might wish to do. The Lord's design in that frightful period to come is for a remnant in Israel to consider once again the testimony of the prophets in the written Word. The pressure of the times will be such that, as people seek for genuine answers for their plight, the only place to turn will be to Jesus the Messiah as proclaimed by the two witnesses, the one hundred forty-four thousand, and their followers.

The Redemption of Israel

Physical Redemption. I am grateful that God will not abandon Israel in this situation. He has a purpose for Israel reflected in many of the promises of the prophets. But it will be through Israel's greatest darkness that her redemption and glory will come. Messiah will come to initiate the fullness of the Messianic kingdom, and God will institute all that man has ever hoped for in his dreams of utopia. But all these ultimates in blessings revolve on what Israel will do in relation to the Lord. Therefore, as we come to the end of the darkness period, with two-thirds of the Israelis gone (Zechariah 13:8), with no one to turn to for help, and with no ideology or religious Judaism to guide them in their greatest distress, the only place to turn is to the Lord. Zechariah points this out:

> "They will call on My name,
> And I will answer them;
> I will say, 'They are My people,'
> And they will say, 'The LORD is my God' "
> (Zechariah 13:9b).

The key phrase is the first line where the one-third left will call upon God for help. In view of the circumstances, this is no polite call in prayer, but this will be a shriek for God to intervene in such a situation of peril for Israel.

This is the moment for which God has been waiting. He will immediately aid Israel because He regards them as His people. The Messiah comes with the armies of Heaven, and the antichrists and the power blocs brace for battle along the line already indicated in the battle of Armageddon. But this show of strength by Satan and his armies cannot in any way deter Messiah and His armies from coming to earth:

> And in that day His feet will stand on the Mount of Olives, which is in front of Jerusalem on the east; and the Mount of Olives will be split in its middle from east to west by a very large valley, so that half of the mountain will move toward the north and the other half toward the south (Zechariah 14:4).

This Scripture is to be coupled with the passage in Revelation 19 which describes the coming of Jesus as the Word of God, riding on the white horse, so as to fight His enemies. The feet of the Messiah will touch the Mount of Olives, exactly as the angels had announced at the ascension of Jesus (Acts 1:11). This event is definitely not to be understood as the rapture of the Church, since on that occasion it is the dead in Christ who will be raised, living Christians will be changed and then join the resurrected dead in Christ, all to meet the Lord in the air (see chapter eight). But on the occasion of the return of the Messiah to earth, there is a violent change in the topography in the land: the Mount of Olives is split in two, and then the battle is fought with the antichrists and their armies.

The passages to which we have referred already in the battle of Armageddon, Revelation 14:19-20 and Isaiah 63:1-4, describe one treading grapes in the winepress. When grapes were placed in the winepress, they were squeezed, the juice ran off, and the liquid was collected. This becomes the picture of the judgment of the nations. The armies of Heaven will, in a sense, tread the life out of the enemies of Israel who have dared to lift up a finger against God's ancient covenant people. The end result will be that while in God's permissive will He permitted Satan through the political antichrist to organize the strategy of trying to squeeze the life out of Israel, yet the Lord will stop it at a certain point and judge Israel's enemies for such an action. The armies of the antichrists will be utterly crushed.

Zechariah describes the battle action of God:

Then the LORD will go forth and fight against those nations, as when He fights on a day of battle (Zechariah 14:3).

And it will come about in that day that I will set about to destroy all the nations that come against Jerusalem (Zechariah 12:9).

On this occasion the Messiah will make certain that the sovereignty of God will not be questioned; in the battle of Armageddon in the land of Israel the nations of the earth will recognize that the God of Israel is also the God of all the earth. The military action of the Messiah will finally insure the *physical* redemption of Israel.

When I talk to many Israelis today about redemption they generally will say that it has already taken place. When asked to explain their reply, they answer, "Well, we are here." Now this is correct in part. As we pointed out in chapter two concerning the return of Jewish people to the land, God has been working in modern history, effecting the process of the redemption of the land and the people of Israel. But it is a mistake to think that redemption is already accomplished by the mere presence of Jewish people in their ancient land. Total redemption begins, first of all, with the turning of Israel to God, and the nation's recognition of this very God as sovereign. Obviously, physical redemption is a necessary dimension but its *fullness* will come only after the battle of Armageddon. Yet spiritual redemption is the other necessary dimension which we need to consider.

Spiritual Redemption. It is interesting to see that when God is ready to begin the Messianic kingdom, it must start with Israel:

And I will pour out on the house of David and on the inhabitants of Jerusalem, the Spirit of grace and of supplication, so that they will look on Me whom they have pierced; and they will mourn for Him, as one mourns for an only son, and they will weep bitterly over Him, like the bitter weeping over a first-born (Zechariah 12:10).

When Israel will turn to the Lord for help, the spirit of God will be poured out on the one-third of Israel who remain. But a peculiar response occurs at this point. Those in the redeemed remnant lament for a number of reasons. Obviously they lament over what has been lost of the nation, although many of those who died have no doubt perished as martyrs for the truth and will be resurrected. Such a lament would be quite natural over the frightful diminishing in the ranks of the household of Israel.

But there appears to be another reason for the lament. In the "fountain opened for . . . sin" (Zechariah 13:1), and with this remnant "born anew as in a day," those of the remnant recognize their Redeemer. The prophet described him as "the pierced one."

Now we need to understand what is meant by the phrase, "the pierced one." Why was such a one pierced? And what is more important: When was He pierced? The only viable answer is the one which comes from history. The pierced one is Jesus the Messiah who, when He was on earth the first time, came to be our sin-offering; furthermore, in His death He gives us His life. But of course this is dependent upon a personal acceptance by faith. While thousands upon thousands accepted Jesus as Messiah in the first century, and multitudes of Jewish people have done so in the ensuing centuries—even though at times a pseudo-Christianity completely misrepresented the New Testament message, yet not all the household of Israel acknowledged Him.

However, at the time of the coming of the Messiah to redeem Israel in its direst hour, all of Israel then will recognize the identity of their redeemer: Jesus the Messiah. He will be recognized by His wounds, still visible even though He has a glorified body. Israel will know that the wounds are a testimony to the reason why the Messiah had to die. No wonder the household of Israel will lament. They will probably ask, "Why did not all of our forefathers see Him for who He is? It would have spared us all this heartache."

I need to comment at this time on the interpretation of "all Israel will be saved" (Romans 11:26). Some people feel that every last one of Israel who ever lived will come to a saving knowledge of the Lord, even though this means a second chance for those who have died without an atonement for their sins. Perhaps this feeling comes from a sentimental wish that Israel as a people of God should also be spiritually redeemed. On the other hand, there are those who think that Jewish people can find salvation in their religious system in spite of the fact the religion does not have the concept of substitute in the atonement for sin; rather, the Jewish idea of atonement is based on self-effort through repentance, prayers, and good deeds. But whatever the reason for this "universalism" where every Jewish person will find his way to the presence of the Lord, it is not a scripturally based idea. The Abrahamic covenant does guarantee that there will always be a people Israel in the long history of man (Genesis 17:7). But we must be precise in what God has promised to Israel. He has: 1, promised the seed of Jacob that He will guarantee their continuity within human history; and He also, 2, made it quite clear that there is a need for every person, Jewish person included, individually to find an atonement for his sins. Moses taught the concept of substitute in the sacrificial system in the Mosaic covenant, and the New Covenant continues this emphasis which presents Jesus as the Substitute who died for our sins. Except for this Messiah, who is the Substitute who has died on our behalf, there can be no other basis of atonement for sin (John 14:6).

The presence of "all Israel" has a specific historical context. Zechariah indicated that it is at the *end* of the darkness experience when the one-third remnant of Israel calls for help from the Lord and finds salvation and redemption. We need to note that this is an event which can occur only at the time of the coming of the Redeemer to earth. He is the one who makes it possible for Israel to enter into its physical *and* spiritual redemption.

Paul also makes this clear:

> And thus all Israel will be saved, just as it is written,
> "The Deliverer will come from Zion,
> He will remove ungodliness from Jacob."
> "And this is My covenant with them,
> When I take away their sins" (Romans 11:26-27).

The apostle carefully makes two points associated with the salvation of "all Israel": 1, it is in the day when the entire remnant of Jacob will have their sins taken away, and 2, it is the Deliverer who comes, at a specific historic point, to provide spiritual redemption. Obviously, from what we have already seen as to the concept of the darkness of the day of the Lord and the reason and purposes for it, "all Israel" refers to an entire particular generation, at the end of their darkness period, or better yet, at the inception of the fullness of the kingdom of Messiah.

The coming glory of Israel, however, represents a context that we shall have to explain in chapter nine when we shall see how the full effects of the Messianic constitution become a reality. Figure 23 describes some of the events and their sequence in relation to Israel's plight in the darkness of the day of the Lord.

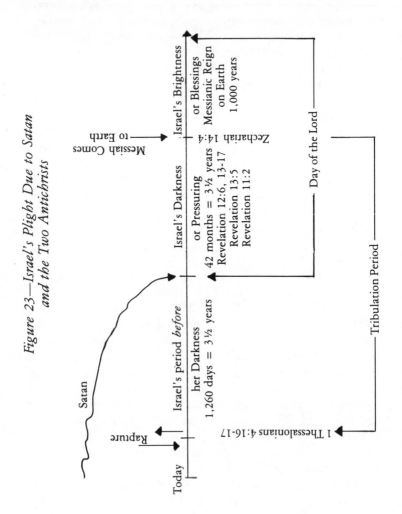

Figure 23—Israel's Plight Due to Satan and the Two Antichrists

Events Associated with the Day of the Lord
(see chapter two)

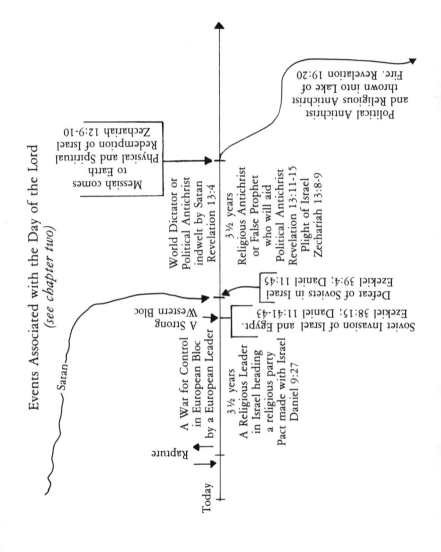

Satan

Rapture

Today

A War for Control in European Bloc by a European Leader

A Strong Western Bloc

3½ years
A Religious Leader in Israel heading a religious party Pact made with Israel Daniel 9:27

Soviet Invasion of Israel and Egypt. Ezekiel 38:15; Daniel 11:41-43

Defeat of Soviets in Israel Ezekiel 39:4; Daniel 11:45

World Dictator or Political Antichrist indwelt by Satan Revelation 13:4

3½ years
Religious Antichrist or False Prophet who will aid Political Antichrist Revelation 13:11-15 Plight of Israel Zechariah 13:8-9

Messiah comes to Earth Physical and Spiritual Redemption of Israel Zechariah 12:9-10

Political Antichrist and Religious Antichrist thrown into Lake of Fire. Revelation 19:20

8

CHRISTIANS AND THE JUDGMENT SEAT OF CHRIST

O blessed hope! The rapture nears!
Today, perhaps! We hail the dawn,
Of Heaven's glad, eternal morn;
Above earth's turmoil, strife, and fear,
Christ's, "Lo I come!" His children hear.
All things declare the time's at hand!
God's schedule will mature as planned.
Ann Lind-Woodworth

Some years ago when in Israel my wife and I went to Kibbutz Tirat Zvi, which is a religious kibbutz in the Beit Shean valley some thirty miles south of the Sea of Galilee. It is a beautiful region situated almost on the border between Israel and Jordan. At the time this was a political hot spot, and many of the communal farms in the region were suffering from sporadic bombardment by the Palestinian Arabs in Jordan. One of Israel's press officers had suggested that I go there and live with the people for several days to see how they fared, trying to live normal lives in spite of constant harassment. On my part, I was interested in this kibbutz because I wanted to see how religious Jewish people lived as they were shelled by guerrilla forces. What would be the sensitivities of people who, while seeking to live pious lifestyles as they followed a traditionally Jewish worship, had to kill when infiltrators would come across the border into the kibbutz to do them harm? How would they understand their actions if the situation became desperate enough that they would have to defend themselves by shooting at terrorists and invaders?

I vividly remember talking to many secular Israeli youth who had great misgivings in their hearts when they had to shoot to kill in combat, although they understood the necessity for self-defense when Israel was attacked. It was difficult for them to rationalize their inner feelings as to their misgivings.

With religious Jewish youth living on the borders, I found a different attitude. They had a deep faith in God's promises to Israel, especially concerning the land. While the religious folk sought no harm to Arabs across the border in Jordan, yet they had a sense of God's providential care that, since He gave them this particular land, they were within divine rights to protect it. And if they had to kill in self-defense, then they felt they were within the will of God in sustaining the title deed to this land in the name of God. The religious Jews had an ideology to fall back on to sustain themselves under the constant pressure and harassment.

It was an interesting experience for my wife and me as we stayed on this kibbutz for six days. We interviewed many of the people living there, including one gentleman who was running for a seat in the knesset (parliament) at the time. We had opportunity to see how these religious Jewish people apply their insights concerning Scripture and the traditions to the entire range of problems facing Israel in the modern context.

One evening there was a wedding on the kibbutz. The reception afterwards was held outdoors under many lights strung up for the occasion. The Palestinian Arabs on the other side of the Jordan River decided to "join us," that is, by way of firing several rounds of their Katyusha rockets into the kibbutz. We all ran for the shelters, leaving the food on the tables. But that was not the end of the reception, however, because we stayed below ground for only about forty-five minutes, and then when the all clear sounded, we trooped out and carried on from where we had left off. The people were used to such an interruption in their daily lives, and did not let it bother them.

This wedding was very interesting and we saw some beautiful lessons from the Bible come to life. About two hours before the actual wedding ceremony, we all went over to the bridegroom's house. There sat the handsome bridegroom in the living room of his parent's home, flanked by his father and father-in-law to be. We all wished the bridegroom well and chatted with him a bit. Then everyone went to the house that belonged to the parents of the bride. The beautiful bride sat in her seat of honor and on one side there was the bride's mother and on the other side the mother-in-law to be. We greeted the bride, wished her well also, and stood about having fellowship with her and her friends. What we were waiting for, of course, was the coming of the bridegroom for his bride before they were to go to the synagogue for the wedding. At the moment it suited the bridegroom, he left his father's house, followed by his father and father-in-law to be, and walked to the bride's house. When he arrived, he greeted his bride with a kiss, stood for a few moments with her, and then went on to the synagogue. After a few minutes the bride arose, followed by her mother and mother-in-law to be and many of the fellows of the kibbutz who sang songs of joy as they walked along behind her. We all walked to the synagogue where the wedding ceremony took place under the canopy as the rabbi read the marriage contract. The reception followed the ceremony.

As my wife and I watched and took part in the various proceedings, we looked at each other and remarked what a revealing illustration it was of how the Old Testament depicts the time when all Israel as the bride will be united with the Father as the bridegroom at the beginning of the brightness of the day of the Lord; and also how in a unique way the New Testament pictures the wedding of the Church (the bride), and Jesus the Messiah (the bridegroom) at the marriage supper of the Lamb (Revelation 19:9). For the purposes of this chapter, however, we will discuss primarily the latter.

The One Coming of the Messiah Is In Two Phases

We need to consider carefully that the Scriptures do teach that the appearance of Jesus is in two phases: one in connection with the Church, and the other which relates to Israel.

Some of the differences in the phases are pointed out as follows:

Reason. A very different reason can be seen in the coming of Jesus in the two phases:

1. Then we who are alive and remain shall be caught up together with them in the clouds to meet the Lord *in the air* (1 Thessalonians 4:17).

2. For I will gather all the nations against Jerusalem to battle, and the city will be captured. . . . Then the LORD will go forth and fight against those nations, as when He fights on a day of battle (Zechariah 14:2-3).

In His first phase, Jesus comes to catch away those in Christ and He takes them to Heaven. In the second phase, Jesus comes to defeat the enemies of Israel so as to make possible the inception of the Messianic kingdom.

Those involved in the two phases. One needs carefully to study the contexts to see who are the participants in connection with the two phases:

1. And the dead in Christ shall rise first. Then we who are alive and remain [living Christians at the time of the rapture] (1 Thessalonians 4:16-17).

And it was given to her to clothe herself in fine linen, bright and clean; for the fine linen is the righteousness of the saints (Revelation 19:8).

2. And the armies which are in heaven, clothed in fine linen, white and clean, were following Him on white horses (Revelation 19:14).

"They [Israel] will call on My name,
And I will answer them;
I will say, 'They are My people,'
And they will say, 'The Lord is my God' " (Zechariah 13:9b).

Those involved in the first phase when Jesus returns are resurrected Christians, those who have "died in Christ," who will be joined by a generation of Christians living at the time of this resurrection. As the resurrected Christians will receive bodies similar to the body with which Jesus arose after His resurrection, so Christians living in this phase of Messiah's coming will likewise experience a change in their earthly bodies to glorified ones when they ascend to meet the Lord. At the marriage supper of the Lamb all of the body of Christ will be clothed in white linen, enjoying the grand occasion of blessed fellowship with the Lord Jesus, exulting in the reunion with parted loved ones, and beginning the enriching experience of relating and sharing with the multitudes in the body.

But in the second phase of the coming of Christ, He comes at the call of the remnant of His people Israel to redeem them, nationally and spiritually, an entirely different context from the Church.

The *Specific Place To Which Jesus Comes.* We also need to examine carefully the principal localities with each of the phases in Jesus' coming:

1. Caught up together with them in the clouds to meet the Lord *in the air* (1 Thessalonians 4:17).

2. And in that day His feet will stand on the *Mount of Olives,* which is in front of Jerusalem on the east (Zechariah 14:4).

In the rapture, the dead in Christ and living Christians meet the Lord in the air to be taken with Him into Heaven. In the second phase of the return, Jesus descends to the Mount of Olives to wage His battle with the antichrists and their armies.

Results. What occurs in time immediately after these two phases is also different. For Christians there is the very real experience of the judgment seat of Christ, when rewards will be given or withheld (1 Corinthians 3:10-15). We shall be discussing this judgment, those involved, and the basis for it in greater detail later on in this chapter; it is sufficient here to mention that this situation is different from what will happen just after the second phase of Christ's coming. In the latter, there is the resurrection of Old Testament and tribulation saints, and the rewards for the labors of these particular people. There is the judgment of the nations as well. These latter experiences we shall touch on in chapter nine when we discuss the Messianic constitution. But each of the results after the two phases of Jesus's coming merit the closest attention to detail so that the Word of God can be rightly divided.

See Figure 24 for a comparison of the two phases.

Imminence. I feel that I need to make some observations concerning the imminent coming of Jesus for His body in His timing. One important consideration of imminency is that there are no specific signs that point to the return of Jesus for the Church or, for that matter, the end of the church age. Please note what Paul had to say about the attitude and expectancy of believers in our age:

> And to *wait* for His Son from heaven, whom He raised from the dead, that is Jesus, who delivers us from the wrath to come (1 Thessalonians 1:10).

> So that you are not lacking in any gift, *awaiting eagerly* the revelation of our Lord Jesus Christ (1 Corinthians 1:7).

> *Looking* for the blessed hope and the appearing of the glory of our great God and Saviour, Christ Jesus (Titus 2:13).

There are other passages, but we have enough to indicate that believers are to have their eyes, expectations, and hopes set on the appearing of Jesus. We have been delivered from the wrath to come (the experiences of the events of the tribulation and the experiences of a lost eternity), and so we wait for His appearing with great eagerness and anticipation. No signs are indicated in these verses concerning the coming of Jesus in His first phase.

To understand this matter of signs, we need a deeper perspective of God's program. From an Old Testament point of view, there is no mention of the Church, or a first and second coming of the Messiah. The prophetic outlook for those who longed for the kingdom in Old Testament days was the coming of Messiah to institute His Messianic reign on earth. When Jesus began His public ministry, and in the first part of it, He talked about the coming kingdom and sought to elicit Israel's response to Him as the King and that they also should repent to have their part in the kingdom.

In the second part of Jesus's ministry, there is a shift of emphasis as the Messiah sought to prepare His disciples for their ministry in the future. After the death, burial, and resurrection of Jesus, and the subsequent explanations by Paul as to the mystery of God's purposes, there is to be a period when the people of God are the Church (Romans 16:25f; Colossians 1:26f). In the age in which we live, the message goes out to all peoples, Jewish and Gentile alike, but the fullness of the kingdom when the people of Israel are restored in their land and when Messiah will reign over them is a future event.

From our point of view today, we can talk about a first and second coming of Messiah, the first one which is history already, and the second one in its second phase, which is still to come. What we must recognize therefore is that all the signs of which the Old Testament spoke actually relate to Israel when its promises refer to the kingdom of peace on earth, when the seed of Jacob will be in special relationship to Jesus the Messiah, and when Jesus will reign in Jerusalem, the city of the great King. Accordingly, it is not acceptable exegesis to take passages in Scripture which speak of signs for Israel and apply these very signs as significant for the Church and its rapture.

In other chapters of this book we have been considering the signs that relate to Israel and the alignment of the nations just prior to the coming of Messiah to earth. Even more specifically, signs will have special meaning for the believers during the tribulation period. They will see the rise of the European leader who will become the political antichrist, his horrible transformation as the abomination of desolation (Matthew 24:15) when he demands worship, the invasion and devastation of Israel by the Soviet Union and the ultimate defeat of the latter, and the pressurization of Israel by the political antichrist and his armies. In describing this period Jesus issued a warning to believers to be on the alert (Matthew 23:42), but the warning relates to signs of the tumultuous times of the tribulation.

For the believers of the body of Christ, while we see the gathering storm about to break loose in the subsequent period of the tribulation, and certainly these signs concerning Israel and the nations make us aware that our age is drawing to a close, yet we are to wait for the coming of Jesus to take us to the home of the Father. In our context, for now, we anticipate the imminent appearance of Jesus, and to hear the shout of the archangel and the blast of the trumpet of God. The believers of the tribulation period look for the second phase of this coming of Jesus with the armies of Heaven to institute the fullness of the Messianic kingdom. We conclude that the coming of the Christ for His body is not to be specifically conditioned by signs or prerequisite events.

The Judgment Seat of Christ and the Great White Throne Judgment

At the same time that we differentiate between the two phases of the coming of Jesus, we also should distinguish carefully between two judgments: where Christians are judged, and where the unsaved appear. The Scriptures do indicate a difference:

1. For we shall all stand before the judgment seat of Christ (Romans 14:10).

2. And I saw a great white throne and Him who sat upon it (Revelation 20:11).

And if anyone's name was not found written in the book of life, he was thrown into the lake of fire (Revelation 20:15).

In the passage in Romans Paul addressed himself to the Roman Christians, in particular, and to all Christians in general, with the pronoun "we." All believers in Jesus will stand one day at this judgment seat of Christ to receive their rewards or, unfortunately, the withholding of rewards.

But the great white throne judgment is another matter altogether. The point is specifically made concerning those who stand before the latter judgment: it is because their names are not written in the Lamb's book of life! When people receive the truths of the Lord, either in the days of the Old Testament, in this present age, in the period of the tribulation, or even in the kingdom age, their names are recorded in the Lamb's book of life. The inscription becomes the guarantee on the part of God that anyone trusting in Him is forever recorded in God's book and his name will never be removed. But if one's name is not included in this book of life, it is proof that a person was never born anew, and had therefore never become God's child. The great white throne judgment is for the unbelievers of all ages, and the results of that experience are tragic when everyone in this predicament will be placed in the lake of fire. It will be a horror indeed when the ultimate verdict for an unbeliever is the lake of fire! Therefore, concerning these two judgments, there is a difference in time, purpose, and people.

Will We Recognize Our Departed Loved Ones?

A recurring question in Bible classes, conferences, and private consultation is whether we shall recognize departed loved ones and have fellowship with them again. Certainly the question comes out of a deep concern on the part of Christians who yearn someday to see again departed members of families and friends who have died as believers. While God does not give a lot of information in this area, I feel that He does give us enough so that our hearts can be assured.

In the account of Mary Magdalene at the tomb, after the resurrection of Jesus (John 20:13-16), she stood there, distressed and weeping, because He was not to be found in the tomb. As she turned away from the tomb, she saw a man whom she presumed to be the gardener and asked him where the body of Jesus had been taken. The person to whom Mary was talking was actually Jesus in His postresurrection appearance, but the point is that Mary simply could not imagine for one moment that she was talking to someone who had risen from the dead. Her mind could not break out of the mold of this worldly orientation and realize that she was talking to someone who already had His part in the world to come. All it took, however, was one word by Jesus: "Mary!" It was probably in the special way He spoke her name that it immediately clicked in Mary's mind that this One standing in front of her was actually Jesus Himself. She had no problem recognizing Him then.

In another instance, there is the account of the two disciples of Emmaus returning home, and Jesus joining them at some point along the road (Luke 24:15-31). This was nothing unusual since the road would have been filled with travelers returning from Jerusalem after the Sabbath, just as it occurs even today in Israel. These disciples were taken up with the events of that weekend when Jesus had been arrested, tried, condemned, crucified, and then buried. They spoke of their hope that perhaps Jesus could have been the one to redeem Israel, but now their hopes were dashed to the ground and they were returning home, dejected in mind and spirit. They had left Jerusalem at the crack of dawn on the first day of the week and were aware that some strange events had occurred at the tomb where Jesus had been buried, but the testimony then of an empty tomb seemed too farfetched to give credence to the report (Luke 24:22-24). Even when Jesus explained the Scriptures to them concerning the claims of Messiah, their minds were so preoccupied with their disappointment that they could not imagine the resurrected Jesus, much less that they were actually talking with Him, who already had His part in the glory of the next world. It was only after they entered the house where the two disciples lived and sat down to supper that, in the blessing and breaking of the bread by Jesus as the guest, they finally realized the identity of their traveling companion. Again, it was in that special way Jesus blessed and broke the bread that they recognized Him. Like Mary, they too could not break away from the context of an earthly existence, especially in their discouragements, to realize that it is possible to recognize and talk with One from another world.

We are not any different in many ways. But we will know our loved ones who have gone into the presence of Jesus. Someday when we have joined them, freed from the pull of this world, it will be with a special inflection of the voice, a specific mannerism, a special look, that we will recognize and remember a loved one. Our basic traits of personality will not change and these will prove to be the features by which we will remember and know members of families and dear friends.

Every Christian Is Involved with the Judgment Seat

Every believer without question will appear before Jesus, who will assess our service. While we have already pointed out this experience in which Christians will participate, we take it up now in more detail. Paul provided us with the specifics of this context:

> But you, why do you judge your brother? Or you again, why do you regard your brother with contempt? For we shall all stand before the judgment seat of God. . . . So then each one of us shall give account of himself to God (Romans 14:10,12).

And again Paul repeats this information in slightly different words, but with the same meaning:

> For we must all appear before the judgment seat of Christ, that each one may be recompensed for his deeds in the body, according to what he has done, whether good or bad (2 Corinthians 5:10).

The apostle stressed that this is an experience in which every Christian must participate. Jesus, as the examiner, will go over every detail of our service. No one escapes this scrutiny!

I remember one time when I had explored this aspect of encounter with Jesus Christ in a Sunday morning message. After the meeting I stood with the pastor at the church exit, and greeted the people as they left. One very well-dressed woman stopped in front of me and said, "I don't believe a word of what you said this morning." She added, "All of us will make it into Heaven someday and there will be no such tomfoolery as an examiner who pries into our lives." Of course, I doubted whether she was really a child of God, but she would not permit me to talk to her about her salvation experience. I could only finally say at that point, "Madam, it makes no difference what people think or feel. What the Lord has spoken must be accepted at its face value!"

It is all too often a tragedy that the Scriptures are judged by people's ideas and feelings, rather than that the Scriptures stand as objective truth, directing all our thoughts and deeds. We live in a day of permissiveness and many simply will not accept moral or value absolutes. Sometimes this attitude or permissiveness has even invaded the body of Christ and we are not too careful with our lifestyle. But moral absolutes form the basis for upright, equitable, and impartial justice at the judgment seat with Jesus as the examiner. We do have an inescapable appointment with Jesus.

We Are Examined As To How We Build

At the judgment seat of Christ, we shall be proved as to our responsibility as believers.

Building on the Foundation. Paul explains to us the basis for our examination:

> For we are God's fellow workers; you are God's field, God's building. According to the grace of God which was given to me, as a wise master builder I laid a foundation, and another is building upon it. But let each man be careful how he builds upon it (1 Corinthians 3:9-10).

The important point to remember is that we are God's fellow workers in the ongoing of His program. The apostle challenged the Corinthians that he had laid a foundation among them. He had surely presented the gospel to them and they had responded and come to know the Lord. It was not to stop there, however. The Corinthians were to build on that foundation. In the same way, someone laid a foundation within us when the seed of the Word was sown and we were presented with the gospel. After accepting Christ, we have the responsibility to build on the foundation that was begun in us. That does not mean that we hire pastors in our churches as a substitute for the work we are supposed to do. A pastor provides guidance so that, in one way or another, we develop to become spiritually mature believers, and also use the gifts that the Lord has given to us for an outreach through our local churches or societies in which we serve. But in our development and in the outreach we really must build on the foundation that someone laid in our lives.

Therefore a superstructure must rise on the foundation implanted in us. In BeerSheva (Beersheba) in Israel, there was a synagogue where the walls were left to stand only three-fourths of the way up. All around it were new buildings springing up, handsome structures reflecting the genius and hard work of the Israelis. To say the least, this incomplete building looked strange, set in the midst of other buildings long since completed. I asked a guide what happened, and he described the immigration in the early 1950s when Israelis felt that all Jewish people could, upon settling in BeerSheva, worship in that one particular synagogue. Israeli government planners thought that all Jewish people, no matter where they came from, would be glad to mingle together in the same house of worship.

Well, it was an ideal but Israelis found out that it was not possible to put all the various ethnicities of Jewish people together. English, American, and German Jews could not worship with Moroccan and Iraqi Jews; the ethnic origins of the Jewish immigrants were much too diverse in their cultural backgrounds. Today Israeli planners are far wiser and they work with the second generation children, who would be more pliable to mingle with one another to begin building a homogenous social structure in Israel.

I wonder whether some believers' lives look just like that synagogue: an unfinished superstructure. We may have started well but, arriving at a certain point, we then stop without ever finishing the superstructure on the foundation. Or considerable time elapses before the work is taken up again, but precious opportunities have been taken by another believer. We need to be constantly reminded that we should be careful how we build upon the foundation and be faithful at the task.

Paul adds further:

> Let no man deceive himself. If any man among you thinks that he is wise in this age, let him become foolish that he may become wise (1 Corinthians 3:18).

In this matter of building on the foundation, we had better be wise with God rather than wise with the world. To have the wisdom of God means that we do not fool ourselves as to what He wants accomplished with our lives. He is saying to us, "Build upon that foundation which someone has started in you." We do well not to become spiritual monstrosities by leaving incomplete our spiritual development.

The Materials With Which We Build. Furthermore, the very material that we use in the building will be examined:

> Now if any man builds upon the foundation with gold, silver, precious stones, wood, hay, straw (1 Corinthians 3:12).

The two different kinds of materials used in the building of the superstructure are very apparent. The gold, silver, and precious stones are references to lasting materials and, come what may, the ordinary ravages of time will never destroy them. But wood, hay, and straw? These materials do not last;

wood can rot away, and hay and straw can be fired easily. It is not too difficult to recognize the degree of quality involved in building the structures in our lives.

The Lord makes it even more urgent to make the right decision as to how to build wisely and adequately:

Each man's work will become evident; for the day will show it, because it is to be revealed with fire; and the fire itself will *test* the quality of each man's work (1 Corinthians 3:13).

For the individual believer there is a very pointed question as to how one builds. What kind of decisions are made whereby the lifework of a believer will last? Is a believer's labor translated into lives that have come to know the Lord? Do teachers live and talk in such a way that this is also shared with young lives who will in turn grow up and be productive believers? Is money invested wisely to insure proper training for young people to propagate the gospel to the ends of the earth and advance the cause of Christ? If this is so, then these are wise decisions to insure that one builds with lasting materials. Someday in the glory we shall meet people who have been won to the Lord and have been encouraged for His service because of our building with indestructible commodities.

On the other hand, unfortunately, believers can make wrong and foolish decisions whereby resources, time, and talents are squandered on self, on possessions, and on selfish interests. Questionable spiritual and moral activities can produce only a superstructure with the perishable items of this life and, tragically, people who build in this way will arrive in the glory with nothing in their hands. Because these folks make the wrong decisions and do not place the Lord's interests first, they will have nothing to show for all the labor that was expended during their earthly lives. How sad when no precious souls will greet selfish believers on their arrival in Heaven because no money, or very little of it, was used for the work of the gospel to win people. Foolish decisions mean that, if all our investments are for self and this world, they will be lost or burned up, and ultimately we will arrive in the glory as spiritual paupers.

Involved in the material we use for our superstructure are even the motives and priorities by which we seek to serve the Lord. This is obviously an examination into our innermost being, where the wellsprings of our choices are made. We all have reasons for choosing the activities in which we are engaged. We want people to think the best of us, and we make decisions so that we can be seen in the best possible light.

What can be the proper motive for our ministry among Christians? Do we serve so as to be noticed by people and therefore receive praise from men? Or do we serve as servants of the Most High, seeking to please Him? At times we can be well thought of by both men and the Lord, but at other times we will be unpopular with people when we have to make choices that honor God. The latter must always be first in our hearts, however, and this only comes as we are rightly motivated by the will of God to make the right choices. When we honor God and His concerns, we build lastingly. But when our motives are mere self-seeking, when our priorities are self- and man-centered, then we build with materials that will decay, rot, and rust, or which will quickly burn up. We then have nothing lasting to show for all the effort that has been expended.

Take for example a situation in a church. Every member in a congregation is a component part to help the group move out and reach a community for Christ, or send missionaries to various parts of the world for service. But in order to make a church work, it is necessary to have time, talents, and money, all three, in a consecrated arrangement that entails proper motives and priorities. People in congregations sometimes ask, as they listen to their pastors plead for a combined consecrated witness, ''What is the preacher driving at? I come to church on Sunday morning; I come on Sunday evening; I even come sometimes for the prayer meetings. What more does he want from me?'' The point is that we don't come to church to serve ourselves. Rather, we come to be refueled by listening to the Word of God. We should establish our priorities as to what comes first, and check out our motives for service. Then we can all work together in reaching a community for youth and children, cook in the kitchen, work in the church office, go on visitation, and invest in the work to make sure that it will have the widest possible outreach. This is lasting service for the Lord.

I want to address myself to the young reader. I feel that every young person should check out the Lord's will as to whether or not specialized work for the Lord is for him or her. Obviously, God does not call everyone to this specific service, inasmuch as some are going to be farmers, some factory workers, some will work in offices, stores, universities, and the multitude of jobs available in modern society. But before a young person sets his or her mind on a job or position, he should ask, "Does God want me in a particular way?" This is checking out the priorities and motives for the decisions where we ask the Lord as to what is His will for our lives.

Perhaps we say, "Oh, the ministry, the mission field, there is no money in that. Look at how some of these people have to live. No, that is not for me!" This is already a wrong motive and it just might lead to building the superstructure with wood, hay, and straw. Especially is this so if the Lord is really calling a young person who has his eye on making all the money he possibly can. While a lot of money can be made in the course of a lifetime, yet if one misses his calling, all or part of his work will be lost. That is why this examination of our priorities and motives is such a serious business, and if we don't check them out, we shall be tried at the judgment seat of Christ for our lack of sensitivity.

For the last generation of the Church, just before the rapture, the situation becomes even more critical. Paul speaks of "the day" and of the fire that will try a person's works. This is again a reference to the darkness experience in the first part of the day of the Lord, and will include also the period prior to this darkness. The time period refers generally to the tribulation, which in reality will be a hell on earth, and an experience of mass destruction of property and materiel as armies move about and are deployed to gain military advantage. The supernatural events described in the book of Revelation will also create havoc beyond degree. Property and wealth amassed by believers will be misused by the enemies of the gospel.

What happens when Christians live for this world only and amass wealth and property which is not at all used for the Lord? Obviously the misuse of property or the destruction of it means that selfish Christians were dealing only with hay, wood, and straw, and that their priorities and motives were sadly misdirected. The last generation of the Church just prior to the rapture has even a greater responsibility to the things of the Lord than many generations preceding it, in the preaching of the gospel to save people from the tribulation, and to sow the seed of the Word to prepare those who will enter the tribulation period with all its horrors. The latter is especially true for Israel, when many evangelized before the rapture will become believers during the tribulation period.

The Rewards or Lack of Them

Some Christians feel that all believers will enjoy the same degree of awards and share equally in the glory. I must confess that I cannot see the logic behind these statements. The justice of God must take into account an examination of the quality of one's service and work. To treat everyone alike when evaluating rewards for one's service would mean that quality, responsibility, and conscientiousness of believers would be emptied of all meaning; it would not make any difference between one who served the Lord with his whole being, another who is only partial in his service, and one who is merely playing with his beliefs. No, the Scriptures do say that God will respect dedication, concern, and wholehearted service, and will reward this kind of meaningful activity.

Paul spells out the matter of selectivity in rewards:

If any man's work which he has built upon it remains, he shall receive a reward. If any man's work is burned up, he shall suffer loss; but he himself shall be saved, yet so as through fire (1 Corinthians 3:14-15).

God does take note of the kind of superstructure we are building for ourselves, its lasting quality, our motives and priorities; if our works withstand the tests of time and the ravages of the fire, we are then promised a reward. Careful Christian responsibility carries with it a commendation by God. If on the human level there is recognition for an employee's dependability on his job, then on the divine level the recognition for work well done by the believer is of even greater value.

But if the Christian's work is shoddy, partial, and lax in many ways, or if the believer has been self-seeking, then he loses the possibility of a reward. A Christian does not receive any commendation from the Lord when all his labor is destroyed, burned up, or wastes away. Yet that person can be *saved!* In other words, supposing all of a believer's efforts are lost and all that is left is the foundation; yet God does not take away the foundation because this is the very basis for the salvation of that person. Salvation is not the issue at the judgment seat of Christ; rather, this judgment tests the quality of one's work either to offer or to withhold the reward.

What is disheartening is when Christians rationalize, "Well, if I can be saved just by the skin of my teeth, I will be satisfied." The point is, however, that that kind of person will not be happy or content with such a result. The loss of reward is a very real possibility, which means tears and remorse for lost opportunities. We all know how it is when we have played on an athletic team and, even after we have tried our best, have lost the game. At least we tried. But think of a Christian who did not try his best, simply sloughed off his opportunities, and then will have to answer for it. Never is it God's intention that we be saved by "the skin of our teeth." God wants people with vision in service and faithfulness in labor. That kind of devotion will bring with it an everlasting reward and an increased responsibility for service in the kingdom of God to come.

One more observation needs to be made. Some could have the notion that the great preachers and well-known missionaries will receive most of the rewards, and everyone else will receive less recognition. But the judgment seat is going to reveal a lot of surprises. Obviously, if a minister has served well, he will be appropriately recognized. Yet there will be "little" people, about whom the body of Christ has never heard, and they can receive some of the greatest rewards. I am thinking of a couple who were never great speakers and they had little money. However, they spent time and whatever they had caring for hundreds of young people. They have been a dad and mom to these young people, listened to their heartaches, cooked for them at all hours when they came to their home, stood with them in their trials, counseled with them in the things of the Lord, and led many to salvation. As a result, many of these young people were spared lives of sin, were made into useful members of society, and some have become missionaries. Will this couple receive a great reward? Of course, as much as any great preacher. All that God asks is that we be faithful with the capacities which He has given to us, use what he has equipped us with, and we shall never lose our reward.

I am reminded of a builder who once worked for a contractor. He had labored many years as a builder, erecting homes, office buildings, schools, and so on. As the years went by, this man felt that he wasn't receiving his fair share of the wages paid out. One day the contractor gave this builder the plans for a house and told him to build it. The builder decided that this was his opportunity to gain something for himself. He planned to put into this house the cheapest of all materials, and pocket the difference between the best and least valuable goods. So the concrete was not mixed right, the wood was the cheapest kind, and the plaster was not prepared according to

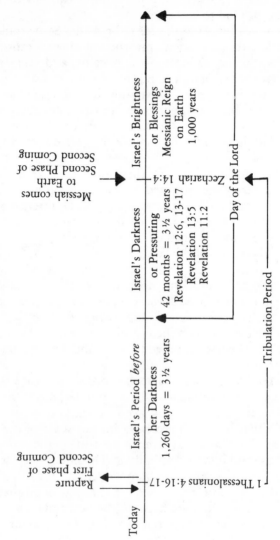

*Figure 24—The Day of the Lord and
The Two Phases of Messiah's Second Coming*

Events Associated with the Day of the Lord
(see chapter two)

	First Phase	Second Phase
Reason	Comes for His Church	Comes to Defeat Israel's Enemies
People	Believers Who Died in Christ Living Generation of Christians	Comes at Call by Israel in Their Darkest Hour
Place	Meets His Church in the Air	His Feet Will Stand on the Mount of Olives
Results	Judgment Seat of Christ Marriage Supper of the Lamb	Resurrection of Old Testament Saints Judgment of the Nations Beginning of the Kingdom of Peace on Earth

specifications. In every way the builder shortchanged the materials and labor that went into that house. When the house was completed the contractor came to inspect it. After looking over the structure, the contractor said to the builder, "You know, you have worked for me these many years. I have tried to do the best for you. There were times when it was hard for me to pay you all you were worth, but I have tried to be fair. So, in token for all you have done for me, I am giving you this house. This house is my gift to you." Suddenly the builder realized that he had built a house for himself that would quickly fall apart.

May the Lord help us that at the judgment seat of Christ we will be able to give a good account of our trusteeship and live well in the superstructure we are erecting at this very moment.

9

ISRAEL'S MESSIANIC CONSTITUTION

Definition of Utopia: from Greek, *ou*, not, no + *topos*, place; therefore: no place!

And the wolf will dwell with the lamb,
And the leopard will lie down with the kid,
And the calf and the young lion and the fatling together;
And a little boy will lead them.
Also the cow and the bear will graze;
Their young will lie down together;
And the lion will eat straw like the ox.
And the nursing child will play by the hole of the cobra,
And the weaned child will put his hand on the viper's den.
They will not hurt or destroy in all My holy mountain,
For the earth will be full of the knowledge of the Lord
As the waters cover the sea.
Then it will come about in that day
That the nations will resort to the root of Jesse,
Who will stand as a signal for the peoples;
And his resting place will be glorious.   Isaiah 11:6-10

During the days of the Old Testament, or what is known as the Old Testament historical kingdom, Israel had a constitution which I choose to call the Mosaic constitution (see chapter one). It had three elements to it primarily: the moral, which was largely the ten commandments; the sacrificial, which provided for a person's atonement and the opportunity to worship and serve the Lord; and the juridical, which consisted of the civil and criminal laws that governed the people within that society. The third element was primarily tailored for a rural setting, but as time progressed and the nation became more urbanized these laws were adapted to provide for the combination of rural and city society.

Actually there was also a fourth element which spelled out

the models of worship and lifestyle for the nation; for example, holidays, dietary, family relations, and so on. However, for the purpose of this book I shall not pursue the study of this element, which is really an independent study of culture as a part of the way one expresses his belief and lifestyle.

In the first century, when Jesus died for our sins, His death as the atonement for sin was proclaimed by the early believers as the fulfillment of the sacrificial element of the Mosaic constitution. God was gracious to Israel. He provided some forty years after the death of Jesus for the transition in thinking and acceptance by Israel that Jesus indeed is the Messiah and that His death and resurrection herald a new day in God's purposes.

But once the temple was lost in 70 A.D., the Mosaic constitution ceased to exist. This document can be in force only when all of its three elements exist side by side simultaneously; when any one of these elements is taken away this document cannot remain as it was originally ratified. The loss of the sacrificial element is the indicator that the New Covenant is now in force; all spiritual blessings can be enjoyed when one receives the atonement provided by Jesus.

I am suggesting, however, that at least two of the elements of the Mosaic constitution do have significance for today. 1, The moral-absolutes element is in effect, written on the heart of every believer (Hebrews 8:10). 2, The sacrificial emphasis is inseparably connected with the death of Jesus on the cross (tree) and provides the very basis in this age for becoming a part of the body of Messiah. 3, We also have numerous civil and criminal laws in modern society, some of which can be traced to the Mosaic constitution. The juridical element of this document, however, is not specifically a part of the New Covenant inasmuch as the body of Christ does not function as a nation. Israel was constituted as a nation with laws to govern its legal codes but the Church is not structured in this way.

We now come to the modern scene and in chapter three we have described the providential hand of God regathering His people to the ancient soil of the homeland. In 1948 Israel issued its declaration of independence and then began to constitute itself as a state. At the time of the signing of this declaration, the hope was expressed that a constitution for the new state would be drawn up shortly. It was an optimistic hope, but it never was realized. Almost as soon as the state was born, Jewish people began to pour into the land, even during the progress of the War of Independence, when Israel was fighting for her survival. After the armistice was signed in the spring of 1949, immigration picked up in earnest, especially from Arab countries. The extraordinary set of circumstances meant that, right from the beginning, all the energies of the leaders of the state were taken up with the conduct of the war and subsequently with the real strain of trying to establish the thousands of immigrants entering the country. It was not possible to finish a constitution by the end of 1948, and in fact it is still in the process of being written.

There is another reason why a constitution remains unfinished. In 1948 the people who comprised the state were largely European in background, Ashkenazim, who came from northern and eastern Europe. From 1948 to about 1960, however, the large influx came from Arab Middle East (Oriental Jews) and the Mediterranean countries (Sephardim Jews). Most of these peoples had developed in centuries past a rich cultural and religious heritage. The Oriental Jews in Iraq had as their ancestors the Babylonian Jews who had developed their Talmud by 500 A.D. The Sephardim Jews had their golden age in literature in Spain, as we saw in chapter four, but they were finally expelled in 1492; those who managed to survive did so under the most difficult circumstances in other Mediterranean countries to which they had fled.

The first generation of Oriental and Sephardim immigrants to Israel after the founding of the state found it generally difficult to fit into a technically advanced society of the twentieth century, although many did well in agriculture and with small trades. However, the mix of technically advanced European Jews and the lack of modern technical skills of the Oriental and Sephardim Jews was bound to produce dislocations as everyone tried to work together, live together, and begin the process of establishing a homogenous culture. Even though the modern state is comprised of about 42 percent Oriental and Sephardim Jewry, yet the pattern of cultural mix is still fluid in many ways. For this very important reason it is difficult to draw up a constitution that will satisfy all the people of the state, but step by step the basic laws, or articles, are being written. So far, there are basic laws for electing the knesset (parliament), the determination of what constitutes Israel lands, the election of the president, and provisions for the government.

The lack of a finished constitution does not mean that Israel has no laws to govern her society. There are laws still left from the days when there was an Ottoman (Turkish) dominion prior to 1917. Many laws are still on the books from the days when Great Britain exercised her mandate over the land. Of course, the knesset has enacted major statutes and other laws since 1948 on behalf of the state.

But this attempt to draw up a constitution can be quite critical at this juncture of history. For example, the prophetic implications, the power bloc in formation exactly as the Bible predicted for the end of the age, the presence of the modern State of Israel, and all the rest of the conditions that mark the time for the Messiah's return, only raise the question whether Israel will be able to complete her constitution. Even if modern Israel were almost to conclude this document, while religious leaders attempt to ratify again the Mosaic constitution in the days prior to the darkness period for Israel, that is, the first part of the tribulation (see chapter seven), all these efforts will be short-lived. The point is that God has something better in store for Israel when she finally recognizes her Messiah: *the Messianic constitution.*

Once Israel has experienced its physical and spiritual redemption, God will put into operation a constitution, which the prophets already spelled out, for the days of the fullness of the Messianic kingdom. In the period of the day of the Lord, Israel will have a document which will bring about a utopian set of conditions in which all nations will participate. The modern Israelis have done admirably in reconstituting the state and sustaining it, trying to fit into the world community of nations, although unwanted in many quarters. Yet Israel can never escape its destiny of divine rendezvous. God permitted the present Israel to come to pass, but it is for the purpose of ultimately uniting His people under a constitution which He Himself has drawn up. Just as there was a Mount Sinai experience for the sons of Jacob, so there will be a Mount of Olives experience in the complete redemption of the nation, and then a Mount Zion experience when the Messianic constitution is enacted. Our purpose now is to examine the various articles of this forthcoming document.

Redemption of Israel and the Nations

The prophet Jeremiah spelled out the redemptive feature of the Messianic constitution, which has both the material/physical and spiritual emphases. While I have pointed out that Zechariah emphasized this combination when Israel will be redeemed and call for Messiah (Zechariah 12:9-13; 14:1-4; see chapter seven), yet Jeremiah goes into more detail concerning these features of the New Covenant.

Physical-Material Features. Jeremiah first pictures the future for the nine clans[1] who had ceased to be a political unit

---

[1] While Judah was dominant in the southern kingdom, the official three clans present were Judah, Benjamin, and Simeon scattered among Judah, since they had no claim to land because of the curse placed upon them; also, Levi had no claim to land, a word that was never rescinded although they served as priests (Genesis 49:7; Deuteronomy 10:9). I have included Levi among Israel and Jacob.

in 721 B.C. Even though the prophet ministered at about 600
B.C., approximately one hundred twenty years after the
northern kingdom was no more, God never forgot them, and
He therefore issued His word through His man:

> Hear the word of the LORD, O nations,
> And declare in the coastlands afar off,
> And say, "He who scattered Israel will gather him,
> And keep him as a shepherd keeps his flock."
> For the LORD has ransomed Jacob,
> And redeemed him from the hand of him who was stronger
>   than he,
> And they shall come and shout for joy on the height of Zion,
> And they shall be radiant over the bounty of the LORD—
> Over the grain, and the new wine, and the oil,
> And over the young of the flock and the herd;
> And their life shall be like a watered garden,
> And they shall never languish again (Jeremiah 31:10-12).

The promise for physical blessing is specifically for the nine
clans, called Israel and Jacob. There was no such restoration
for them as a national unit alongside Judah after the Babylonian exile and therefore we can say only that Jeremiah insists
that, in any partial physical redemption in the modern scene [1]
and total aspect in the Messianic kingdom, all nine clans must
be present.

But the prophet also declares the physical restoration of
Judah as well. It was a word to the people of the southern
kingdom as to the future experiences of its three clans:

> Thus says the LORD of hosts, the God of Israel, "Once again
> they will speak this word in the land of Judah and in its cities, when
> I restore their fortunes,
>   'The Lord bless you, O abode of righteousness, O holy hill!'
> "And Judah and all its cities will dwell together in it, the farmer
> and they who go about with flocks" (Jeremiah 31:23-24).

---

[1] While Jewish people today cannot declare with certainty their tribal origin, except in some
special circumstances the Levitical clan who have names as Cohen or Levi, yet God will one day
make the grand separation to declare who of Israel belongs to which clan.

I don't believe that Jeremiah had in mind only the restoration from Babylon in 538 B.C., when a remnant of Judah returned and started the second commonwealth of Israel that was to last into the first century A.D. The total scope of the prophet's message goes far beyond the physical restoration from a Babylonian exile; the recall is occurring in our day and must even be regarded for the future as well.

So as to tie together both prophecies for all twelve clans, and not leave us in any doubt as to the future historical context, the prophet adds:

"Behold days are coming," declares the LORD, "when I will sow the house of Israel and the house of Judah with the seed of man and with the seed of beast. And it will come about that as I have watched over them to pluck up, to break down, to overthrow, to destroy, and to bring disaster, so I will watch over them to build and to plant," declares the LORD (Jeremiah 31:27-28).

The implication is that in the modern immigration movement to the land of Israel, and in the future involvement as well, God restores both houses of the seed of Jacob and unites them together on their land. While the Old Testament historical kingdom ruptured because of an impulsive drastic decision by King Rehoboam (1 Kings 12:12-16), and each kingdom went its own way, yet all of the descendants of Jacob will once again be brought together, never again to be plucked away from their homes. These are the prospects for the house of Israel in the brightness of the day of the Lord in the Messianic kingdom. We shall have more to say about the many features of material/physical blessings further on in this chapter. But these are factors which cannot be spiritualized away, made to refer to heavenly bliss, or relegated to experiences within the Church. We need to guard with care what a proper interpretation of Scriptures has to say, to avoid needless confusion.

Spiritual Features. As we have seen, redemption also has to include the spiritual change of people and Jeremiah makes this point in the New Covenant as well (see chapter one) (Jeremiah 31:33-34).

The one-third remnant of Israel that will be left after the darkness-pressurization experience will realize that, as the Spirit of God is poured out of the house of David (Zechariah 13:8-9; 12:10), everyone will know the Lord. At least in the first generation of the second part of the day of the Lord it will not be necessary for one to preach within the ranks of that generation to know the Lord. The law will already be written on their hearts because they will all be believers. Indeed, it will be a new Israel at the dawn of the brightness of the day of the Lord; she will have her peace in a land of plenty in the day when she enters into her spiritual redemption.

One note is necessary concerning how we can speak of a kingdom where both spiritual and material blessings are involved. Most will dispute that somehow spiritual blessings can be enjoyed only in Heaven, removed from this earth's scene. To describe material enjoyment along with spiritual benefits seems to detract from the latter. But why is it not possible to have both together? In the garden of Eden certainly both sets of blessings were entirely possible, and as long as Adam and Eve were obedient to God's commandment, they not only enjoyed total consecration and fellowship with the Lord, but also entered into every physical and material blessing and delight. The same was true in the Old Testament historical kingdom concerning the relationship between Israel and the Lord. As long as Israel was sensitive to the elements of the Mosaic constitution, there was every spiritual and material blessing. Conversely, when there was a drought and physical loss in the land, it was also a sign that the spiritual contact between Israel and the Lord was broken.

It is only in our age that there is the enjoyment of all spiritual blessings, but not necessarily material blessings (except for our needs, Philippians 4:19).[1] But the context of our

---

[1] The body of Christ is not constituted as a nation, as was Israel. While we mingle with the people of this world, and are citizens of nations, we don't as believers in the body operate as a nation with all its pomp and ceremony. Most of the time, we as believers will have our part with poor and disadvantaged brethren among the nations and therefore material wealth should not be our desire or goal of life.

age is not the entire guide for what will be the rule in the future; therefore, in the brightness of the day of the Lord there should not be any surprise when both sets of blessings will be the order of relationship between the people of the Messianic age and the Lord. After all, if Christians can enjoy the feasting at banquets today, along with a fine spiritual message, why quibble when we talk about the combination of spiritual and material blessings in the kingdom of peace?

The Gentile Nations. We have already seen how the Israelis will shout for divine intervention in their day of greatest pressurization and how Messiah will respond to rescue a remnant of Israel. This redemption of Israel, all twelve clans, becomes the key as to when the brightness of the day of the Lord will begin, and the utopia among men will become a reality. But the reader may very well ask: What about the rest of the nations? Will they not also have a part in the brightness phase of the day likewise to enjoy physical and spiritual redemption?

In order for all the nations to take part in the blessings of the kingdom (for it is promised that this will be the case, Isaiah 42:6; 49:6), it will be necessary to purge out unregenerate nations, and we see how God proceeds to accomplish this separation. By the end of the tribulation period, while two-thirds of Israel will perish, so will one-third of mankind (Revelation 9:15, 18), marking the beginning of separation of righteous from unrighteous people. The process is frightful, but men who curse God, even after He will use drastic means to speak and correct them (Revelation 9:20-21; 16:8-11) do not deserve to join the saints in the Messianic kingdom.

Leaders of nations with many of the military forces will also be involved in the battle of Armageddon where the conflict climaxes when ungodly men will actually fight against the Lord of lords, Jesus the King (Revelation 19:19-21). The predictable result of this battle is the slaughter of an untold number of rebels who will then await in Sheol their sentence

on the day of judgment, along with the rest of the unbelievers of all the ages (Revelation 20:11-15). The political and religious antichrists will not even be given the benefit
of a hearing before the Judge on that day but rather, immediately upon the conclusion of the Armageddon conflict,
they will be hurled into the lake of fire. In a tragic but
necessary action, God purges most unregenerate people of
the tribulation period to bar them from any presence in the
brightness of the day of the Lord, the Messianic kingdom.

Yet God is merciful. Every one in the tribulation period
will have opportunity to hear the message of life and to know
the Lord. Even in the worst hell of humanity's history, God
will never let go of anyone willing to listen to the message of
life. Many will refuse to bear the mark of the beast (Revelation 13:17; 20:4) and will maintain their testimony to reach
others. God will aid in this endeavor; in a very visible way the
message of life will be preached by angels in the attempt to
evangelize people and encourage them to seek out the
believers (Revelation 14:6). Others as believers will be martyred for their faith (Revelation 6:9).

However, by the end of the tribulation period, there is still
the prospect that many among the nations will survive the
awesome judgments and wars and arrive at the threshold of
the kingdom's fullness, still to reject God's sovereignty. The
Lord will take steps to remove this final body of unre-
generates. At the very beginning of the kingdom of peace, a
judgment of the nations will purge out all remaining
unbelievers as well as those nations and leaders who have opposed the will and Word of God. The Prophet Joel provides
the warning in his prophetic message:

> "For behold, in those days and at that time,
> When I restore the fortunes of Judah and Jerusalem,
> I will gather all the nations,
> And bring them down to the valley of Jehoshaphat.
> Then I will enter into judgment with them there
> On behalf of My people and My inheritance, Israel,

> Whom they have scattered among the nations;
> And they have divided up My land" (Joel 3:1-2).

What we note first of all is the time frame of the prophecy: when the fortunes of Judah and Jerusalem are restored. This also refers to the time when all the clans of Israel are settled and are safe in their homeland, nevermore to be plucked from it. Furthermore, additional evidence for the time of the judgment of the nations is also given; Joel 3:1-2 occurs after the dreadful, that is, the first part of the day of the Lord in the tribulation period (Joel 2:31).

Of all the many reasons God could use to judge the nations—ungodly and immoral leaders, unjust expansionism, cruel slaughter of conquered peoples, God-defying systems of ideology which lead people away from God, and so on—one reason stands out in particular. The charge against the ungodly leaders calls them to account: what did they and their nations do to Israel, particularly in the darkness of the day of the Lord?

While Joel describes the injustices to Judah and Jerusalem by the nations in terms of what happened in his day—the plunder of people and land (Joel 3:5), the partitioning of the land (verse 2), selling inhabitants into slavery for the slightest whim of pleasure (verses 3 and 6), sending people into exile (verse 2), and the slaughter of people—yet he also pictures these and other horrible deeds which will yet be perpetrated against Israel in the future and for which God will judge the nations.

Jesus Himself taught that there will be a judgment of nations at the inception of the kingdom. Nations were pictured as sheep and goats, and the references to these animals were well known in the rural scenes of Jesus's day. No one ever made a mistake as to which are sheep and goats because they are as diverse as any set of opposites, not only in appearance but in nature as well. In the same way, nations which are righteous and unrighteous are also diverse in God's sight. At the judgment throne the sheep nations, who are sensitive to

God's leadership and will (Matthew 25:35-36), are the ones which will have their part in the kingdom (Matthew 25:34). Those nations described as goats spurn God's sovereignty and will, and are involved in religious systems which deny Him and His concerns (Matthew 25:42-43). Their destiny will be separation from Christ and they have their horrible experience in eternal fire (Matthew 25:41). Once more, this verse applies to ungodly leaders of nations, and the people within these nations who choose to follow their immoral political guides.

Asked how God's sovereignty was rejected, Jesus's reply concerns itself with how the nations treated His brethren. In the immediate Scripture context, the Messiah was describing the day of the Lord, particularly the pressuring of Israel in her darkness experience. What initiated this discussion in Matthew 24—25 were questions the disciples had asked Jesus: the sign of His coming, and the end of the age (Matthew 24:3). The context in which these Jewish disciples were speaking was the coming of Messiah for the inception of the kingdom of peace. No mention is made of any Church here since, as was discussed in chapter eight, this was a mystery which Paul brought forth at a later date, after Israel's leadership had made the fatal decision concerning Jesus's claim as Messiah and King, and after His ascension and Pentecost. Furthermore, the Church is to be taken from this earth's scene before the tribulation period and God then specifically prepares Israel for her role in the kingdom.

Some will want a wider context for the identity of Jesus's brethren to include believers in general or any people in need, and admittedly there can be an *application* which demonstrates genuine compassion and care for a ministry of concern. But we must keep in mind the questions the disciples had asked and the answer Jesus gave to them, and the context, which has to do with Jesus's brethren as the people of Israel, and the scope of preparing Israel for the kingdom. It is Jesus's brethren, the Jewish people (Matthew

25:40,45), who are slaughtered, imprisoned, persecuted, made destitute when they have to wander without food or clothing (Matthew 24:29-30; 25:31-46) in the time of Israel's greatest pressurization. But as with Assyria who had attempted to defeat Israel and one hundred eighty-five thousand troops (Isaiah 37:36), and with Babylon who had destroyed the first temple and sacked Jerusalem and then found themselves in their death throes as a nation (Jeremiah 50:18-46), so the Judge of nations will bring about a just retribution for the antichrists, the nations, and peoples who will yet so shamefully treat Israel.

The purge of ungodly nations is real; they will not be permitted to enter the kingdom, and possibly the very names of these nations could be eradicated from the community of nations in the brightness of the day of the Lord. At least in the first generation of the kingdom there will be the presence of a redeemed Israel as well as the sheep nations who have also found spiritual redemption. It is staggering even to imagine the force for good in a world where all are believers! But this is God's purpose and goal for the world community of nations within human history.

The Political Context of the Kingdom

Since the fullness of the Messianic kingdom does involve Israel as a redeemed nation, and the presence of other redeemed nations as well, it will be necessary to have a political structure by which the nations will cooperate as a cohesive unit. God's purposes for the kingdom call for a monarchy, as already described by the agreement with David (see chapter one), but it will be desirable to mention again some of the features of this covenant (2 Samuel 7:16).

Type of Government. The first of the terms is a promise made by God to David concerning his house. With the promise of the kingship for Israel (Deuteronomy 17:15f) God indicated that He would select the regent king for the people of

Israel because, after all, in the theocracy, God as *the* King has the right to make the choice. David was selected to be the person to rule over Israel, and the promise is extended whereby the line of David will continue this leadership. Eventually in the fullness of time the line focuses on the Messiah: Jesus of the line of David.

The second term insists that the throne of David never will cease to exist as long as there is a history of man. However, because of the curse placed on Coniah, or King Jehoiachin (Jeremiah 22:28, 30), no king has sat on the throne of David during the second commonwealth (538 B.C.—70 A.D.); yet it did not mean that the throne of David was abrogated. Rather, the throne was vacant until the appearance of David's greater son, when He can exercise the right to sit as king.

The crucifixion scene becomes highly significant when some authorities in Israel objected to the description of the identity of Jesus. The full inscription of the cross (tree) of Jesus read:

"JESUS THE NAZARENE, THE KING OF THE JEWS" (Matthew 27:37; John 19:19).

Pilate was urged by some to change the sign to read, "He said, 'I am King of the Jews' " (John 19:21). The Roman governor did not acquiesce to these demands; providentially the description of His office remains as a testimony throughout the centuries. Jesus is the King, destined to sit on the throne of David when in the fullness of the kingdom Israel will acknowledge Him.

There are Christians today who say that Jesus is now, during the course of the church age, sitting upon the throne of David at the right hand of the Father (Hebrews 1:3). But in no way can we say that this seat of authority is the throne of David. If we take literally the Scriptures which spell out the usage and context of the phrase, "the throne of David," they are always associated with a throne here on earth and in a specific place, Israel in general and Jerusalem in particular. Actually, as we have seen, Jesus is waiting until Israel calls for

Him to rule over the nation, but until then the throne of David remains unoccupied until the brightness of the day of the Lord.

In addition, God's promise for optimum government is the *kingdom* of David when, in the fullness of the kingdom, both spiritual and material blessings will be the order of the age. God's man, the benevolent King Messiah, will rule with equity and justice to insure all the most favorable conditions on earth which man has most desperately desired.

The World Capital. One of the terms of the New Covenant described Jerusalem as important to Israel as well as to the whole world. Even in the modern setting this city is regarded with extreme interest. It has always been considered by Jewish people as their chief city and capital of the land of Israel since the days of David. But Jerusalem is also important to Christians because so many of the events, lives, and sites of the New Testament, in addition to the Old Testament, are associated with this key city. The Muslims as well regard Jerusalem as important since it is their third most holy city; the Dome of the Rock mosque, set on the site of the former temples, also marks the point, according to the Koran, from which Muhammad ascended to Heaven and returned. Yet Jerusalem will play a far greater role in the future because it is the city of the great King (Matthew 5:35).

The Prophet Jeremiah declared concerning Jerusalem:

''Behold, days are coming,'' declares the LORD, ''when the city shall be rebuilt for the LORD from the Tower of Hananel to the Corner Gate. And the measuring line shall go out farther straight ahead to the hill Gareb; then it will turn to Goah. And the whole valley of the dead bodies and of the ashes, and all the fields as far as the brook Kidron, to the corner of the Horse Gate toward the east, shall be holy to the LORD; it shall not be plucked up, or overthrown anymore forever'' (Jeremiah 31:38-40).

Jeremiah describes Jerusalem by taking a counterclockwise walk around it, starting with the tower of Hananel at the

northeast corner. In going west from this point we arrive at
the corner, probably at the northwest point. From here we
encompass an area bounded by the hill Gareb and the region
of Goah, locations not known today, but they somehow
depict the northwest, west, and southwest regions of the city.
The valley of dead bodies is at the south end and is called Ge
(Gay) Hinnom (Valley of Hinnom), but which in time came
to refer to the area where there was always a smoke going up
from the burning of the leftovers and ashes of the sacrifices
used on the temple altar. The brook Kidron is at the east side
of the city and the Horse Gate at the southeast corner or in
the general east region. Interestingly enough, Jeremiah's
description of the city does not specify an eastward expan-
sion, but rather it does grow northward, westward, and
southwestward.

At the end of Jeremiah's ministry in Judah, the Babylonians sacked the city and burned the first temple (586 B.C.).
After the Babylonian exile and in the days of Nehemiah (444
B.C.), the city had an area smaller than that in Jeremiah's
day, but by the time of Jesus, in the first century A.D.,
Jerusalem had expanded to the area generally bounded by
the Old City of Jerusalem, as we know it today (except that
the present Old City walls, the work of Turkish engineers and
builders in the 1500s, omit a large area on the south side
which was enclosed in Jesus's day).

In the prophet's projection of Jerusalem, he described it as
a time of peace when Israel will never again be plucked from
the land. From our point of view, we certainly cannot look
back to any such time in the context provided by the prophet.
Over and over again across the centuries the streets of
Jerusalem have run with blood as it was subjected to the
violent assaults of man's wars. The experiences of history have
only made a mockery of the concept of the city of peace. But
in the days of the brightness of the day of the Lord, Israel will
be at rest, Jerusalem will be peaceful, and God will protect
this city.

God has also indicated that in the Messianic kingdom the administrative center of the world community of nations will have a specific location:

> And many peoples will come and say,
> "Come, let us go up to the mountain of the LORD,
> To the house of the God of Jacob;
> That He may teach us concerning His ways,
> And that we may walk in His paths."
> For the law will go forth from Zion,
> And the word of the Lord from Jerusalem (Isaiah 2:3).

In considering the passage, we cannot see only the spiritual sense. True, the gospel did begin in Jerusalem, and then was heralded to the nations of the earth, and individuals have accepted Jesus as Saviour and Redeemer. But the context of the passage also gives us a physical dimension and hence a clue as to the timing of this prophecy. The scope is still future when Jerusalem will be the world capital and nations will acknowledge and accept all legal, moral, and spiritual pronouncements which issue from it. What Isaiah said about 700 B.C. will be applicable in the brightness of the day of the Lord when Jerusalem's authority is recognized among the nations.

The Ecclesiastical Element of the Kingdom

The Messiah as King-Priest. The Mosaic constitution was very careful to distinguish between the regal and priestly functions in the affairs of the nation Israel. The house of David provided the kingship while the clan of Levi was responsible for leading the nation in worship. There was a definite reason for this arrangement; God as the Lawgiver recognized that, in the course of a nation's experience, it is necessary to protect the state of affairs when unregenerate men seize both religious and political power for themselves. An ungodly leader, acting in both of these capacities, then has total power and becomes the worst kind of tyrant. Nations have, in the course of their history, found this to be true.

There are many examples through the centuries where

great church systems have also sought to dominate the political arena, only to fall into the greatest corruption and become tyrannical over the lives of people. For this reason, there has been to a lesser or greater extent the desire in western countries to separate the affairs of state and church. But this was nothing new. The Mosaic constitution already separated these functions and is a testimony to the wisdom of God, who knows what is best for man in his sinful condition.

But in the fullness of the Messianic kingdom, there will be a union of both regal and priestly affairs in the person of the Messiah:

> The LORD says to my Lord:
> "Sit at My right hand,
> Until I make Thine enemies a footstool for Thy feet."
> The LORD will stretch forth Thy scepter from Zion, saying,
> "Rule in the midst of Thine enemies" (Psalm 110:1-2).

> The LORD has sworn and will not change His mind,
> "Thou art a priest forever
> According to the order of Melchizedek" (Psalm 110:4).

Only because the Messiah has a divine nature, in addition to His humanity (Psalm 110:1; Matthew 22:41-46), is it possible to unite the functions of a perfect spiritual leader and perfect political authority, and not corrupt national Israel and the outreach into world government or pervert the worship system. In fact, this unique arrangement is one of the most desirable features of the fullness of the Messianic kingdom in that a perfect person will protect all the features of the political and spiritual processes.

We shall now see the divine design for the best possible ecclesiastical arrangement, although with the limitations on space in this book, I will be able to discuss this area only in a general way.

The Center of Worship. The Messianic temple will be the nucleus of worship in the kingdom, but this aspect of worship is probably one of the thorniest problems of a kingdom rule on earth. However, the Scriptures themselves provide the guide for a discussion on this topic.

First, there is the Messianic temple, presented in the principal passage, Ezekiel 40—43. The prophet described the total worship area to be a square, about seven hundred and fifty feet on a side, enclosing the space for courts and temple building. The distance on each side is about two-and-one-half football fields. The details the prophet provides for the dimensions is amazing. An outer wall surrounds the entire complex and three entrances—north, east, and south—provide access through the outer wall. To enter, one ascends seven steps from the ground level to pass through gate houses in the outer wall, into an outer court where any and all people may come to worship. In this area, against the outer wall are a series of rooms, and at each corner are kitchens where the people can prepare their food when partaking of sacrificial meals.

There is an inner wall surrounding an inner court area, and from this inner wall on each of its three sides—north, east, and south—the distance to the rooms against the outer wall area is about one hundred and fifty feet. This is about one-half the length of a football field for each of the three sides and does provide room in the outer court area for crowds of people.

The same arrangement exists to enter the inner court. Three entrances are on the north, east, and south sides, and one ascends, this time eight steps, from the outer court level to the inner court level. Another set of gate houses exists in the inner wall, leading into the inner court.

In front of the temple building in the inner court area stands the massive altar of burnt offering; at the north side of the altar there is space for the killing of the sacrificial animals and their preparation for offering. Ten steps then lead from the inner court level into the temple itself, which is a building about one hundred and fifty feet long and ninety feet wide. The building is divided into two parts, the holy place and the most holy place (holy of holies).

In the holy place only one article of furniture is mentioned: the table before the Lord (Ezekiel 41:22). In the Mosaic legislation the holy place had three pieces present: the seven-branched candlestick, the table of showbread, and the table of incense (Exodus 40:22-24). No furniture or veil is mentioned for the inside of the holy place, according to Ezekiel, whereas Moses placed in it the ark of the testimony and the mercy seat on top of the ark, and also installed the veil to separate the holy place and the holy of holies. All of these changes suggest a new worship system altogether in the kingdom, as we shall soon see.

Now when we examine the commentaries on Ezekiel 40—43, we find that Bible scholars struggle with the meaning of these chapters, and at least three possibilities are suggested: 1, the Zerubbabel temple following the Babylonian exile (although very few hold to this view); 2, this passage depicts the church age;[1] 3, the vision of Ezekiel is a representation of the consummation of all things which is connected with the eternal state of bliss of Revelation chapters 21—22.[2]

The first view can hardly be the case because the temple area Ezekiel envisioned is much larger than what was constructed upon the return of Israel from Babylon. It is also a matter of record that the furniture of the Zerubbabel temple (and the Herodian reconstruction) were as Moses prescribed, different from Ezekiel's instruction. In the second view, we can only point to the message given to Ezekiel as he addressed himself to the house of Israel, and *not* to the Church; the description can be fulfilled only in the day when Israel is finally settled in the land (Ezekiel 40:4). Israel is not the Church and specifically the Church is not confined to a special land area. The third view has an extreme difficulty with it. The detailed analysis of Ezekiel's temple indicates a literal structure, but John in the Revelation views a new Jerusalem where there is *no* temple building (Revelation

---

[1]P. Fairbairn, *Ezekiel, An Exposition* (Edinburgh: T. & T. Clark, 1855), page 435
[2]Carl Friedrich Keil, *Biblical Commentary on the Prophecies of Ezekiel, Vol. II* (Grand Rapids, Eerdmans, 1950), pages 416-434

21:22) but instead the Lamb is the temple of it. So many other differences in the third view exist between what Ezekiel describes and what John depicts that the two passages can only be regarded as incompatible insofar as temple structure is concerned.

If we take what Ezekiel writes on a literal basis, one major consideration becomes impressive: the maze of detail in the dimensions provided for every aspect of the temple. The point of the numerous dimensions is to enforce the idea that the prophet was talking about a literal temple and all the areas surrounding it. He meant that the multiplied figures of length and width, and some concerning height, are to be taken literally and not spiritualized or allegorized into intangible concepts of the Church or the bliss of the eternal state. The old adage is true: where Scripture makes sense, we are not to use any other sense, even though we may not understand all the implications.

The Question of Sacrifices. Granted that we have a temple building and that we need to take Ezekiel's dimensions seriously, how shall we understand the description of sacrifices offered by a priestly family called Zadokites and also observances of holidays according to Israel's religious calendar? Obviously, many believers today are going to raise some serious objections to what appears to be a renewal of the law, especially in view of what Hebrews says:

> For by one sacrifice He [Jesus] has perfected for all time those who are sanctified (Hebrews 10:14).

Therefore, how can we talk about another temple and sacrifices after Jesus has already died for our sins? These are perplexing problems when attempting to understand Ezekiel and we shall consider some pertinent details to help us see what the prophet has in mind.

1. The first consideration is that this worship procedure is *not* a return to the Mosaic legislation! There are so many differences between what we choose to speak of as the Ezekiel

legislation and the Mosaic specifications that the rabbis at one point, when considering the canonicity of the books of the Old Testament, actually spoke out against Ezekiel.

For example, in the liturgical calendar, of the three pilgrimage festivals—the Feast of Unleavened Bread, the Feast of Weeks (Pentecost), and the Feast of Ingathering (Tabernacles; Exodus 23:14-16)—Ezekiel omits the Feast of Weeks altogether (Ezekiel 45:21-25). In addition, the Sabbath offerings of the Ezekiel legislation are greatly increased over that of Moses (Ezekiel 46:4-5; Numbers 28:9-10). In the daily burnt offerings, Moses prescribed offerings for morning and evening, but Ezekiel specifies the burnt offering only for the morning (Ezekiel 46:13-15; Numbers 28:3-5). The new moon offerings of Ezekiel are decreased in comparison with what Moses prescribed (Ezekiel 46:6-7; Numbers 28:11-13). We can point to many other differences, but these are enough to indicate that the prophet was calling for a new arrangement in the kingdom. See Figure 25, which compares the differences between Ezekiel and Mosaic temple specifications for worship.

These differences were not merely omissions for brevity. If the prophet wanted to emphasize the reinstitution of the Mosaic constitution, all he had to do was to point out its reestablishment and not go into such detail concerning his view of the worship system. Some of the rabbis eventually recognized what God was saying through Ezekiel and the book was kept as a part of the Old Testament canon, a testimony to the purposes God has in mind.

2. But the problem of sacrifices still remains. We shall consider briefly one of the offerings, the sin offering, in order to try to understand its meaning.[1]

It is necessary to realize that under the Mosaic sacrificial system the animal itself did not take away sin; rather, the

---

[1]See Louis Goldberg, *Leviticus, A Study Guide Commentary* (Grand Rapids: Zondervan, 1980) for a more in-depth study of the Levitical sacrifices and their relationship to the sacrifice of Jesus the Messiah.

animal became the object lesson as to what the exchange-of-life principle means. The animal was regarded as (a) taking the sin of the offerer and therefore (b) it was put to death. But in the death of the animal (c) its blood was offered upon the altar to cover the sin of the offerer, where he would never see it again; (d) but, since blood and life are considered synonymous in the Old Testament (Leviticus 17:11), the animal's blood symbolized its life that was to be received by the offerer.

If the offerer did not internalize these truths, then the whole procedure was just a ritual. But if he did commit himself to the principles associated with the sacrifice as the object lesson, God worked in his heart to regenerate him and make him a new man. The important point is that God wanted the Old Testament worshiper to realize the exchange-of-life involved between the offerer and the animal; if the Israelite caught this great lesson, he had an atonement for sin and a real assurance of his forgiveness.

In time Jesus came, and from God's point of view His sacrifice is the means by which the beliefs of the people in the Old Testament were validated. The Messiah's unique sacrifice at that point in history was the sure guarantee of acceptance for every person's belief in the exchange-of-life principle when he personally appropriated principles of the object lesson. But in addition, in the age in which we live people are regenerated when they also relate to and believe in the exchange-of-life principle with respect to Christ. When we believe in Jesus, He takes our sin, whereby we will no longer have to face it; His blood covers our sin so that God no longer sees it, and we as believers have His life. The Old Testament object lesson brings out all the more clearly the salvation ministry of Jesus. Sometimes people feel that there is no more use for the sacrificial system of Moses now that the Mosaic constitution has been set aside. But this is a mistake. The sacrificial system still makes clear Jesus's unique salvation ministry offered at the cross.

*Figure 25—Differences in Specifications
for Worship by Moses and Ezekiel*

Holidays	Passover; Leviticus 23:4-8 Pentecost; Leviticus 23:15-21 Tabernacles; Leviticus 23:33-36	Passover; Ezekiel 45:21 Pentecost; Omitted Tabernacles; Ezekiel 45:25
Offerings	Sabbath; Numbers 28:9-10 2 lambs 2/10 ephah flour	Sabbath; Ezekiel 46:4-5 6 lambs 1 ram Flour offering with no restriction on amount
	Burnt Offering; Numbers 28:3-5 2 lambs, one for morning and one for evening 1/10 ephah flour offering	Burnt Offering; Ezekiel 46:13-15 1 lamb each morning 1/6 ephah flour
	New Moon; Numbers 28:11-13 2 bulls + 3/10 ephah flour 1 ram + 2/10 ephah flour 7 lambs + 1/10 ephah flour for each lamb	New Moon; Ezekiel 46:6-7 1 bull + 1 ephah flour 1 ram + 1 ephah flour 6 lambs + flour with no restriction on amount

Only a few of the differences are indicated between Ezekiel and Moses as to temple and worship. Other differences include: the furniture of the temple, the family of priests permitted to serve, their consecration, and the cleansing of the altar.

In the day of the fullness of the kingdom, with the presence of the Messianic temple and its reinstitution of sacrifices, we once again have the sin-offering animal as the vivid object lesson which will signify what the exchange-of-life principle means for the people of the kingdom. However, this lesson will refer to the work of Jesus on the cross as the fulfillment of the object lesson. Never should it be regarded that the Ezekiel legislation does away with the unique sacrifice of Jesus. The sin-offering sacrifices of the Messianic temple will be one graphic way to preach the gospel as to what the death of Jesus means, encouraging visitors who are unbelievers to act on what they see. By object lesson and by message during the offering of a sin-offering, testimony will be given that there is only one way by which hearts can be changed, and that is by looking to Jesus and receiving His life. Believers viewing this entire procedure will have cause for a glorious song of praise in thankfulness for what Jesus accomplished in his death.

3. We need to remember that, although the first generation of people in the brightness of the day of the Lord—Israel and the nations—are believers, yet it will be necessary for succeeding generations in the thousand-year reign of Messiah to make the decision to become believers. In a day of perfect conditions the worldwide preaching of the truth of the Word of God will be unhindered. The greatest opportunity will be provided to present what it means to know God. Not only will there be preachers and teachers of the Scriptures present everywhere; people will also have unprecedented opportunities to visit Jerusalem and see by object lesson and preaching what is meant by the death of Jesus the Messiah. It is in this sense that we need to recognize what the Ezekiel sacrificial system will mean in the Messianic kingdom.

In addition, the nations will send their representatives to worship in Jerusalem:

Then it will come about that any who are left of all the nations that went against Jerusalem will go up from year to year to worship the King, the LORD of hosts, and to celebrate the Feast of booths (Zechariah 14:16).

Booths are the tabernacles, one of the pilgrimage festivals, and the nations' representatives will make their pilgrimages to Jerusalem. Some of many of their duties will be to observe the many sacrifices in the temple and at the altar. The sin-offering in particular will be the object lesson to remind people that they need salvation to be right with the Lord in the total sense.

4. Worship will take place in only one way: the Ezekiel legislation of the Messianic temple.

And it will be that whichever of the families of the earth does not go up to Jerusalem to worship the King, the LORD of hosts, there will be no rain on them (Zechariah 14:17).

There will be teeth, in a sense, to protect the only sanctioned temple worship and prevent any rival temple worship among the nations. If it is necessary to shut off a nation's water supply, the Messianic kingdom will have the authority to see to it that the Lord's will is observed.

5. Finally, there will be no possibility for freedom of worship to start a degeneration of a valid approach to God. In the past, and even in our day, pagan worship exists because men's unregenerate hearts have taken the things of God and perverted them. Satan stands behind every one of these false systems, tempting men to turn away from the Lord to follow false worship procedures. In the day of the brightness of the Messianic kingdom, Satan will be locked up and will be unable to create any havoc in the divine way of worship; it will be guarded by God, who will prevent any start of false worship systems (Revelation 20:1-3). We see therefore the mercy and grace of the Lord who takes pains that men will not miss the way to approach Him. God's deepest desire is to help people find salvation for their souls, and make it possible that His own can worship Him in spirit and truth.

If people in the kingdom do not want to accept the way laid out by the Lord for salvation, they will not be forced into it. But if folk persist in private and personal dislike for the things of the Lord, then at the end of the kingdom, as we pointed out in chapter six, Satan will be loosed to gather up all the rebels and God will have His way with them in the battle of the Little Season. It is not the Lord's wish, however, that any should perish in this way, even as today, where God's grace is held out for men to accept if only they desire it.

Specific Blessings of the Messianic Kingdom

We cannot discuss here at length the many-faceted dimensions of utopia which man will enjoy in the Messianic kingdom. A few of the blessings can be enumerated so that we can have some insight as to the greatest day, short of the new heavens and new earth, for man and his enjoyment in a God-instituted utopia on earth.

The Moral Sphere. One tremendous dimension in the moral sphere is that the nations of this world will be ruled by the King-Messiah from Jerusalem. There will be an authority in this world capital which will have the greatest political and social effects this earth has ever seen. While man has his substitute in the United Nations in New York, we see the weakness of man's efforts to control the pride and greed of nations when human decencies and national sovereignties are violated. The authority which issues from the world capital is spelled out by the prince of prophets:

> And many peoples will come and say,
> "Come, let us go up to the mountain of the LORD,
> To the house of the God of Jacob;
> That He may teach us concerning His ways,
> And that we may walk in His paths."
> For the law will go forth from Zion,
> And the word of the LORD from Jerusalem (Isaiah 2:3).

God will give the community of nations in the Messianic kingdom an honest rulership and make the nations toe the line according to His moral absolutes.

A parallel dimension to the moral authority which issues from Jerusalem, particularly in the first generation of the kingdom when everyone will be believers, is that finally we will have a control on the arms race. God will underscore His control, through His King-Messiah, and no more during the course of the kingdom on earth will there be the resort to force between vested interests and national groups. This will be because:

> And He will judge between the nations,
> And will render decisions for many peoples;
> And they will hammer their swords into plowshares, and their
>   spears into pruning hooks.
> Nation will not lift up sword against nation,
> And never again will they learn war (Isaiah 2:4).

We can never begin to estimate the loss in human lives, the anguish to families and nations, and the horrible loss of possessions because of war. One of Satan's most prized enticements is to inveigle nations into war where millions of people are hurled into a lost eternity. On the other hand, we cannot even estimate the beneficial effect of using the vast sums of money involved in the arms race, the billions of dollars, for the purpose of peace, uplifting people from social and economic degradation, and the greatest advance in technical and social spheres, rather than squandering these monies for war. It staggers our minds, even from today's point of view, to imagine what could be done for the alleviation of hunger, the caring for economically disadvantaged people, the development of new energy systems, and so on, with the billions of dollars earmarked for armaments, war, and so-called defense. The future in a kingdom age will already be made brighter beyond man's wildest dreams when the problem of war will be eradicated.

The Removal of the Curse. One of the dimensions in the physical aspects of the kingdom will be the removal of the curse God placed upon the world. Nature itself from the days of our first parents to this very day carries upon it a heavy burden of judgment:

> Cursed is the ground because of you:
> In toil shall you eat of it
> All the days of your life (Genesis 3:17b-18).

Man's constant struggle with nature is the attempt to arrest the debilitating forces in the very soil with which he works, and the fight still goes on.

It is quite likely that man's efforts were not merely to control the weeds of the ground. He struggles with dangerous diseases, fungi, rot, and so on, which have attacked his very crops. But there is also evidence that the curse covers even wider areas than what is confined to the ground itself. Also included are the diseases which affect man, even involving the defects in the genes which he carries that can bring about deformities in his offspring. Man himself eventually succumbs to diseases, inherited from generation to generation, that can be traced back to the judgment by God on nature. What confronts us by the curse is actually the physical evil which permeates this entire planet. Besides disease, this evil is seen in the ruin caused by earthquakes, hurricanes, tornadoes, and all the rest of unexplained horror. The curse has far-ranging consequences.

But in the kingdom all this disfunction will be removed. All of nature is awaiting the day when its burden will be lifted:

> For the anxious longing of the creation waits eagerly for the revealing of the sons of God. For the creation was subjected to futility, not of its own will, but because of Him who subjected it, in hope that the creation itself also will be set free from its slavery to corruption into the freedom of the glory of the children of God. For we know that the whole creation groans and suffers the pains of childbirth together until now (Romans 8:19-22).

How can we begin to measure the beneficial effects of blessings upon this planet when all of the disorders have been rectified: the diseases which affect man, the diseases which affect the ground, and the elimination of all physical evil including earthquakes, tornadoes, hurricanes, etc. No longer will man have to struggle with his environment. Instead, he will be able to devote his energies to positive and uplifting benefits for himself as well as the world in which he lives.

Elimination of Physical Disease and Death. When the curse is removed, the consequences will be immediate concerning body wholeness:

> Then the eyes of the blind will be opened,
> And the ears of the deaf will be unstopped.
> Then the lame will leap like a deer,
> And the tongue of the dumb will shout for joy.
> For waters will break forth in the wilderness
> And streams in the Arabah (Isaiah 35:5-6).

The Scriptures cannot even begin to spell out all of the diseases and the ill effects upon the human body. The prophet, however, makes very clear there will be no deafness, blindness, crippling, or any impairment of speech or mind. Both mankind and animals will be able to enjoy life to the fullest.

Even death will be removed in most instances. The Jerusalem which is created for rejoicing, when people will live in gladness and joy (Isaiah 65:18-23), is indicative of all burden and sorrow being lifted from men's hearts. The prophet also says something about the longevity of life:

> No longer will there be in it an infant who lives but a few days,
> Or an old man who does not live out his days;
> For the youth will die at the age of one hundred
> And the one who does not reach the age of one hundred
> Shall be thought accursed (Isaiah 65:20).

In the kingdom, infant mortality will be unknown and men will live long lives. In fact, it will be possible that a person who enters the kingdom at the coming of Christ to earth will be able to live out the entire Messianic kingdom. The prefall situation comes close to describing earth's conditions when Adam could live to be nine hundred sixty-five years of age and when many of the patriarchs prior to the flood lived long lives. But in a state where the curse is removed, long life should not be thought impossible.

The suggestion is, however, that some will die. To emphasize the longevity, a youth who has to die will still be considered a lad if it happens when he is one hundred years of age (a situation hardly the case from today's point of view)! If one has to die, however, the prophet indicates that for one reason or another he is regarded as "accursed." For anyone to be labeled as such could only be in a situation where there is rebellion against the established order of the kingdom. Opportunities no doubt will be provided for people to change their minds and not continue in opposition to authority, but if there is no change, then judgment will be swift and these people will be removed from the society of man. The King-Messiah in Jerusalem has guaranteed that He will have total control over the nations to prevent any political or civil disturbances injurious to the well-being of man and the nations.

Food and Water in Abundance. Again, with the lifting of the curse from the ground, it will mean that the soil will become superproductive and the corollary will be that water will be in abundance:

> The wilderness and the desert will be glad,
> And the Arabah will rejoice and blossom;
> Like the crocus
> It will blossom profusely
> And rejoice with rejoicing and shout of joy.
> The glory of Lebanon will be given to it,
> The majesty of Carmel and Sharon (Isaiah 35:1-2).

The point of the passage is the reference to the "Arabah" (translated "desert" in the King James Version), which refers to the land south of the Dead Sea in modern Israel. At present this territory looks like the moonscape, absolutely lifeless, with not a shred of vegetation. The prophet describes the tremendous change in productivity of the kingdom whereby even this area will be extremely fruitful, even as the plains of Sharon along the Mediterranean seacoast blossom today. Other prophets also describe the extreme fertility of the land—Ezekiel 36:11; Jeremiah 31:12-14,24-25; Amos 9:13-15, to mention only a few.

I would also have to say that the soil productivity and abundant water supply cannot be limited only to Israel. What happens there is in reality the experience of all nations on the earth. This means that the areas of cultivation today will be greatly enhanced, and barren and infertile soil which is presently worthless will become productive. Increased food supply will be necessary in order to care for the increase in world population during the Messianic kingdom. No doubt other foods will be manufactured chemically to supplement natural food for man's sustenance. In short, the hunger problem of today in the nations of the third world will be only a memory of the past.

Change in Animal Natures. After the flood the dread of man became a part of the animals' experiences (Genesis 9:2) as no doubt man sought various animals for food. Animals soon became aware that man sought them as prey and they fled from man. The kingdom, however, will be different. Man and animals will live together in harmony and peace (Isaiah 11:6-8). What is apparent is that man will no longer be carnivorous so as to eat the flesh of animals, fish, fowl, and insects, but rather he will revert again to the situation prior to the flood when he was a vegetarian. The knowledge of food chemistry will be in an advanced state so that food products from grain and other vegetation will be made highly beneficial for man's health and will include all the nutrients he needs.

Social Problems Rectified. It is staggering to contemplate the magnitude of social problems today. Cities employ social workers who struggle with a mountainous load of cases representing economic privation, conflicts with the law, losses poor people suffer because of unscrupulous entrepreneurs, and so on. One cannot begin to list all the needs which reflect the misery of underprivileged people in so many of the have-not nations. The kingdom, however, will rectify these depressing situations. The prophets declare:

"And they shall build houses and inhabit them;
They shall also plant vineyards and eat their fruit.
They shall not build, and another inhabit,
They shall not plant, and another eat;
For as the lifetime of a tree, so shall be the days of My people,
And My chosen ones shall wear out the work of their hands"
   (Isaiah 65:21-22).

"Also I will restore the captivity of My people Israel,
And they will rebuild the ruined cities and live in them,
They will also plant vineyards and drink their wine,
And make gardens and eat their fruit" (Amos 9:14).

While the Scriptures speak concerning Israel, yet the principles relating to these passages are to be extended to the ends of the earth. All nations will be able to enjoy every benefit: their citizens will not suffer loss due to liars, cheats, violent men, the smooth and suave rich whose bank accounts grow fat at their expense, and repressive government regimes which ruin them. The government provided by King-Messiah will be scrupulously fair with everyone; every person, no matter who he is, will have equality before the law and will enjoy all the fruits of his labor. No one will be able to oppress his neighbor, and no special interest groups will oppress or enslave any peoples.

All of these facets in the physical, social, and economic spheres, and many more, will provide the dimensions which will truly make of this kingdom the utopia that men had longed for but have not been able to accomplish with their man-made schemes. Only God Himself can bring this about with a perfect government under His King-Messiah, who Himself is Lord. Only He can insure this kind of utopia, when the nations will do His bidding and be responsible to a moral standard provided in His Word.

The End of the Messianic Kingdom

Alas, even with the best that man can hope for, the Messianic kingdom age will eventually end with a violent rebellion against the rule of God. As successive generations are born, it will be necessary that the gospel be preached, calling for men to make a decision to receive Jesus as Saviour as well as acknowledge Him as King-Messiah and Lord. The tragedy is that in successive generations of the kingdom more and more men will reject the call of salvation. However, as long as men will have utopian conditions there will be no reason to mount a rebellion against the world government of Messiah, Son of David.

As in so many situations today, the true character of a person has to be tested to reveal what is truly in the mind and heart. Such a set of conditions will develop on a massive scale as we come to the end of the kingdom, when the devil will be released from his abyss and allowed freedom to gather up all of the unbelievers (Revelation 20:7-8). Satan will operate in the same way as he always has in the past; he will deceive the nations and the peoples of the nations, those who have *not* made any effort to acknowledge Jesus the Messiah as the Redeemer from sin.

Human nature being what it is, even in the kingdom, there will still be the pride of heart and disdain for God by unbelievers. In some way, when Satan is released, he will put into the hearts of unbelievers that they will be better off if they could but overthrow the sovereignty of King-Messiah and again establish a kingdom dominated by man. It will all be so subtle, since the rebels will not even realize until it is too late that Satan was behind them directing their thoughts.

The outcome has already been noted: God will separate out the believers from the unbelievers. Those, however, who chose to march under the banner of earth's leadership in revolt will receive their just rewards for turning against their true Benefactor after enjoying all the blessings of the kingdom.

The final picture of the unredeemed is their consignment to judgment at the great white throne and eventually to the lake of fire (Revelation 20:11-15). How great will be the remorse and suffering of kingdom residents when, after enjoying the best of what God offers, they will experience torment through the ages, despairing of what could have been theirs if they had only made the right choice. It is frightful to contemplate.

10

THE TURBULENCE OF THE MIDDLE EAST AND YOU

Two Billion Untouched Peoples!
Those who have *not* as yet been
spoken to by Christians!
Consultation for World Evangelism
Thailand, June 1980

We come to the end of our discussion concerning the key for an interpretation of prophecy and its application for understanding the turbulent events of the Middle East at the end of the age. At this point, after finishing such a series on prophetic teaching, I have been asked by Christians: "What difference does it make how we interpret prophecy? Besides, so many good Bible teachers disagree on these issues." Then usually the Christian will add, "What does this all mean to me personally, anyway?"

I have always insisted that prophetic preaching and teaching must be practical. We have to appreciate the note of urgency in the presentation of prophecy. For example, prophecy does relate directly to evangelism. When we realize that we are living in the last days and we know we are in the midst of events leading to the tribulation, then we can insist with urgency on a decision for Christ by unbelievers before this age closes.

There is certainly an urgency in prophecy that can be applied to missions. If we are convinced that the coming of Jesus is close at hand, then how can we keep silent when so many millions in the world have not even heard the gospel even once? How can we justify withholding the message of eternal life, designed for the people in every land?

Obviously there is an urgency for Christians concerning their lifestyle and the impending rapture of the Church. As Christians we shall have to give an account of our lives and service at the judgment seat of Christ, and prophetic preaching reminds us that we need continually to watch over the way we handle our time, talents, and money.

We are living in momentous and fast-moving days. Words such as "countdown" and "space missions" remind us how far we have come in just a few years. Only several decades ago the biplane was a real accomplishment in speed; now modern jet planes take us across vast distances in a matter of hours, and the spacecraft can go around the world in about ninety minutes. It was only a short time ago, comparatively speaking, when the telephone hung on the wall; if we wanted the attention of the operator, we had to crank the magneto to get her attention. Now cross-country dialing is taken for granted and the person who answers has to stop and think for a moment as to the location of the caller. Iceboxes once kept our things cool, and running after the ice truck for chunks of ice in the summer was a treat for a growing boy; refrigerators and freezers have relegated the icebox to oblivion. In many ways we are reminded of the great advance in technocracy in the twentieth century alone.

In another way, however, we are faced with the fact that there is a serious lack in spiritual and moral spheres on a worldwide basis. We have not developed much in these areas; if anything, we have retrogressed. The world has been embroiled in two world wars in our century, supposedly to solve problems among people and nations, but instead we seem to have multiplied the problems, and the solutions have become even more difficult. Since World War II, we have seen innumerable conflicts the world over causing untold death, political and military agressions, the pitiful sight of ever-increasing numbers of refugees on land and sea, an arms race among nations that is morally evil, and on and on we can go as we look at the extremely difficult problems this world faces. Are we going to solve all the complexities of modern life? People in general, and even many Christians in particular, struggle with conditions that are a part of our world today and ask, "Is there any kind of pattern to what is happening? Does God care about what is happening?"

God has provided us the prophetic Scriptures whereby we can realize something of His program. The knowledge He has given us indicates to a great extent where we are in His purposes. Rest assured, in spite of seeming chaos in the world and the turbulence in the Middle East, God is moving to an ultimate goal.

We read in the Old Testament that the men of Issachar had understanding of the times (1 Chronicles 12:32). Without trying to wrench Scripture out of its context, we realize that God can give us also some understanding of the times in which we live. We are not trying to point to every event, a recent Arab-Israeli crisis, or anywhere else in the world, and then say, ''This is it! God is now going to start the next phase of His program.''

But as we already pointed out, we do feel that we can recognize signs that relate to the coming tribulation period and the return of Jesus to earth to reign; for example, the place of Israel in their land, the line-up of the power bloc of nations exactly as the Scriptures describes it, the prominence of the Middle East because of the availability of oil—so important to the well-being of many nations, and the flow of huge amounts of money to the Middle East. Paul also talked about the grievous times which will come at the end (2 Timothy 3:1): the serious lack in the relations between individuals, the breakdown of the home, the insatiable desire for entertainment, the breakdown of law and order, the ungodliness, and by implication the strained relations between nations and major powers that eventually lead to confrontation (2 Timothy 3:2-4). In addition, Paul also mentioned the apostasy from genuine faith to that of mere religious form (2 Timothy 3:5). The great events of the tribulation and the first part of the day of the Lord, however, do cast their shadows before they occur; the signs from the Scriptures concerning these events do have their shadows in our day before the coming of Christ for His Church.

It is the mercy of God that actually delays the rapture,

because God "is patient toward you, not wishing for any to perish but for all to come to repentance" (2 Peter 3:9). God waits for the one who has not yet made the decision to see in Christ the salvation, or atonement, from sin. While I have mentioned Jewish and Gentile people who will live through the close of the church age on into the tribulation period, and some who will even enter the Messianic reign, yet I am not giving comfort to such people to delay their decisions. Why wait to enter the tribulation, one of the most awful periods in earth's history, before responding to God's offer of salvation? Believers will be martyred on a worldwide basis for their faith in the day of God's wrath on earth; if they survive, it will be only with great physical suffering and anguish. Again, why wait?

Even more important, however, is the great uncertainty that one will even live to the time of the tribulation. We have no assurance that God will give us tomorrow. God warns us to make the decision to receive Jesus as our Saviour today:

Behold, *now* is "the acceptable time," behold, *now* is "the day of salvation" (2 Corinthians 6:2).

Should we not be prepared for the eventuality that we may not live out this day, only then to face eternity separated from the Father? Only by having the life of the Messiah within us are we enabled to go peacefully into eternity into the presence of the Father.

Faith in Jesus the Messiah and Saviour is not a mere "fire escape" either. God's mercy is also extended to us to make good decisions to escape from ourselves, our loneliness, our frustrations, our lack of fulfillment, our meaningless lives. The imminency of the rapture in our day, His soon return, only serves to remind us to accept Jesus Christ, who alone can give us eternal life, which in turn makes our lives meaningful, fills our hearts with peace, gives us rest in our souls, and helps us to relate to our world to bring blessing to lives around us.

For those of us who have experienced Jesus as a reality in

our lives, it behooves us to note that God is trying to speak to our hearts through the events of the turbulent Middle East. We should therefore look for His soon coming. As we see some of the picture unfolding, it ought to spur us to live for our Lord and to witness to both Jew and Gentile alike concerning the necessity for salvation. How much more important becomes our witness in the face of present-day circumstances. How especially pressing becomes the burden to plant the seed of the truth of Israel's Messiah in the hearts of Israel before the real holocaust of the tribulation period. May God give us discernment, like the men of Issachar of old, to have knowledge of the times, in "times like these"!

BIBLIOGRAPHY

Selected Books on Israel and the Jews

History—General

Avi—Yonah, Michael, ed., *A History of the Holy Land* (Jerusalem: Steimatzky, 1969; London: Weidenfeld and Nicholson, 1969).

Bamberger, Bernard J., *The Story of Judaism* (New York: Schocken, 1965) (From earliest history up to the present time, including a chapter on American Jewry).

Ben Gurion, David, ed., *The Jews in Their Land* (London: Aldus Books, 1966).

Eban, Abba, *My People, the Story of the Jews* (New York: Berhman House, 1968).

Epstein, Isidore, *Judaism* (Harmondsworth: Penguin, 1968).

Gibb, H. A. R., *Mohammedanism—A Historical Survey* (New York: Mentor Books, 1955).

Parkes, J., *A History of Palestine From 135 A.D. to Modern Times* (London: Victor Gollancz, 1949).

_____, *A History of the Jewish People* (London: Weidenfeld and Nicholson, 1962; Harmondsworth: Penguin, 1969).

_____, *Whose Land? A History of the Peoples of Palestine* (Harmondsworth: Penguin, 1970).

Vilnay, Zev., *Jerusalem—City of Eternity* (Jerusalem: Israel Universities Press, 1969).

_____, *The New Israel Atlas—Bible to Present* (Jerusalem: Israel Universities Press, 1968).

History—Modern

Antonius, George, *The Arab Awakening* (London: Hamish Hamilton, 1938).

279

Bauer, Y., *From Diplomacy to Resistance,* A History of Jewish Palestine, 1939—1945 (Philadelphia: Jewish Publication Society, 1970).

Eban, Abba, *My People—The Story of the Jews* (London: Weidenfeld and Nicholson, 1969).

Harkabi, Yehoshafat, *Arab Attitudes to Israel,* translated by Misha L. Louvish (Jerusalem: Israel Universities Press, 1976).

A. Kac, *The Messianic Hope* (Grand Rapids: Baker, 1975).

_____, *The Rebirth of the State of Israel* (Grand Rapids: Baker, rev. ed., 1981).

Khouri, Fred J., *The Arab—Israeli Dilemma* (Syracuse: Syracuse University Press, 1968).

Kimche, Jon., *The Second Arab Awakening—The Middle East 1914-1970* (New York: Holt, Rinehart, Winston, 1970).

_____ and David, *A Clash of Destinies,* the Arab-Jewish War and the Founding of the State of Israel (New York: Praeger, 1960).

Laquer, Walter, *Confrontation: The Middle East and World Politics* (New York: Bantam Books, 1974).

_____, *The Road to Jerusalem,* The Origins of the Arab-Israeli Conflict, (New York: Macmillan, 1968).

_____, *The Struggle for the Middle East;* The Soviet Union in the Mediterranean 1958-1968, (London: Routledge and Kegan Paul, 1969).

_____, ed., *The Israel/Arab Reader* (London: Weidenfeld and Nicholson, 1969; New York: New York Times Company, 1968).

Lewis, Bernhard, *The Arabs in History* (Hutchinson University Library, 1970).

_____, *The Middle East and the West* (London: Weidenfeld and Nicholson, 1968; New York: Harper, 1968).

Lorch, Netanel, *One Long War—Arab Versus Jew Since 1920* (Jerusalem: Keter, 1976).

Perlmutter, Amos, *Military and Politics in Israel* (London: Frank Cass, 1969).

Sachar, H. M., *The Course of Modern Jewish History* (New York: Delta, 1958).

_____, *The Emergence of the Middle East, 1914-1924* (New York: Knopf, 1969).

_____, *Israel, the Establishment of a State* London: Weidenfeld and Nicholson, 1952).

St. John, Robert, *David Ben-Gurion;* The Biography of an Extraordinary Man (Garden City: Doubleday, 1959).

_____, *Tongue of the Prophets;* The Life Story of Eliezer Ben-Yehuda (Garden City: Doubleday, 1952).

Selzer, Michael, ed., *Zionism Reconsidered* (New York: Macmillan, 1970).

Weizmann, Chaim, *Trial and Error* (New York: Schocken Books 1966).

Yale, William, *The Near East: A Modern History* (Ann Arbor: University of Michigan Press, 1969).

Israel Today

Bernstein, Marver H., *The Politics of Israel: The First Decade of Statehood* (Princeton, 1957).

Eisenstadt, S. N., ed., *Israeli Society* (London: Weidenfeld and Nicholson, 1967; New York: Basic Books, 1968).

Matras, J., *Social Change in Israel* (Chicago: Aldine, 1965).

Perlmutter, Amos, *Military and Politics in Israel* (London: Frank Cass, 1969).

Sachar, H. M., *From the Ends of the Earth—The Peoples of Israel* (New York: Delta, 1970).

Talmon, J., *Israel Among the Nations* (London: Weidenfeld and Nicholson, 1972).

Selected Books on Prophecy

Allis, Oswald T., *Prophecy and the Church* (Philadelphia: Presbyterian and Reformed, 1945).

Anderson, Sir Robert, *The Coming Prince* (Grand Rapids: Kregel, 1954).

Armerding, Carl, *The Olivet Discourse* (Findlay, Ohio: Dunham, 1955).

Berkhof, Louis, *The Kingdom of God* (Grand Rapids: Eerdmans, 1951).

Blackstone, W. W., *Jesus Is Coming* (New York: Revell, 1908).

Bradbury, John W., ed., *Hastening the Day of God* (Wheaton, Illinois: Van Kampen, 1953).

Chafer, Lewis S., *The Kingdom in History and Prophecy* (Philadelphia: Sunday School Times, 1919).

Culbertson, William, and Centz, Herman B., eds., *Understanding the Times* (Grand Rapids: Zondervan, 1956).

DeHaan, M. R., *The Jew and Palestine in Prophecy* (Grand Rapids: Zondervan, 1950).

Douty, Norman F., *Has Christ's Return Two Stages?* (New York: Pageant Press, 1956).

English, E. Schuyler, *Re-Thinking The Rapture* (Neptune, New Jersey: Loizeaux Brothers, 1954).

Feinberg, Charles L., *Israel in the Spotlight* (Chicago: Scripture Press, 1956).

_____, *Israel in the Last Days* (Altadena, California: Emeth Publications, 1953).

_____, *Premillennialism or Amillennialism*, 2d and enlarged ed. (Wheaton, Illinois: Van Kampen, 1954).

Gray, James M., *Prophecy and the Lord's Return* (New York: Revell, 1917).

Gray, James M., *A Textbook on Prophecy* (New York: Revell, 1918).

Guthrie, Donald, *New Testament Introduction* (Downers Grove, Illinois: InterVarsity Press, 1971).

Harrison, William K., *The Time of the Rapture as Indicated in Certain Scriptures*, (*Bibliotheca Sacra,* 114 (1957): 316-25; 115 (1958): 20-26, 109-19, 201-11).

Henry, Carl F. H., *The Christian Witness in Israel*, (*Christianity Today*, 5:22:22-23, August 14, 1961; 5:23:17-21, August 28, 1961).

_____, *Israel: Marvel Among the Nations*, (*Christianity Today*, 5:24:13-16, September 11, 1961; 5:25:15-18, September 25, 1961).

_____, *The Messianic Concept in Israel*, (*Christianity Today*, 7:1:7-12, October 13, 1961; 6:2:11-14, October 27, 1961).

Heubner, R. A., *The Truth of the Pre-Tribulation Rapture Recovered* (Millington, New Jersey: Present Truth Publishers, 1973).

Kligerman, Aaron J., *Messianic Prophcy in the Old Testament* (Grand Rapids: Zondervan, 1957).

Ladd, George E., *The Blessed Hope* (Grand Rapids: Eerdmans, 1956).

_____, *Jesus and the Kingdom* (New York: Harper and Row, 1964).

McClain, Alva J., *The Greatness of the Kingdom* (Chicago: Moody, 1959).

————, "Biblical Eschatology," Unpublished notes (Winona Lake, Indiana: Grace Theological Seminary).

Morgan, G. Campbell, *Behold He Cometh* (New York: Revell, 1912).

Murray, George L., *Millennial Studies* (Grand Rapids: Baker, 1948).

Payne, J. Barton, *The Imminent Appearing of Christ* (Grand Rapids: Eerdmans, 1962).

Pentecost, J. Dwight, *Things to Come* (Findlay: Dunham, 1958).

————, *Prophecy For Today* (Grand Rapids: Zondervan, 1961).

Peters, George, *The Theocratic Kingdom*, 3 vols. (Grand Rapids: Dregel, 1952).

Ryrie, Charles C., *The Basis of the Premillennial Faith* (New York: Loizeaux Brothers, 1953).

Sauer, Erich, *From Eternity to Eternity* (Grand Rapids: Eerdmans, 1954).

Seiss, Joseph A., *The Apocalypse* (Grand Rapids: Zondervan, 1957).

Smith, J. B., *A Revelation of Jesus Christ* (Scottdale, Pennsylvania: Herald, 1961).

Tenney, Merrill C., *The Book of Revelation* (Grand Rapids: Baker, 1963).

Thiessen, Henry C., "Will the Church Pass Through the Tribulation?" (*Bibliotheca Sacra*, April-June, 1935).

Walvoord, John F., *Israel In Prophecy* (Grand Rapids: Zondervan, 1962).

————, *The Millennial Kingdom* (Findlay: Dunham, 1959).

————, *The Rapture Question* (Findlay: Dunham, 1957).

————, *The Return of the Lord* (Findlay: Dunham, 1955).

_____, "Premillennialism and the Tribulation," (*Bibliotheca Sacra,* 112, April, 1955: 97-106).

West, Nathaniel, *The Thousand Years in Both Testaments* (New York: Revell, 1880).

_____, ed., *Premillennial Essays* (New York: Revell, 1879).

Wilkinson, John, *God's Plan for the Jew* (London: Mildmay Mission to the Jew, 1944).

_____, *Israel, My Glory* (London: Mildmay Mission to the Jew, 1894).

Wilkinson, Samuel H., *The Israel Promises and Their Fullfillment* (London: John Bale and Danielsson, 1936).

Wood, Leon J., *Is the Rapture Next?* (Grand Rapids: Zondervan, 1956).

Wuest, Kenneth S., "The Rapture—Precisely When?" (*Bibliotheca Sacra,* 114, 1957: 68-69).

SCRIPTURE INDEX

SUBJECT INDEX